SCM STUDYGUIDE TO THE PSALMS

SCM STUDYGUIDE TO THE PSALMS

Stephen B. Dawes

scm press

© Stephen B. Dawes

Published in 2010 by SCM Press
Editorial office
13–17 Long Lane,
London, EC1A 9PN, UK

SCM Press is an imprint of Hymns Ancient and Modern Ltd
(a registered charity)
St Mary's Works, St Mary's Plain,
Norwich, NR3 3BH, UK
www.scm-canterburypress.co.uk

British Library Cataloguing in Publication data

A catalogue record for this book is available
from the British Library

978 0 334 04342 3

Typeset by Regent Typesetting, London
Printed and bound by
CPI Antony Rowe, Chippenham SN14 6LH

Contents

Acknowledgements

I owe an immense debt to John Eaton who taught me Hebrew and guided me through my first university studies in the Old Testament, as we then called it, without a second thought, in the late 1960s. Since then, colleagues and ministerial students at Trinity College, Legon, Ghana, The Queen's College, Birmingham, and the South West Ministry Training Course; colleagues and part-time students in the Selly Oak Colleges and the Universities of Birmingham and Exeter, together with church groups all over the place, have been stimulating conversation partners and fellow readers of that compelling and challenging book. I am grateful to Natalie Watson and the staff of SCM Press for their encouragement and help with this *Studyguide*. Above all, my deepest thanks are due to Margaret, without whom nothing I have ever done would have been possible.

Abbreviations

ABD	Freedman, D. N. (ed.) (1992), *The Anchor Bible Dictionary*, 6 vols, New York: Doubleday.
ANET	Pritchard, J. B. (ed.) (1969), *Ancient Near Eastern Texts Relating to the Old Testament*, 3rd edn, Princeton: Princeton University Press.
ASB	*The Alternative Service Book 1980* (1980), London: Hodder and Stoughton.
AV	Authorised Version or 'King James Version' (1611).
BCP	The Book of Common Prayer 1662.
BHS	Elliger, K. and Rudolph, W. (eds) (1967–77), *Biblia Hebraica Stuttgartensia*, Stuttgart: Deutsche Bibelgesellschaft.
CBQ	*Catholic Biblical Quarterly*.
CW	*Common Worship: Services and Prayers for the Church of England* (2000), London: Church House Publishing.
DBI	Ryken, L., Wilhoit, J. C. and Longman, T. (eds) (1998), *Dictionary of Biblical Imagery*, Downers Grove: InterVarsity Press, USA.
DBI-SCM	Coggins, R. J. and Houlden, J. L. (eds) (1990), *Dictionary of Biblical Interpretation*, London: SCM Press.
DMBI	McKim, D. K. (ed.) (2007), *Dictionary of Major Biblical Interpreters*, Downers Grove: InterVarsity Press, USA.
DOTT	Thomas, D. W. (1958), *Documents from Old Testament Times*, New York: Harper.
DOTWPW	Longman, T. and Enns, P. (eds) (2008), *Dictionary of the Old Testament Wisdom, Poetry and Writings*, Downers Grove: InterVarsity Press, Academic.

DSSB	Abegg, M., Flint, P. and Ulrich, E. (1999), *The Dead Sea Scrolls Bible*, New York: HarperSanFrancisco.
GNB	Good News Bible (1994).
IDB	Buttrick, G. A. (ed.) (1962), *The Interpreter's Dictionary of the Bible*, 4 vols, Nashville TN: Abingdon Press.
IDBSupp	Crim, K. (ed.) (1976), *The Interpreter's Dictionary of the Bible Supplementary Volume*, Nashville: Abingdon Press.
JB	Jerusalem Bible (1966).
JSOT	*Journal for the Study of the Old Testament*.
LXX	Septuagint.
NCTS	*Newsletter for Targumic and Cognate Studies*.
NDLW	Davies, J. G. (ed.) (1986), *A New Dictionary of Liturgy and Worship*, London: SCM Press.
NEB	New English Bible (1970).
NETS	*New English Translation of the Septuagint* (2007).
NIB	*The New Interpreter's Bible*, various editors (1993–2002), 12 vols, Nashville TN: Abingdon Press.
NIDNTT	Brown, C. (ed.) (1975), *The New International Dictionary of New Testament Theology*, 3 vols, Exeter: Paternoster Press.
NIDOTTE	VanGemeren, W. A. (ed.) (1996), *The New International Dictionary of Old Testament Theology and Exegesis*, 5 vols, Grand Rapids MI: Zondervan.
NIV	New International Version (1978).
NJB	New Jerusalem Bible (1985).
NJPS	*Tanakh*, Jewish Publication Society, 2nd edn (1999).
NKJV	New King James Version (1982).
NRSV	New Revised Standard Version (1991).
OCB	Metzger, B. M. and Coogan, M. D. (eds) (1993), *The Oxford Companion to the Bible*, Oxford: Oxford University Press.
OCCT	Hastings, A. M., Mason, A. and Pyper, H. (eds) (2000), *The Oxford Companion to Christian Thought*, Oxford: Oxford University Press.
OTP	Charlesworth, J. H. (ed.) (1983), *Old Testament Pseudepigrapha*, 2 vols, New York: Doubleday.
REB	Revised English Bible (1989).
Targ	Targum.

TDOT	Botterweck, G. J. et al. (eds) (1974–2006), *Theological Dictionary of the Old Testament*, 16 vols, Grand Rapids MI: Eerdmans.
TNIV	Today's New International Version (2005).
Vulg	Vulgate.

Introduction

The purpose of this *Studyguide*

In the Preface to his 1990 introduction to Psalms, Klaus Seybold states his intention like this:

> Our study . . . [will not] offer any new approach to the Psalms for which the author alone may claim credit. Rather it builds on the results of scholarly exegesis and the accumulated knowledge which this has made available. It seeks to bring its readers to read the Psalms for themselves, and to make their own observations and discoveries.

I will be satisfied if this book does just that.

Elisabeth Schüssler Fiorenza's new book *Democratizing Biblical Studies* argues for a new model of biblical studies that will 'foster collaboration, participation and engagement'. I will be satisfied if readers find this book a helpful step in that direction.

The shape of this *Studyguide*

There are nine chapters in this *Studyguide*, all of which contain many features of other *SCM Studyguides* such as text boxes, bullet points, questions to reflect on and things to do.

Chapter 1, 'Opening the Book', is an introduction which explores what it might mean to read this strange but compelling anthology of ancient religious poems.

From its 'publication' probably some time in the fourth or third century BC the book of Psalms has been in constant use in Judaism and then Christianity. It has given words for worship in different forms and in many different settings from the Temple in Jerusalem and monasteries at Qumran and Cluny to synagogues, parish churches and independent chapels. It has provided prayers for private use in good times and bad, supplying images, sayings and examples to encourage, inspire and nourish believers in their spirituality. It has been a memorable theological resource in both faith communities for instruction, reflection and meditation. Its words and images have passed into common speech and literature. Over the past 250 years it has been studied by biblical scholars as a gateway into and expression of the worship, thought, history and literature of ancient Israel. Its gems, like Psalm 23, have been valued. Its violence, as in Psalm 137, has been both emulated and deplored. In this introduction we look at what psalms are and begin to see how different readers, ancient and modern, have read them.

In Chapters 2–8 we look at the different *voices* found in Psalms and the very different ways they speak about and to God. I have identified seven such voices (praise, shalom, dissonance, penitence, hope, spirituality and theology), but it could have been two, in which case it would be praise and lament, or seventeen. These are the voices I hear when I listen to different psalms, some of which are joyful words of praise, some are complaints and accusations directed at God, some are teaching and instruction, and others are words of confession or dreams of better days. These voices are not, I must stress, categories by which individual psalms can be catalogued, even if I do offer suggestions about psalms which seem to me to be principally voicing one of these things rather than another. I am not suggesting yet another update on Gunkel's 'types' (of which you will learn in due course). I am simply, as one reader to other readers, sharing one way of reading psalms which I find fruitful, in the hope that it might help other readers to read Psalms, and if you have noticed how many times one word has been used in this sentence, then I ask you to hold that word in your mind for a few pages' time. These chapters cover all the ground that is usually covered in first-level introductions to Psalms, and they bear the marks of the biases, blind spots and enthusiasms of its writer, as all introductions should. Each of these chapters divides into four parts:

- a longer or shorter exegesis of a psalm with a particular 'voice'
- an exploration of that 'voice'

- an extended comment of one sort or another, and
- some guides for further reading.

Chapter 9, 'New Studies in the Psalms', focuses on two significantly new movements in Psalms study. In the first part, 'Many psalms, one book', we look, tentatively because this discussion is still in its early-ish days, at the discussions about the shape of Psalms as we have it, how it might have taken that shape, and what that shape might be saying. It could be, of course, that Psalms is a collection of poems put together at random, which is how many scholars thought of it until recently and some still do, though even if that were the case that doesn't necessarily prevent readers reading it as 150 chapters in sequence and benefiting from the experience. Or it could have been put together very carefully with a logic that only the compiler understood and that is now utterly beyond recovery. Or there might be clues in the book's final form which, if followed, help us to see new things in it. That's the agenda for part 1. In part 2, 'Reception history' (well, you've got to have a technical term in here somewhere, haven't you?), we introduce a very new addition to biblical scholars' interests, that of how Psalms has been read and used over the centuries.

After that there are the usual select bibliography, indexes and notes, plus a glossary and a guide to commentaries on Psalms.

Some technicalities

In this *Studyguide*, 'Psalms' always means the book of Psalms. The writers of psalms are often now called 'poets', but what they wrote is a specialized kind of poetry, and so I shall refer to them as 'psalmists' in the same way that we call those poets who write hymns, 'hymn-writers'.

This book will introduce you to some Hebrew words and these are given in transliterated form, but in three different ways: words like 'shalom' or 'Torah' which have passed into common use are usually given in their common forms without either italics or inverted commas, quoted words are given in their quoted forms, and all others are given in italics in one of the standard academic styles (SBL 1999 as in Soulen and Soulen, p. 201).

Quotations are normally from the NRSV, with other translations used for comparison from time to time.

Page numbers are given in all references, except when the reference is to a commentary on a particular verse when the reference can be found in the discussion of that verse. Full bibliographic details for all works mentioned in the text can be found in the General Bibliography (p. 216). Details for specific groups of works can also be found elsewhere: for various 'useful tools', in the section with that heading in Chapter 1; for commentaries, in the Guide to Commentaries on p. 211; for big dictionaries and so on, usually in Abbreviations on p. viii; for books relevant to particular topics, normally in the 'Suggestions for further reading' at the end of each chapter (where books marked * are suggested places to begin).

The divine name is normally written as YHWH.

YHWH

Writing the divine name as YHWH is easy enough and that is how it is often found in modern textbooks. The Hebrew Bible writes this name (sometimes referred to as the *Tetragrammaton* – 'the Four Letters') in a way that can never be pronounced, and substitutes the word *Adonai* ('Lord') for it when it is to be read aloud. Traditional English translations therefore write 'LORD' in small capitals for every occurrence of this divine name. JB (1966) and NJB (1985) print the name as *Yahweh*, which is probably the correct pronunciation, but this is deeply offensive to Jews and should be avoided. 'LORD' is, however, also problematic, because it is a title and not a name, and one with overtones of hierarchy and feudalism that the divine name did not possess. This, some argue, renders it unusable in our contemporary context, as well as making us forget the important Old Testament point that the God of Moses has a name that he discloses. The contemporary hymn-writer Brian Wren, who is deeply committed to using 'good language' in worship, suggests simply writing and saying '*Adonai*' or possibly printing 'NAME' and adding a footnote saying, 'God's name is not spoken: use "*Adonai*," "*El Shaddai*," "Living One" or another reverent substitution' (Wren, p. 251). *Jehovah*, a sixteenth-century and entirely artificial combination of the German forms of the consonants of YHWH and the vowels of *Adonai*, is rarely used today, with one obvious exception.

1

Opening the Book

What is this chapter about?

This chapter introduces two basic questions – What is a 'psalm'? and What is Psalms? – before noting the great name of Mowinckel and reading Psalm 24. It then considers why people read psalms and what readers bring to their reading, important aspects of the modern academic study of Psalms and of the Bible generally. Next it introduces some useful tools before our first major engagement with Psalms, which is to look at the psalm titles.

How is it organized?

- First, we ask the basic question about all reading, which is that of identifying genre: so – what are 'psalms'? Then we ask the same question historically – what were psalms?
- Second, we look at the collection as a whole: what is Psalms and what was Psalms?
- Third, we read a psalm (Ps. 24) and see what we can find in it.
- Fourth, we note how psalms have been read in different ways by different readers, and highlight the role of the reader in contemporary biblical studies.
- Fifth, we introduce some useful tools for studying psalms.
- The 'extended comment' looks at the psalm titles.
- There are explanatory boxes on the title of the book, 'First Temple/Second Temple', the four ancient versions of the Old Testament, and the two minor complications of verse numbers and psalm numbers.

- Throughout the chapter there are a number of 'To do' boxes which, not surprisingly, invite you to do things.
- The chapter ends with suggestions for further reading on introductions to biblical study, different approaches in Old Testament studies, Old Testament introductions, introductions to Psalms, the recent history of Psalms study, the four ancient versions and the psalm titles.

What should I be able to do by the end of it?

- Appreciate the importance of 'genre' in reading psalms and Psalms.
- Identify different speakers and liturgical features in a psalm.
- Understand the place of Mowinckel in Psalms study.
- Recognize the role of the reader in all reading, including academic study.
- Know where to look for more study resources.
- Judge where this *Studyguide* is coming from.
- Describe the variety of components in the psalm titles.
- Understand a number of technical terms.

The genre questions: what are 'psalms' and what were they originally?

If you pick up a scrap of paper with 'Take four ounces of flou ...' scribbled on it you know immediately that your piece of litter started life as a recipe. If somebody tells me that 'There was an Englishman, a Welshman and ...' I know immediately that they are going to tell me a joke, probably a bad one. We know these things because sometime, somewhere, someone explained them to us, but it's all now lost in that long ago time when we learned to 'read' texts, or at least it is for me. When, in my late teens, I first read, 'In a hole in the ground there lived a hobbit ...' I wasn't quite sure what I was reading, but I stayed with it, and my first venture into a new genre had begun. Recognizing the genre of what we are reading is the key to all reading. When it comes to reading the Bible, however, genre is not quite so straightforward. Is Genesis 1 science or theology, for example? I am absolutely certain that it is not science of any kind, but when I was first asked how I knew that, I had to do some hurried thinking and then some careful explaining. Saying that it was blindingly obvious and common sense wouldn't have done. Fortunately with psalms it isn't quite so difficult or anywhere near so controversial, but it is still not easy.

To do

Without opening your Bible: what do you think 'psalms' are?

You have probably just discovered that identifying the genre of psalms is not as simple as it sounds. Depending on our experience, we might think of psalms as music used in worship or on a CD in which the Latin words are lost in magnificent Gregorian chant. Or we might think of a psalm as one of those Bible passages read in church or synagogue like any other 'lesson', or possibly as a more interesting one than usual because this one is sometimes read 'antiphonally' by the whole congregation or by different groups in it. Or we might think of psalms as prayers from the Bible used in private prayer. There are other possibilities too, but these are the big three: psalms are 'worship songs', 'Bible readings' and 'prayers', though if you look it up in a dictionary you will find that the standard definition of a psalm is 'a sacred song or hymn', which only covers the first of these.

To do

Now let's ask the same question historically. What were psalms when they were written and first used? One way to approach this could be to pick ten psalms at random from Psalms and see if they offer any clues.

The chances are that you will have found some psalms which look as if they were written and used as 'worship songs' or 'words for worship' of some kind. You might have found one or two which call themselves 'prayers'. You might also have found some which don't look much like either. And whether they were anything like 'Bible readings' depends on when they became part of any recognizable 'Bible' and whether worship in ancient Israel included anything like 'lessons';

both of which are substantial questions in their own right. What they all have in common, however, is that they are ancient Hebrew religious poetry.[1]

Working definition

A canonical psalm (that is, one of the 150 in Psalms) is an ancient Israelite religious poem which may have begun its life as a worship song, a prayer, an unclassifiable liturgical text or a piece of instruction or teaching, but which in its canonical form (as one of that 150 in Psalms) is a chapter of torah, that is, official instruction in theology and spirituality.

What is Psalms and what was Psalms?

To do

If this was a *Studyguide* to Amos or Genesis, you would be expecting about now to be asked to read that book from beginning to end. I'm willing to bet that you aren't expecting to be asked to do that with Psalms. So before you do exactly that (skim-reading will be fine), you might reflect on why you were not expecting it, and why I might be suggesting you do it.

Psalms is, quite simply, the book that comes at the beginning of 'Writings' in the Hebrew Bible and between Job and Proverbs in Christian Bibles and that consists of 150 psalms or chapters of ancient Hebrew religious poetry which are used in Judaism and Christianity as words for worship, Bible readings and prayers.

Asking what Psalms was is not so simple. The bottom line is that Psalms was an official Jewish collection of 150 psalms or chapters of Hebrew religious poetry, some of which appear to be words for worship, some of which are prayers and some of which don't seem to be either. Many introductions to Psalms or the Old Testament, however, are more specific. They describe Psalms as a 'hymn book' or 'the hymn book of the Second Temple', a title that goes back at least to the great nineteenth-century German scholar Julius Wellhausen (1844–1918) (Kirkpatrick, p. xxxvii); but there are two difficulties with this.

The first is that Psalms doesn't look much like a 'hymn book', even though its title in the Hebrew Bible, *sēper tĕhillîm* ('Book of Praise/s'), might suggest worship songs. Many commentators admit, as Kirkpatrick did in his important commentary early in the twentieth century, that this designation is not entirely accurate (pp. l–li). Some psalms might look like congregational hymns, but others look like choir anthems, liturgical antiphons, cantatas, or material for solo voice and chorus, as well as the various oddments one might find in a cathedral music cupboard. There is also material that doesn't look very singable by anybody or appear to have any obvious place in public worship. And we must also bear in mind that we do not really know all that much about the liturgical or musical traditions of either the First or the Second Temples.

'First Temple' and 'Second Temple'

The 'First Temple' is the one in Jerusalem commissioned by King David, built by his son, Solomon, dedicated in 950 BC and destroyed by the Babylonians in 586 BC, or so the Old Testament tells it. The 'Second Temple' is the one built after the return from exile in Babylon and dedicated in 516 BC. Herod the Great began a complete rebuilding of this one in 20 BC, which was only finished in AD 65. The Romans destroyed it during the Jewish Revolt in AD 70. All that remains of it today is part of the 'Western Wall'.

Psalm 1, however, introduces Psalms as a book to be read, 'meditated' upon and used as an official anthology of 'instruction' (torah) or spirituality. This is certainly how later rabbis approached Psalms and we see the end of the process in the publication of the Midrash on Psalms (*Midrash Tehillim*) in the thirteenth century AD. Among Christians, Athanasius (293–373) called Psalms 'an epitome of the whole Scriptures', Basil of Caesarea (330–79) regarded Psalms as a 'compendium of all theology' and Martin Luther (1483–1546) called it a 'little Bible', the Bible in miniature.[2]

The second difficulty lies with the date because, with the possible exception of Psalm 137, we cannot say with certainty when any of the psalms were written.

Fashions come and go in dating them. There may be signs of the return of a trend to date them later rather than earlier, as Hunter, for example, writes that Psalms is 'both in form and to a large extent in substance, a post-exilic composition' (Hunter, 2008, pp. 43, 136); but most commentators still think that many of the psalms date back to the First Temple period. Crenshaw's cautionary words are important here: 'Every attempt to date psalms encounters enormous difficulty' (Crenshaw, 2001, p. 6; see also Goldingay, 2003, p. 30). The date of the 'publication' of the collection itself is also uncertain and its editors unknown. It is usually thought that the anthology was in its present form by the end of the third century BC, although variant versions of it existed for several centuries after that, as we know from the Dead Sea Scrolls (see Chapter 6).

Reading a psalm

Psalms, *tĕhillîm* and 'the Psalter'

Our English title 'Psalms' comes from the Septuagint title *Psalmoi*, a Greek word for music made on stringed instruments, which it also uses to translate the Hebrew word *mizmôr* found in some of the psalm titles. The title 'the Psalter' comes from *Psalterion*, 'stringed instrument', in the title of Psalms in the fifth-century Christian manuscript Codex Alexandrinus.

Just as hymn books provide a window into the life of a worshipping community, so Psalms provides glimpses into the religion of ancient Israel (Crenshaw, 2001, pp. 72–9). The great name here is that of the Norwegian scholar Sigmund Mowinckel (1884–1965).[3] He is one of the four towering figures in Psalms study in the twentieth century, and his classic, *The Psalms in Israel's Worship*, attempts, among many other things, to identify how psalms were used in what ancient Temple liturgies, rituals and festivals, by whom and why. Following him, others, for example, added to the picture of a great New Year Festival each autumn when YHWH was enthroned as King and in which the king played a major role in all kinds of liturgical dramas. There is, however, a warning to heed here about how much can be reconstructed from Psalms. My much loved teacher John

Eaton was probably Mowinckel's best disciple in Britain and built on his work in a number of books over 30 years (for a summary, see Eaton, 2003, pp. 22–4). Unfortunately, much of that New Year Festival and many of their conclusions are now thought to contain quite a bit more imaginative reconstruction than is warranted. Goldingay puts it a tad too strongly when he concludes that the attempt to make connections between particular psalms and specific acts of worship is 'as much of a failure as the attempt to date them', but the warning does need to be given (Goldingay, 2006, vol. 1, p. 54). Mowinckel's basic observation, however, that most of the psalms are liturgical texts and that appreciating them as such is basic to appreciating them at all, remains an important one in Psalms study.[4]

To do

Read Psalm 24. What speakers and actions can you identify?

See my 'liturgical reconstruction'[5], which is, of course, just a bit of fun, but there is no doubt that Psalm 24 opens a window onto some kind of liturgy involving a procession. The problem is, however, that although this psalm is clearly one giving 'words for worship' it comes without any rubrics. There is nothing to tell us the occasion on which this psalm is to be used; nothing about which actions are to accompany it or which it is to accompany; nothing about how 'the King of glory' is represented in this liturgy and nothing about how many and whose voices are involved. Another good example of this common puzzle of words without rubrics is those psalms in which there is a sudden change of tone. What happened, for example, between verses 29 and 30 of Psalm 69? Was there a big liturgical moment, like a sacrifice? Did someone preach a sermon, a prophet give an oracle, or someone offer a testimony of some kind? Did a priest pronounce a blessing? Was there a piece of liturgical drama or a musical interlude? Were there specific prayers? We can only speculate.

To do

Read Psalm 24 again. What other features can you see in it?

Here is my list made after looking at that psalm in my NRSV. I see a number of literary features:

- there is a title, printed in italics
- a Hebrew word appears twice, also in italics
- it is divided into three sections (verses 1–2, 3–6, 7–10)
- in some verses the second line almost repeats the first.

This lively psalm, therefore, also opens windows onto issues of tradition (the title), translation (that untranslated Hebrew word) and Hebrew poetry (the divisions and the repetitions). There is also the question of the relationship between the first section (verses 1–2) and the other two, for there seems to be no obvious one.

I see that Psalm 24 is theologically rich:

- it names God as 'the LORD' (that is, YHWH) and gives four other names or titles: 'the God of (their) salvation', which we could translate as 'the Saviour God'; 'the God of Jacob'; 'the King of glory', which we could translate as 'the Glorious King', and 'the LORD of hosts';
- it teaches that this God 'created the world' and blesses people; that he has 'saved' a particular group of people and will 'come in' to their temple; that he is 'holy' as well as 'glorious' and that he is a great warrior;
- it teaches what this God expects of his worshippers.

So in this psalm we glimpse something of what was believed and taught in the Second Temple period in Temple circles, what sacred stories were told by Temple preachers, what was thought about right and wrong by Temple prophets, and what 'religious experiences' were offered by Temple worship and Temple spirituality.

I see that there are some words, phrases or ideas that need unpacking, for example the seas and rivers idea in verse 2 and 'the LORD of hosts' title for God; and that there are some particularly odd details, especially in verses 7 and 9: what sort of 'gates' have 'heads'? And why are those doors 'ancient'?

One of the legacies of Ninian Smart (1989), an important twentieth-century sociologist of religion and theologian, was 'the seven dimensions of religion', a schema by which religions can be mapped. He suggested that religions can be described under seven headings:

- doctrine (what is believed and taught?)
- myth (what sacred stories are told?)
- ethics (what is taught about right and wrong?)
- ritual (what practices are involved in worship?)
- experience (what does it offer to its adherents?)
- institutions (how is it organized?)
- material forms (what sacred objects does it use?).

Looking at Psalm 24 I can see something on each of Smart's headings, so the psalm opens a window too onto the religion of ancient Israel.

Then, there is the other title and its number: 'Psalm 24'. That reminds me that this individual psalm is part of a collection (Psalms), which is itself included in a larger collection we know as the Hebrew Bible/Old Testament. At the very least that inclusion gives everything in the psalm an 'official' status. Because Psalms is an 'authorized' or 'canonical' text, its anonymous voices raised in praise or protest now speak in the name of the community; its images and metaphors now receive official sanction; its religious, moral and theological understandings are now 'torah', that is teaching, guidance and instruction, to be learned and lived, as the introduction to this official anthology (Ps. 1) makes clear.

Reading psalms requires that we are alert to all of these possibilities.

Reading Psalms

In its turn Christianity accepted the canonical status of Psalms and valued the book for many reasons, not least because of the way in which some Jews had begun to read it as a 'prophetic' book which spoke of what God was going to do to 'redeem his people' (see Chapter 9). Christians gave this their own twist and so, for the early Church, Psalms was a book that was seen to write of Christ, a book of 'prophecies' in which the first Christians read much to help them understand and express their emerging belief that 'Jesus is Lord'. After that, in both Judaism and Christianity, as canonical Scripture and liturgical text, Psalms was a 'spiritual classic' providing resources for public worship and private prayer as well as for doctrine and catechesis. In due course, it freed itself from ecclesiastical control and became popular literature in which believers could meet their God, study their Bible and celebrate their faith. Reading Psalms provided a theology to sing and pray with heart and mind, one written in the evocative and earthy language of poetry, image and metaphor. Psalms supplied words in which to express the struggle of faith with doubt and confusion amidst the harsh realities of life, and ones in which to voice joy and delight. Such 'devotional reading' of Psalms continues to this day and whatever may be said about it, for example that some of it is decidedly odd, it points to the 'living' nature of the book. Psalms, perhaps uniquely in Scripture, does not belong to its authors, editors, translators, publishers, historical exegetes, official interpreters, teachers or preachers but to its users, however much critical academic or ecclesiastical voices may sometimes grumble at what they do with it.

It is sometimes said that 'academic' reading of the Bible is an alien and destructive reading which denies the Bible its real authority. Some academic reading may be like that and some will certainly have a negative side-effect on certain kinds of religious faith. For many academics, however, reading the Bible seriously (which is a better word than the usual 'critically' and means exactly the same) is about 'faith seeking understanding', to use the well-known phrase of Anselm, and always has been even if some religious communities and a few academics have not always seen it like that. Academic reading of the Old Testament itself, however, is now much more varied than it was.

- The older 'historical-critical' method still has a place, and its convictions that the meaning of a Bible passage lies in what the original author intended and what the original readers or hearers would have understood is to be respected, even if we can't be as confident as we used to be that we can know what that actually was.[6] We need to recognize, this method insists, that Psalms is an ancient book of ancient texts, coming from a real time and place, and its historical base, context and features are an important part of what it is. There is a world 'behind' this text, the world that produced it and that it addressed, which needs to be taken into account.
- 'Literary-criticism' is a term with a bit of a history in biblical studies, but the modern version from the 1970s on has opened up new ways of reading texts which recognize that they are 'literature'. Psalms is a book of poetry, in which each poem exists in its final form and is accessible to us as it is. It can therefore be read as any poetry can be read and appreciated for what it is without enquiring into its origins, checking for signs of editing or drafting, or asking about the biography of the poet. There is a world 'of' or 'in' the text itself, the

world of its words, shapes, constructions, images, styles and forms, in front of us as we open the book and read.

- Then we come to you and me, readers of Psalms. Contemporary academic study now recognizes that we exist and that the reader is the third and very active participant in the reading process. As readers we bring our contexts to our reading, our interests, passions, enthusiasms and questions. There is a world 'in front of' the text, the world of the reader who engages with the text and makes meaning out of what he or she reads.

There have always been 'schools of thought' in academic Bible study, with competing or complementary ideas and methods, and today is no exception. Broadly speaking today's scene invites us to recognize these worlds 'behind', 'of/in' and 'in front of' the text, and to recognize the complementarity of Author, Text and Reader (the 'Diagram of Biblical Interpretation' at the end of Soulen and Soulen is the neatest summary of all this that I know). There are still some squabbles about which of these is 'proper' academic study, which is cutting-edge and which is old-hat, and there are also different sub-sets within these three 'methods', but in the main we seem to be moving to a place that recognizes that each of these approaches is legitimate, that each has its place, that each is a good tool for doing what it does and that each is doing a different job (Barton, 1996, pp. 237–46, and 2007, pp. 187–90). So:

- Psalms has a history. It is an ancient anthology of ancient texts from an ancient culture. Historical criticism recognizes that and explores it.
- Psalms is a work of literature. Its poetry is open before us, crafted, rich in images. Literary criticism enjoys that and explores it.
- Without readers, Psalms, just like the Bible or any other book, remains closed and silent. 'Reader-response' criticism recognizes that and invites readers to read in a committed and involved way.

In this *Studyguide*, we will encounter these interests and approaches, but, before we go further, honesty demands that in these postmodern days I declare my interest as its writer. I am a white, ordained, married, sixty-ish, English Christian of the Methodist variety, who climbs mountains, rides a big motor scooter and lives in Cornwall. I value Psalms as an anthology of ancient religious literature, despite the dud bits, which addresses God in voices from exuberant praise to angry complaint, testifies to God's goodness and reliability and deplores his absence and silence. I read Psalms as a window into the fascinating world of ancient Israelite faith to which I, as a Christian, am heavily indebted. I do not read Psalms or the Old Testament, and I must stress this, as a book which 'points to Christ' (and here the contrast between this *Studyguide* and Bullock's introduction could not be greater). My view is that the New Testament must be read in the light of the Old, rather than vice versa, and that later Christian readings are precisely that, later Christian readings. As such, they have a place (see Chapter 9 on the reception history of Psalms), but to me a secondary one. Above all, I appreciate Psalms as a compendium of Old Testament theology where the big questions about God, faith and life are explored with passion and commitment. I therefore read Psalms as an 'insider': but I do not read it uncritically. Although I read it 'with the grain', I am not blind to its knots. Although I read it with a 'hermeneutic of trust', I also recognize the need for a 'hermeneutic of suspicion'. And so I believe that this text of 'Holy Scripture', like all of the Bible, must be read with full academic rigour, that there are serious consequences for faith communities when it isn't, and that those who, from either side, are currently trying to drive a wedge between 'the Church' and 'the Academy' are fundamentally misguided. Now you know where I am coming from.

To do

What are you, as Reader, bringing to your reading of Psalms?

Some useful tools

A Bible is good. Several are better. This *Studyguide* uses NRSV as our base translation, and an edition with the Apocrypha and footnotes is essential. I use *The New Oxford Annotated Bible (NRSV) with the Apocrypha* (1991). This contains useful brief introductory notes on how to use this edition profitably, introductions to the major groups of books in the Old and New Testaments, introductions to each book and some general articles at the end, including one on modern approaches to biblical study and one on Hebrew poetry. Beside this, I highly recommend *The Jewish Study Bible*, edited by Berlin and Brettler, which contains the NJPS translation. This too has introductions to each book, two informative sets of articles on Jewish interpretation of the Bible and the Bible in Jewish life and thought, and a series of 'backgrounds for reading the Bible', which include ones on 'the development of the Masoretic Bible' and the modern study of the Bible. The articles in these two Bibles are a studyguide in themselves. In addition you should collect as many other translations as possible.

There are now a good number of introductions to the Old Testament readily available. I particularly commend:

Barton, J. and Bowden, J. (2004), *The Original Story: God, Israel and the World*, London: Darton, Longman and Todd.
Collins, J. J. (2007), *A Short Introduction to the Hebrew Bible*, Minneapolis: Fortress Press.
Drane, J. (2000), *Introducing the Old Testament*, Oxford: Lion.
Holdsworth, J. (2005), *SCM Studyguide to the Old Testament*, London: SCM Press.

You can't go far without Bible commentaries, which come in all shapes and sizes, so see the 'Guide to commentaries on Psalms' at the back of this book (p. 211).

It is also useful to have a good one-volume Bible commentary. I suggest one of these:

Barton, J. and Muddimann, J. (eds) (2001), *Oxford Bible Commentary*, Oxford: Oxford University Press.
Dunn, J. D. G. and Rogerson, J. (eds) (2004), *Eerdmans Commentary on the Bible*, Grand Rapids MI: Eerdmans.
Mays, J. L. (ed.) (1990), *Harper's Bible Commentary*, San Francisco: HarperSanFrancisco.
Carson, D. A., France, R. T., Motyer, A. and Wenham, G. J. (eds) (1994), The *New Bible Commentary: 21st-Century Edition*, Nottingham: InterVarsity Press.
Brown, R. E., Fitzmyer J. A. and Murphy R. E. (eds) (2000), *New Jerome Biblical Commentary*, New Jersey: Prentice Hall.

Bible Dictionaries are helpful resources. It is worth finding out where you can consult the four volumes plus Supplement of *IDB* or the six volumes of *ABD*. One-volume dictionaries are available, and any serious student probably needs one on their shelf, for example:

Achtemeier, P. (ed.) (1997), *HarperCollins Bible Dictionary*, San Francisco CA: HarperCollins.

Freedman, D. N. (ed.) (2000), *Eerdmans Dictionary of the Bible*, Grand Rapids MI: Eerdmans.

Millard, A. R., Packer, J. I. and Wiseman, D. J. (eds) (1996), *New Bible Dictionary*, 3rd rev. edn, Nottingham: InterVarsity Press.

OCB covers the same sort of ground well, as do Fee and Hubbard (eds) in *The Eerdmans Companion to the Bible*, but Chilton *et al.* (eds), *Cambridge Companion to the Bible*, is not a dictionary.

Then there are more specialized dictionaries. *DBI* is 'an encyclopaedic exploration of the images, symbols, motifs, metaphors, figures of speech and literary patterns of the Bible'. *DOTWPW* has articles on anything you are ever likely to need to know about Psalms. Then, not so readable, there are the big 'theological dictionaries', which concentrate on the meaning of words and ideas: *TDOT* in 16 volumes and *NIDOTTE* in 5.

Soulen and Soulen's *Handbook* is the best handbook on technical terms used in biblical studies there is, and it will answer almost any technical query you have.

A concordance is an indispensable tool to find words or passages. My favourite, the nineteenth-century Young's *Analytical Concordance to the Holy Bible* was reissued in 2002 by Hendrickson. Zondervan publish a *New International Bible Concordance*, and *Strong's* still appears in various guises. Be careful of 'concise' or 'pocket' editions, which are usually too concise to be useful. The drawback with concordances is that they are translation specific, so if you are searching for verses that use a 'modern' word found in NIV or NRSV, for example, you will have to think what the AV word might have been, if you are using Young's, which is based on the AV. There are various free online concordances and two particularly easy to use ones are available at http://www.bibletab.com and http://bible.oremus.org.

There is much Bible stuff available on the web, of course, most of which needs a health warning. There are huge resources available at www.textweek.com, though even there you need to be wary. Click on 'Index by Scripture', which opens up a page where you click on 'Psalms' (or Amos or Romans or whatever); then when that opens click on 'general resources' just under the book heading and there you are. The Society for Old Testament Study site (www.sots.ac.uk)

is more limited and the Old Testament Gateway site (www.otgateway.com) is a poor relation of its excellent New Testament namesake. My own webpage at www.stephendawes.com contains some of the teaching material I use, plus the text of a number of my previous books.

The psalm titles

In 1919 the famous *Peake's Commentary* called the psalm titles a 'barren subject' and gave them only half a column out of its 15-column introduction to Psalms (Addis, p. 373). For most of the twentieth century, they loitered on the periphery of academic studies and commentaries and introductions devoted few pages to them, though things are changing and the new *DOTWPW* gives them a substantial 15-column entry. Devotional readings of psalms rarely make use of them, except by taking the 'David' headings literally, and versions of psalms for liturgical use always omit them. They are often obscure and frequently problematic: but that itself makes them useful in this introductory chapter. Of the 150 canonical psalms, 116 have titles, which 'would have been added in the second Temple period' (Gillingham, 2008, p. 5). They range from two words (for example 'Of Solomon') to six lines, as in Psalm 60:

> To the leader (1): according to the Lily of the Covenant (2). A *Miktam* (3) of David (4); for instruction (5); when he struggled with Aram-naharaim and with Aram-zobah, and when Joab on his return killed twelve thousand Edomites in the Valley of Salt (6).

This long title conveys six pieces of information or instruction, though not every translation prints it and some add their own. The translations vary considerably. We will look at each of its six parts.

The four ancient versions

The *Septuagint* (LXX) is the most important of the old translations, but that definite article is misleading. The term is best understood as an umbrella or 'family' term for the translations of the Hebrew Bible into Greek which began in Alexandria in the third century BC for the benefit of the Greek-speaking Jews of the Dispersion and continued for a couple of centuries. The title and abbreviation come from the legend that 72 (or 70) translators worked in complete isolation and produced 72 (or 70) identical translations. There is a new English translation, the *New English Translation of the Septuagint* (*NETS*), published by Oxford University Press, with an online version available at http://ccat.sas.upenn.edu/nets. Most LXX references here are to that, though occasionally I quote the 1844 translation by Brenton. For the complexity behind the deceptively simple designation 'LXX', see 'Septuagint' by Peters in *ABD*.

Targums are explanations, summaries and translations of the Hebrew Bible, which exist in a variety of versions, some going back to the second century BC. They appear to have been primarily educational in their purpose, almost like a commentary, and are structured to be read alongside the Hebrew Bible version of each passage. The version used here is the translation of the Psalms Targum by E. M. Cook produced by the International Organization for Targumic Studies, available online from the *Newsletter for Targumic and Cognate Studies*. See 'Targum, Targumim' by Alexander in *ABD*.

The *Vulgate* is the Latin translation of the Bible completed by Jerome in AD 405. It replaced an older Latin version and took careful note of the Hebrew as well as the Septuagint and other Greek translations. However, just as the BCP of 1662 retained the older translation of the psalms by Coverdale rather than use the one from the AV of 1611, so the version of psalms in the Vulgate is not Jerome's but an older Latin version known as the 'Gallican Psalter'. This was heavily dependent on the Septuagint rather than the Hebrew Bible and so is of little independent value in establishing the meaning of the Hebrew text. The version used here is available online at http://www.latinvulgate.com. See 'Vulgate' by Parker in *ABD*.

The *Peshitta* is the Bible of the Syrian Church, and its translation of the Old Testament into Syriac probably dates from the third century. Psalm titles do not appear in the original version of this translation and were added in the fifth century. See 'Versions, Ancient (Syriac)' by Brock in *ABD*.

In the Septuagint, where this psalm is Psalm 59, the title is:

1. Regarding completion (*eis to telos*). For those that shall yet be changed. For a stele inscription. Pertaining to David. For teaching. 2. When he set on fire Mesopotamia of Syria and Syria Soba, and Joab returned and struck the Ravine of Salt, twelve thousand (LXX-*NETS*)

In the Targum it is:

1. For praise. *Concerning the ancient* testimony *between Jacob and Laban. A copy made* by David, for instruction. 2. *When David had gathered troops and passed by the Heap of Witness and fought* with Aram-on-the-Euphrates and Aram Zobah, and afterwards Joab returned and smote the Edomites in the Plain of Salt, *and* twelve thousand from the army of David and Joab fell.[7]

In the Vulgate, where this psalm is also Psalm 59, it is:

1. Unto the end, for them that shall be changed, for the inscription of a title, to David himself, for doctrine. 2. When he set fire to Mesopotamia of Syria and Sobal: and Joab returned and slew of Edom in the vale of the saltpits, twelve thousand men.

Note the differences between the Hebrew Bible, represented by NRSV, and the Septuagint and Targum; also the dependence of the Vulgate on the Septuagint.

Two minor complications: verse numbers and psalm numbers

English Bibles do not include the titles in the verse numbering, so in them Psalm 60 has a title plus 12 verses. The Hebrew Bible, however, counts the title as the first verse, or in the case of Psalm 60 as the first two verses because it is so long. This means that psalm verses are numbered differently in the Hebrew Bible and English Bibles. Most commentaries follow the English Bible verse numbers, but not all.

The NRSV, most English Bibles and the Targum follow the numbering of the psalms in the Hebrew Bible: but the Septuagint and Vulgate use a slightly different numbering system, in which Psalm 60 appears as Psalm 59. In the Septuagint, which the Vulgate follows, Psalms 9 and 10 are one psalm, and so this throws the numbering out by one until you get to NRSV Psalms 114 and 115. The Septuagint combines these two psalms as Psalm 113, but then divides NRSV Psalm 116 into two, which brings it back to being out by one until we get to NRSV Psalm 147, which it also divides into two, and so the remaining few psalms are the same number in both collections. The latest Roman Catholic version, NJB, avoids this confusion by following the Hebrew Bible numbering and putting the numbering of its parent translation, the Vulgate, in the margin.

1 'To the leader' (that is, the preposition *lĕ* + the definite article + a noun. Note this for later!) (NRSV, NJPS, REB).

Minor variations are 'choirmaster' (NJB), 'director of music' (TNIV, NIV) and 'chief Musician' (AV, NKJV), quite different from the ancient translations. The titles in the Septuagint represent another stage in the 'reception history' of Psalms and the translators either did not know the meaning of this Hebrew noun or ignored it in favour of their own theological agenda which was to see psalms pointing forward to God's climactic intervention in history. The Hebrew noun (*mĕnaṣēaḥ*) occurs in the titles of 55 psalms and at the end of the prayer that concludes Habakkuk (3.19). It is found mostly in Books 1—3 of Psalms and mostly in psalms that use the first person singular, but it is not confined to psalms of any one style or mood. Majority opinion thinks it refers to the leader of worship responsible for the music, so Alter translates it as 'To the lead player'. Goldingay has a slightly different suggestion, translating the term as 'The Leader's' and thinking that this might refer to a collection of psalms, that is, 'The Leader's Collection'. Following Mowinckel, Eaton suggests that the term is more likely to refer to what these psalms are *for*, and he suggests that it was 'for propitiation' (Eaton, 1967, p. 16) or 'for favour' (Eaton, 2003, p. 70), somewhat akin to the Targum's 'for praise'. Few have been convinced. None of the remaining 95 psalms have any equivalent to this term in their titles.

2 'According to the Lily of the Covenant'

Minor variations are: 'To the tune "The decree is a lily"' (NJB), 'Set to "The Lily of Testimony"' (NKJV, REB) and 'To the tune of "The Lily of the Covenant"' (NIV, TNIV). Goldingay accepts that 'Lily' is probably a tune, but separates it from 'Testimony', so there are seven items in his heading of this psalm. AV, NJPS and Alter (2007) offer no translation and have 'Upon/On *shushan-eduth*'. A footnote in NJPS explains that the meaning of the Hebrew is uncertain. What all nine recent translations have in common is that they understand this part of the title to specify the tune or musical setting which is to be used to accompany this psalm, an idea not found in the ancient versions. Most commentators agree, dividing only on whether or not to attempt to translate the obscure Hebrew phrase. None have taken up Mowinckel's suggestion that this refers (here and in the titles of Psalms 45, 69 and 80 which also mention these flowers) to some kind of divination ceremony in which omens are taken from lilies (Mowinckel, vol. 2, p. 214).

The following are also generally taken to be instructions about the tunes, musical settings or styles to which these psalms are to be played or performed:

'According to "The Deer of the Dawn"' (Ps. 22)
'According to *Mahalath*' (Ps. 53) and 'according to *Mahalath Leannoth*' (Ps. 88)
'According to The Dove on Far-off Terebinths' (Ps. 56)
'According to *Muth-labben*' (Ps. 9)
'Do Not Destroy' (Pss 57, 58, 59, 75).

3 A *Miktam*

This is found in the headings of five other psalms (Pss 16, 56, 57, 58, 59). Five of the six are in a sequence and 'Do Not Destroy' features in the titles of three of them. Facts like this will feature in Chapter 9 when we look at collections of psalms within the anthology. NJB translates the term as a musical direction, 'In a quiet voice'. The rest simply give the Hebrew term and NJPS has its usual 'Meaning of Heb. Uncertain' footnote. A footnote in NIV and TNIV says, 'Probably a literary or musical term'. Alter is brief in his introduction to Psalm 16, 'What sort of composition is indicated by this term remains uncertain.' The

Septuagint thinks it was an inscription incised in stone ('A stele inscription') and this is Goldingay's preference too. The Targum of Psalm 16 has 'An honest inscription' and in the other four psalms the word is translated by the phrase 'humble and innocent'. The term is usually taken to identify a particular type of psalm, though what it means is understood differently among those commentators who attempt to explain it. It may be a musical term, as in NJB, or denote the occasion for the psalm such as a service of 'atonement' (Eaton, 2003, p. 96). Or it might be something else entirely. The six psalms in this category are all prayers for protection and help, but so are many more psalms which do not have this term in their titles. Lucas includes *miktam* in his list of terms in the psalm titles which indicate different types of psalm, so we will consider other such terms in the psalm titles here (Lucas, 2003, pp. 23–4).

'Psalm' occurs in the headings of 57 psalms, where it translates *mizmôr*. All our translations use 'psalm', which began life as a Greek word for music made with strings. The Hebrew verb means 'song', whether accompanied or not. It may be that, just as 'psalm' has passed into English as a technical term for a certain kind of religious music, so *mizmôr* was a technical but all-purpose term for 'temple-music'.

Twenty-nine psalms are called 'Songs', and the Hebrew *šîr* is every bit as everyday a term as our English one.

Thirteen psalms have *maśkîl* in their titles (Pss 32, 42, 44, 45, 52–55, 74, 78, 88, 89, 142). Most translations leave the word untranslated, but NJB has 'Poem' everywhere apart from Psalms 78 and 142 where it has 'Psalm' and NKJV has 'A Contemplation'. NIV and TNIV repeat the bland footnote, 'Probably a literary or musical term'. The term appears in the instruction to 'sing (the verb related to *mizmôr*) a *maśkîl*' in Psalm 47.7. In NRSV this appears as 'sing praises with a psalm', but others try harder: 'sing ye praises with understanding' (AV, NKJV), 'learn the music, let it sound for God' (NJB) and 'sing psalms with all your skill' (REB). Despite surface differences, at a deeper level these four are attempting to express the sense of the verb *śākal*, which is to do with being clever, wise, prudent, knowing, skilful (cf. LXX, 'understanding' and the Targum variations on good 'counsel', 'understanding', 'lesson' and 'teaching'). So some suggest that these psalms should be classed as 'contemplative poems' (cf. the title in NKJV), 'skilful psalms', especially carefully crafted ones or 'teaching psalms': but most translators are properly cautious.

Five psalms are headed 'prayers' (Pss 17, 86, 90, 102, 142) and all are psalms which cry out to God for help. Why these five are singled out is not easy to see, for they are obviously not the only prayers in Psalms. A similar question hangs round the marker at the end of Book 3 of Psalms that 'the prayers of David, son of Jesse, are ended' (Ps. 72.20).

Shiggaion in the heading of Psalm 7 is left untranslated in all our versions except NKJV ('A Meditation') and NJB ('Lament'), which is clearly what the psalm is. The Septuagint and Vulgate have 'Psalm' and the Targum, 'A rendition of thanksgiving'.

4 'Of David' (*lĕdāwīd*)

A hundred psalms contain a name in their headings: David (73), Asaph (12), Korah (11), Jeduthun (3), Solomon (2) and once each for Ethan, Heman and Moses.[8] This is where some find things controversial. We will look at Psalm 90 before we get to the question of David. For the Korahite psalms, see Chapter 9.

Psalm 90 is entitled 'A Prayer of Moses, the man of God', a title with no trans-lation problem at all. REB has 'A prayer: ascribed to Moses, the man of God'. In his 1972 commentary, Anderson speaks for the mainstream of biblical scholar-ship when he writes:

> The Psalm is attributed to Moses, and as such it is unique in the Psalter. Few . . . would accept the Mosaic authorship of this lament; most scholars agree that the composition is of a post-Exilic date, late rather than early. The ascrip-tion of the Psalm to Moses may be (at least partly) an appreciation of the poem by later generations. (A. A. Anderson, vol. 2, p. 649)

Tate, in his 1991 commentary in the *Word Biblical Commentary* series, which comes from a more conservative position, says much the same: 'Though the context(s) of the psalm's composition and use cannot be absolutely fixed, the ascription of the psalm to Moses in the title is undoubtedly the result of later (probably post-exilic) scribal exegesis . . .' (Tate p. 438, where he goes on to offer a possible explanation of what that unknown scribe or scribes was trying to do and why).

Seventy-three psalms are headed *lĕdāwīd* in the Hebrew Bible, which increases to 85 in the Septuagint. NRSV, AV, NIV, NJB, NJPS, NKJV and TNIV translate this as 'of David' while REB has 'for David'. Alter opts for the neutral 'a David psalm', Goldingay has 'David's'. LXX-*NETS* usually has 'Pertaining to David' and its translator explains his choice:

> Since the Greek translator clearly did not assign authorship per se to such Psalms, I have opted for the reasonably neutral phrase, 'Pertaining to David' (et al), since it allows for a range of perceived connections with the person(s) in question. (Pietersma, p. 545)

The Targum usually has 'of David'. The Vulgate usually translates the term with '*canticum David*', and in Douay-Rheims (the English translation produced by the Roman Catholic Church in the early seventeenth century) this becomes 'of David' 14 times, 'to David' 4 times and 'for David' an overwhelming 55 times.

This is, of course, the feature in the psalm titles which does create controversy and which most commentaries and introductions feel the need to address. The usual translation of *lĕdāwīd* by 'of David' raises the question of the Davidic authorship of these 73 psalms. This is a point where two worlds collide. Alter writes that 'The Davidic authorship enshrined in Jewish and Christian tradition has no credible historical grounding' (Alter, 2007, p. xv), and while that summarizes the view of many scholars much of the world of 'traditional Christian devotion' doesn't see it like that and neither does some evangelical scholarship (for example, Bullock, pp. 23–6, which can be contrasted with the excellent summary of the issues by Tucker in *DOTWPW*, pp. 578–9). All students studying the Bible in university contexts experience this clash of worlds sooner or later. Obviously, questioning the Davidic authorship of 73 psalms is not as high on the trauma scale as issues around the resurrection of Jesus or the historicity of Abraham or the Exodus, but the clash is real.

Lucas summarizes the translation possibilities of the preposition *lĕ* (which we have already met in '*To* the leader') as authorship ('by'), ownership ('belonging to'), dedication ('to/for') or subject ('about') (Lucas, 2003, pp. 19–20). Goldingay adds 'on behalf of' and separates 'to' and 'for' (Goldingay, 2003, p. 27). In the title of Psalm 88 it occurs 3 times (*of* the Korahites, *to* the leader, *of* Heman). In the case of *lĕdāwīd*, the 13 psalms which have a 'when he . . .' in their titles might be thought to strengthen the argument for 'authorship'. The fact, however, that the Septuagint adds situations to two more (Pss 96 and 97), the Targum to another two (Pss 9 and 58) and the Vulgate to another two (Pss 27 and 143) suggests caution, as do the variety of additions and subtractions of a David reference in headings in these ancient versions and in the headings of the psalms at Qumran. There is clear evidence of a growing 'Davidization' (or, to use Seybold's phrase, 'auto-biographisation', Seybold, p. 36) of the psalms, which is seen at its clearest in an otherwise unknown note called 'David's Compositions', which is found at the end of the 'Great Psalms Scroll' from Qumran (11QPs[a] = 11Q5):[9]

> And David, son of Jesse, was wise and a light like the light of the sun, and a scribe, and discerning and perfect in all his ways before God and men. And the Lord gave him a discerning and enlightened spirit. And he wrote 3600 psalms; and songs to sing before the altar over the whole-burnt perpetual offering for every day, for all the days of the year: 364; and for the Sabbath offerings, 52 songs; and for the offering of the New Moons and for all the days of the festivals, and for the Day of Atonement: 30 songs. And all the songs that he uttered were 446, and songs for making music over the possessed, 4. And the total was 4050. All these he uttered through prophecy which had been given him from before the Most High.

This view clearly understands the David in question to be the historic king, successor to Saul and father of Solomon, the 'sweete singer of Israel' (2 Sam. 23.1, Geneva Bible, 1560) and 'father of liturgical psalmody' (Ecclus. 47.8–10) and it is this position that became firmly established in the tradition of both Judaism and Christianity, indeed the Talmud attributes all of the psalms to David (Baba Bathra 14b, 15a; Pesahim 117a)! Goldingay points out, however, that the word 'David' is capable of other meanings than that of the historical shepherd-turned-king; it can refer to any of the kings of David's line, and after the demise of that royal line it could refer to the future king, the Anointed One, the 'Messiah' who was to come, at least in the hopes of some (Goldingay, 2003, p. 27). The 'academic consensus', however, is that *lĕdāwīd* is not to be understood as a statement about authorship and that it is probably best taken to denote dedication or ownership, 'for David' or 'belonging to David', with 'David' being understood to mean the old royal house of Judah. My preference, therefore, is to translate the term as 'belonging to the Royal Collection' or 'dedicated to the King'.[10]

5 'For instruction'

This heading, unique in the psalms, indicates the purpose of Psalm 60 and although translations vary the sense of them all is the same; though why this psalm is singled out to be taught or learnt, possibly by heart, we cannot know. Two other psalms include a note about their purpose in their headings: Psalm 100 ('A Psalm of thanksgiving') and 145 ('Praise').

6 'When he . . .'

Psalm 60 is one of those 13 'David psalms' that contain either an editorial addition attributing the psalm to a particular point in David's life, or an historical note referring to the circumstances that gave rise to David singing the psalm. The cross reference here is to 2 Samuel 8.3–8 and 10.6–18 (cf. 1 Chron. 18.3–11 and 19.6–19. What stands out among the translations is that in the Targum the 12,000 fallen are Israelites!

7 Musical instruments?

The heading of Psalm 60 contains no instructions about any musical instruments to be used. Instructions about this are found in the headings of eight psalms (Pss 4, 6, 54, 55, 61, 67 and 76 require 'stringed instruments'; Ps. 5 is for the flute or 'pipes'), though none of the ancient versions interpret the wording here to refer to musical instruments. The following three untranslated words are also usually taken to refer to musical instruments: *Sheminith* (Pss 6 and 12), *Gittith* (Pss 8, 81, 84) and *Alamoth* (Ps. 46), though what kind of instruments they are elude identification.

8 Occasions?

The heading of Psalm 60 does not indicate the occasion on which the psalm is to be used. Such markers are found in the titles of a few psalms: 'at the dedication of the Temple' (Ps. 30), 'for the memorial offering' (Pss 38 and 70) and 'for the Sabbath Day' (Ps. 92). Psalm 102 is headed 'A prayer of one afflicted', which is to be used 'when faint and pleading before the LORD'.

We have spent time and gone into some detail on this traditionally peripheral area of Psalms study. We have seen:

- the ancient versions had problems translating these titles;
- few of the modern translations seem to relate to the ancient ones;
- how many different interpretations there are;
- how often the footnotes to NJPS say 'Meaning of Heb. Uncertain';
- how important it is to read footnotes;
- how often the Hebrew is left untranslated;[11]
- the meaning of 'Psalm of David' is one of those 'academic/church and synagogue' flashpoints for some people;
- the psalm titles do not provide any reliable historical information about who wrote these psalms, when, where or why;
- the titles tell us little about what functions particular psalms might have originally served or how they might have been used;
- even if they do tell us the names of tunes or musical settings we are still without those musical scores or instruments.

Modern Bible translations do their best to read like modern books, which, together with the absence of footnotes in many Bibles intended for general use, makes it easy to overlook the fact that our Bibles are translations of ancient texts. The obscurities and difficulties of the psalm headings are, at the very least, a reminder of that and of all that that implies. In Bible study, as in anything else, it is wise to admit what we don't know and recognize the limitations of what we do.[12]

To do

Has anything in this introduction excited you? What? Why? Has anything in it challenged you? What? How? Has anything in it worried you? What? Why? Has anything in it influenced the way you will read the Old Testament in future?

Suggestions for further reading

Different approaches in Old Testament studies

Barton, J. (1996), *Reading the Old Testament*, London: Darton, Longman and Todd.
Barton J. (ed.) (1998), *The Cambridge Companion to Biblical Interpretation*, Cambridge: Cambridge University Press.
Barton, J. (2007), *The Nature of Biblical Criticism*, Louisville KY: Westminster John Knox Press.
*Berlin, A. and Brettler, M. Z. (2004) (adapted), 'The Modern Study of the Bible', in Berlin and Brettler (eds), *The Jewish Study Bible*, pp. 2084–96.
Collins, J. J. (2005), *The Bible after Babel: Historical Criticism in a Postmodern Age*, Grand Rapids MI: Eerdmans.
*Gooder, P. (2009), *Searching for Meaning: An Introduction to Interpreting the New Testament*, London: SPCK. Although the full title shows that this book has a New Testament focus, most of it is directly relevant to the search for meaning in the Old Testament too, and it can be most warmly recommended.
*Hunter, A. G. (1999), *Psalms*, London: Routledge, Old Testament Readings, part 1.
McKenzie S. L. and Haynes, S. R. (1999), *To Each its Own Meaning: An Introduction to Biblical Criticisms and their Applications*, Louisville KY: Westminster John Knox Press.

Introductions to biblical study

*Brown, M. J. (2000), *What They Don't Tell You: A Survivor's Guide to Biblical Studies*, Louisville KY: Westminster John Knox Press.
*Moyise, S. (2004), *Introduction to Biblical Studies*, 2nd edn, London: T&T Clark, Continuum.
*Rogerson, J. W. (2002), *Beginning Old Testament Study*, 2nd edn, London: SPCK.

Introductions to Psalms

*Bullock, C. H. (2001), *Encountering the Book of Psalms*, Grand Rapids MI: Baker Academic.
Crenshaw, J. L. (2001), *The Psalms: An Introduction*, Grand Rapids MI: Eerdmans.
Dillard, R. B. and Longman, T. (1995), *An Introduction to the Old Testament*, Leicester: Apollos, pp. 211–34.
Gerstenberger, E. S. (2001), 'The Psalter', in Perdue, *The Blackwell Companion*, pp. 402–17.

Hempel, J., 'Psalms, Book of', in *IDB*, vol. 3, pp. 942–58.

Hunter, A. G. (2008), *An Introduction to the Psalms*, London: T&T Clark.

Limburg, J., 'Psalms, Book of', in *ABD*, vol. 5, pp. 522–36.

*Longman, T. (1988), *How to Read the Psalms*, Downers Grove IL: InterVarsity Press USA.

*Lucas, E. (2003), *Exploring the Old Testament, vol. 3: The Psalms and Wisdom Literature*, London: SPCK, chs 1 and 2.

*McCann, J. C. 'The Shape and Shaping of the Psalter', in *NIB*, vol. 6, pp. 641–77.

*Murphy, R. E. (1993) 'Psalms, The Book of', in *OCB*, pp. 626–9.

Seybold, K. (1990) *Introducing the Psalms*, Edinburgh: T&T Clark.

Tucker, W. D. (2008) 'Psalms 1: Book of', in *DOTWPW*, pp. 578–93.

Westermann, C. (1976) 'Psalms, Book of', in *IDBSupp*, 705–10.

Some commentaries on Psalms begin with lengthy introductions, others don't. Those of Anderson (though dated now in parts), Broyles, Curtis, Eaton (2003), Goldingay (especially good) and Mays are particularly useful.

Old Testament introductions (excluding those mentioned in 'Some useful tools')

Brueggemann, W. (2003), *An Introduction to the Old Testament: The Canon and Christian Imagination*, Louisville KY: Westminster John Knox Press.

*Coogan, M. (2008), *The Old Testament: A Very Short Introduction*, Oxford: Oxford University Press.

*Dillard, R. B. and Longman, T. (1995), *An Introduction to the Old Testament*, Leicester: Apollos.

Gillingham, S. E. (1998), *One Bible, Many Voices*, London: SPCK.

McKenzie S. L. and Graham M. P. (eds) (1998), *The Hebrew Bible Today*, Louisville KY: Westminster John Knox Press.

Psalm titles

Brueggemann, D. A. 'Psalms 4: Titles' in *DOTWPW* pp. 613–21.

*Lucas, *Exploring*, pp. 19–25.

Kraus, *Psalms*, vol.1, pp. 21–32.

Recent history of Psalms study

During the twentieth century the Society for Old Testament Study produced regular updates on the state of Old Testament scholarship. There are dedicated chapters on what was happening in Psalm scholarship by A. R. Johnson, in H. H. Rowley (ed.), *The Old Testament and Modern Study*, Oxford: Oxford University Press, 1951; and John Eaton, in G. W. Anderson (ed.), *Tradition and Interpretation*, Oxford: Oxford University Press, 1979. After that the Society for Old Testament Study produced a set of Study Guides on particular books (see Day, 1990). A new set is in the pipeline.

Beal, L. W. (2008), '5. Psalms in the Modern Period', in *DOTWPW*, pp. 608–13.

Howard, D. M. (1999), 'Recent Trends in Psalms Study', in Baker and Arnold, *The Face of Old Testament Studies*, pp. 329–68, a reworked and shortened version of which appears as Chapter 1 in Johnston and Firth (eds), *Interpreting the Psalms*.

The four ancient versions

Alexander, P. (1992), 'Targum, Targumim', in *ABD*, vol. 6, pp. 320–31.

Brock, S. P. (1992), 'Peshitta' in 'Versions, Ancient (Syriac)', in *ABD*, vol. 6, pp. 794–5.

Edwards, T. M. (2005), 'The Targum of Psalms', in Johnston and Firth (eds), *Interpreting the Psalms*, pp. 279–94.

Parker, D. (1992), 'Vulgate', in *ABD*, vol. 6, pp. 860–2.

New English Translation of the Septuagint (*NETS*) at http://ccat.sas.upenn.edu/nets.

Newsletter for Targumic and Cognate Studies at http://www.targum.info.

Peters, M. (1992), 'Septuagint', in *ABD*, vol. 5, pp. 1093–104.

2

Voicing Praise

What is this chapter about?

Praise is a core component of worship in both Judaism and Christianity, 'the outward expression of the believer's worship and adoration of God' (Peter Selby – see the full quote on p. 39 below). As the title *sēper tĕhillîm* (Book of Praise/s) suggests, many psalms voice praise. In this chapter we shall examine the last psalm in the book, and explore what it means to 'praise' God. The chapter includes a guide to doing an exegesis and an introduction to Hebrew poetry.

How is it organized?

- The psalm for exegesis is Psalm 150.
- In 'Voicing praise' we explore the dynamics of praise.
- The extended comment is an introduction to Hebrew poetry.
- There are boxes on exegesis and how to go about it, Hallelujah and Hosanna, which in the Old Testament mean different things, and on some of the technical terms used in discussions of Hebrew poetry.
- There are a number of 'To do' boxes.
- The chapter ends with suggestions for further reading on exegesis, praise and Hebrew poetry.

What should I be able to do by the end of it?

- Understand what is meant by 'praise'.
- Recognize the key features of 'psalms of praise'.
- Do a basic Old Testament exegesis.
- Value the contribution of Walter Brueggemann to Psalms study.
- Distinguish between *Hallelujah* and *Hosanna*.
- Appreciate the main features of Hebrew poetry and understand the common technical terms used in discussions of it.

Exegesis and how to go about it

An 'exegesis' is simply an explanation of a Bible passage. It will normally consist of five or six parts:

1 An introductory sentence (or at most two or three short sentences) that describes the passage and sets it in its literary and, if necessary, historical contexts (for example, 'Psalm 65.9–13 is . . .').
2 A sentence that summarizes or explains the passage (for example, 'It . . .' or 'In it . . .').
3 If your exegesis is of a whole psalm or a complex passage you might need a sentence on its structure, and you might do the following two parts on a section-by-section basis.
4 The main part of an exegesis is the explanation of any difficult words, phrases or ideas it contains. If there are few or none of these, take that as an indication that the passage has been chosen because of the following.
5 An explanation of the key themes or ideas it contains. How much space you devote to this depends on how much was taken in doing part 4.
6 A short concluding paragraph that points out the place of the passage and its ideas in the Old Testament.

A good way to go about it is:

1 Look up the passage in NRSV and as many other translations as possible and compare their readings.

---

2 Make your own notes on the five (or six) points above.

3 Only then turn to the commentaries, Bible dictionaries and handbooks to see what they say about the key words, phrases or ideas that you have already identified and tried to puzzle out for yourself.

4 Write up your notes.

5 Add a bibliography at the end that includes the Bible translations you have used as well as the commentaries and any dictionary or handbook entries.

See the reading suggestions at the end of the chapter.

Psalm 150

To do

Without looking anything up, jot down what you think you might need to include in the five points (because there would only be five here, wouldn't there?) in your exegesis of Psalm 150.

1. Psalm 150 is the fifth in a series of five Hallelujah psalms and the final psalm in the book.

2. It is both an extended 'call to praise', in which the worshipping community is called to praise God for what he is and what he has done and express that praise by using all the musical instruments they have, and a doxology, a song which is itself an expression of praise to God. As such it forms a powerful crescendo to Psalms, crowning the shorter doxologies found at the end of Books 1—4.

3. This psalm doesn't divide into sections though it does have a pattern, moving from 'who' is to be praised (verse 1), through 'why' (verse 2) and 'how' (verses 3–5) to who is to offer that praise (verse 6) (Mays).

4. Every verse begins with 'hallĕlû-' (see the text box on pp. 37–8). NRSV catches the strength of this imperative with its exclamation marks. In six short verses, that command is repeated 12 times with a thirteenth in a different

grammatical form which changes from imperative to invitation to 'everything that breathes' to praise YHWH (verse 6a).

God's 'sanctuary' (verse 1) is either his heavenly throne sanctuary or the Temple in Jerusalem. The 'firmament' (verse 1) is the 'dome of the heavens', familiar from the creation parable in Genesis 1. Many commentators write that the two ideas in parallel here suggest that the heavenly sanctuary is meant, and therefore that those who are called to praise God or who are praising God in the psalms are his heavenly 'aides' (for example Goldingay). On the other hand the picture of God's praise going out from one particular spot and also filling the whole of his creation is a powerful one.

We cannot identify the instruments of verses 3–5 but the impression is clear that full orchestra of wind, strings and percussion is to be used.[1]

'Everything that breathes' (verse 6a) usually refers only to human beings (Deut. 20.16; Josh. 10.40) but in Genesis 7.22 it includes all animals, so a 'green' reading of this verse would opt for the widest interpretation here. If we confine the interpretation to humanity, the ending of this psalm is still noteworthy in its address to all humanity.

5. Verse 2 gives the reasons for such praise (for what is meant by 'praise', see the central part of this chapter). YHWH is to be praised 'for his mighty deeds' (Pss 145.4, 12; 106.2). He is a 'God who acts',[2] as seen in both Exodus and Exile. God can act to punish as well as to bless! It was a common idea in the ancient Near East that the gods operated in history, and the Moabite Stone gives us an excellent example.[3] Everyone agreed that your national god or gods brought you prosperity in your harvests and victory in your wars, and Israel shared this theology, as can be seen almost anywhere in the Deuteronomic History. The best example in Psalms is Psalm 105 with its theme of 'making [YHWH's] deeds known among the peoples' and 'tell[ing] of all his wonderful works' (Ps. 105.1–2). The Ten Commandments are introduced by a statement that the God who is giving them is YHWH, 'who brought you out of the land of Egypt, out of the house of slavery' (Ex. 20.2; Deut. 5.6). A similar recital is found in the possibly ancient introduction to the offering of firstfruits in Deuteronomy 26.5–10, and the Song of Hannah, which has passed into Christian usage as Mary's 'Magnificat' in Luke 1.46–55, does the same (1 Sam. 2.1–10). Popular though this idea is in the Old Testament, and in much later theological thinking, it is open to serious questioning, as we see in the psalms of 'lament' in Chapter 4.

> **To do**
>
> Read Psalms 91 and 113, which are two psalms used in worship I attended recently. How do you react to Psalms 91.3–7 and 113.7?

Verse 2b uses a phrase found only here in the Old Testament: God's 'surpassing' (NRSV), 'exceeding' (NJPS) or 'immeasurable' (REB) 'greatness'. Given the parallel in this verse it is likely that this 'greatness' is the greatness of God's power as seen in his 'mighty deeds', an idea that can be found elsewhere in the Old Testament (for example, Pss 66.3; 147.5; Isa. 40.26; 63.1). Another sense of God's 'greatness', however, speaks of his goodness, of what he is rather than what he does, a theme that we shall address in Chapter 8.

6. The Old Testament is not a 'missionary' book. If Psalm 150.6 is anything more than a glorious rhetorical flourish then this psalm can be added to the shortlist of Old Testament passages that explicitly include all humanity in YHWH's final purposes: the blessing of Abraham (Gen. 12.3), the 'light to the nations' work of God's 'Servant' (Isa. 42.6; 49.6), and two rather different pictures of the future of the nations (Isa. 2.2–4/Micah 4.1–4 and Zech. 14.9–19). Otherwise its references to other nations are almost all condemnatory, as in the 'oracles against the nations' (Amos 1—2; Isa. 14—23; Jer. 46—51; Ezek. 25—32).

> ## Hallelujah and Hosanna
>
> 'Hallelujah' (*hallĕlû – yāh*) is a shout of praise which is usually and correctly translated by 'Praise the LORD'. The first Christians used it (as we see in the heavenly hymn in Rev. 19.1–8) and it has featured in Jewish and Christian liturgies down the centuries. In Christianity it has often been replaced by its anaemic Greek nephew, 'Alleluia'.
>
> 'Hosanna' is, in the Old Testament, something quite different. It is a combination of the strong form of the imperative of the verb 'to save' plus the word for 'please' and in this form occurs only at Psalm 118.25 where NRSV translates it as 'Save us, we beseech you, O LORD'. Without the 'please' it is simply a cry for help: to the king at 2 Samuel 14.4 and 2 Kings 6.26, to God at Psalms 12.1 and 28.9, and for God to save the king at Psalm 20.9 and the speaker at Psalms 60.5 and 108.6.

The expression appears in the 'Triumphal Entry' scene in the Gospels where, however, it is usually understood as a shout of praise (Matt. 21.1–17; Mark 11.1–10; Luke 19.28–38; cf. John 12.12–18). Vincent Taylor, in his classic commentary on Mark, writes that Torrey's rendering of the expressions as 'God save him' (Mark 11.9) and 'God in heaven save him' (Mark 11.10) 'probably correctly interprets the sense of the original' (Taylor, 1966, p. 456). Pope, in a full and technical explanation, suggests that the three sayings should be translated as 'Save us please', 'Save us please, O Son of David' and 'Save us please, O Highest' respectively (*ABD*, vol. 3, pp. 290–1). This is not, however, how the Church has understood it and this original meaning has been lost. 'Hosanna' has become a shout of praise, and despite their original differences 'Hosanna' and 'Hallelujah' have become conjoined twins and complete synonyms in Christian tradition, so that GNB can simply translate the Palm Sunday cries of the crowd as 'Praise God'.

Voicing praise

The singular form of the title word for Psalms, *tĕhillîm*, is found at Psalms 33.1, 40.3, 65.1, 119.171 and 147.1. Psalm 145 is headed 'a song of praise', with the same Hebrew word opening the last of its verses. Psalms ends, as we have seen, with *hallĕlû – yāh*, 'Praise the LORD', and that whole psalm is a call to praise God. The preceding four psalms, Psalms 146—149, similarly begin and end with *hallĕlû – yāh*, and counting backwards so do Psalms 135, 117 (*hallĕlû 'et YHWH*), 113 and 106; with Psalms 115 and 116 ending with that exclamation and Psalms 111 and 112 beginning with it. Psalms 113—118 are known as the 'Egyptian Hallel' and Psalms 120—136 as the 'Great Hallel'. We should note for reference in Chapter 9 that only one of these psalms occurs outside Book 5 of Psalms, and that is Psalm 106, which is the concluding psalm of Book 4. While the voice of praise is not silent in Books 1–4 (counting forwards it is found for example in Psalms 8, 9, 18, 19, 21, 30 etc.) it is widely observed that while there are other voices in the psalms in Book 5 the voice of praise predominates there in a way that it does not in the other Books, and that it is that voice which brings Psalms to its powerful and positive close.

Calling the anthology of a varied set of psalms 'Praises' is making a bold statement about the collection as a whole, not least because of the powerful ways in which that anthology also expresses 'lament', the opposite voice to praise (see Chapter 4). And so is shaping the anthology to end so powerfully on the note of praise. There was much in their experience that forced a 'no' from the psalmists, whose poems gave congregations words by which to challenge God and express their anger at the way things were. But as we have it in Psalms, both in its title and its ending, it is a 'yes' which predominates. In his important *Praise and Lament in the Psalms*, Claus Westermann, the third of the towering figures in Psalms study in the twentieth century (see the next chapter), writes that 'Praise of God gives voice to the joy of existence' (Westermann, 1981, p. 11), even 'out of the depths' (Westermann, 1981, p. 5). Liturgists see nothing surprising in 'Praise' as an overall title for Psalms, for they see 'praise' as the default mode of worship and 'central to the Christian tradition of prayer and worship' if not to the 'Judaeo-Christian tradition as a whole' (A. M. Allchin, in *OCCT*, p. 554). Selby sums it up:

> [Praise is] the outward expression of the believer's worship and adoration of God in words, music and ceremonial. The focus of praise is not only on God himself, as in adoration, but above all on his mighty acts in nature and history. Hymns and acts of praise are a common feature of all liturgy, and frequently the distinction between it and adoration on the one hand, and thanksgiving on the other is not clear cut. (*NDLW*, p. 442)

The priority or centrality of praise in Psalms should not therefore surprise us.

Since Gunkel, psalms of praise have been divided into two categories: psalms of thanksgiving and hymns.[4] The 'psalms of thanksgiving' are also commonly subdivided into those of the individual and those of the community, and subgroups appear among the 'hymns' such as 'Songs of Zion' and the celebrations of YHWH's kingship. Westermann offered a new way of describing or defining these psalms which has become widely used, suggesting 'Declarative psalms of praise' for what had been called 'psalms of thanksgiving' and 'Descriptive psalms of praise' for the 'hymns' (Westermann, 1981, book one, part one):

> Since the essential occurrence in both of these groups of Psalms is the praise of God, I propose to call them both Psalms of praise. The difference between

the two groups lies in the fact that the so-called hymn praises God for his actions and his being as a whole (descriptive praise), while the so-called song of thanks praises God for a specific deed, which the one who has been delivered recounts or reports in his song (declarative praise; it could also be called confessional praise). (Westermann, 1981, p. 31)

Declarative psalms of praise ('psalms of thanksgiving') are psalms in which the singers 'declare' how God has helped them in a crisis. They praise God in direct speech ('you') for what he has done, and give that testimony in public. Most use the first person singular, 'I', though there are some corporate ones (for example, Ps. 124). They are often specific and focused. They may originally have been used to tell the worshipper's story at a 'Thank Offering', and the verb they often use is *hôdāh*, which translates into English normally as 'thank'. The core of these psalms is the account of the crisis out of which God has saved the singer. The usual list is Psalms 9—10, 18, 32, 34, 67, 92, 116, 118, 124, 129 and 138. The Song of Moses (Ex. 15) and Jonah's psalm (Jonah 2) are also 'declarative' praise songs.

   Descriptive psalms of praise ('hymns') are psalms in which the singers praise God in more general terms for who he is and what he has done, for his greatness demonstrated in creation and nature and in history and his 'mighty deeds'. These psalms speak about God, rather than to him, and normally use the third person. They use the verb *hālal*, which we have already encountered in various of its forms, and which normally translates into English as 'praise'. The core of these psalms is often a statement of why God is to be praised. The usual list is Psalms 8, 19, 29, 33, 68, 100, 103, 104, 105, 111, 135, 136, 145—150. The Song of Hannah (1 Sam. 2) is a 'descriptive' praise song. Psalms 48, 76, 84, 87 and 122 form the 'Songs of Zion' subgroup, and Psalms 47, 93 and 96—99, which celebrate YHWH as King, constitute the 'Enthronement Psalms' subgroup.

To do

Psalm 111 belongs in the 'descriptive praise' group and Psalm 116 in the 'declarative praise'. Compare these two psalms and see if you recognize both the overall and the detailed differences between these two categories of praise psalms.

Two words of caution:

- If you look through the psalms in the two lists you will notice that things are not as neat as the textbooks suggest. These psalms might divide into two roughly recognizable groups, but few of them are 'pure examples' of their group which contain every feature we named.
- Three English verbs occur prominently in these praise psalms – 'praise', 'thank' and 'bless' – translating three Hebrew ones – *hālal*, *hôdāh* and *bārak*. They are often found in combination or parallel and obviously belong to the same semantic field, but whether they are as interchangeable as some English translations suggest is open to question. For 'bless the LORD' see the exegesis of Psalm 103 in Chapter 8.

In 1988 Walter Brueggemann published *Israel's Praise: Doxology against Idolatry and Ideology*, and a subsequent essay appeared with the title, 'Praise and the Psalms: A Politics of Glad Abandonment' (W. Brueggemann, 1995, pp. 112–32). As always, the colon and what comes after it are important in Brueggemann. He accepts the standard definitions, descriptions and conclusions of Old Testament study but then with passion and conviction introduces other questions. His fundamental conviction is that the Bible creates a new world and that readers can be remade in the vision of that new world by the renewing of their 'imagination'. He rarely quotes Romans 12.2, but Paul's appeal for 'transformation by the renewing of our minds' is at the heart of his agenda. So Patrick Miller, who edits that collection of essays, writes:

> Anyone familiar with his work will not be surprised to hear him speak about 'doxological, polemical, political, subversive, evangelical faith' (in this essay). These are all catchwords in Brueggemann's theology. What this chapter uncovers is how, quite precisely, such faith is enacted in the church's praise. (W. Brueggemann, 1995, p. xv)

In the essay, Brueggemann propounds 11 theses on the nature of praise, arguing that praise is

- a liturgical act that helps us, as all liturgy should, to embrace an alternative image of reality;
- a poetic act which opens us, as all poetry should, to wider visions of reality which make new visions possible;

- an audacious act, not only because it is loud and boisterous, but because in doing it we are adding something to God, giving him something he doesn't yet have;
- an act of 'basic trust', which can be made because the singer has found God to be utterly reliable;
- a knowing act, one which is possible because God has been challenged and forced to act in a way that has demonstrated his reliability;
- a doxological act, in which God is blessed and praised in 'self-abandonment' and without restraint;
- a polemical act, which is prepared to offer praise only and solely to YHWH;
- a political act of social protest, social criticism and social delegitimation, which dethrones all other sources of authority and power;
- a subversive act, which destabilizes all oppressive systems;
- an evangelical act, which enacts the good news of God's rule;
- a useless act (by this he doesn't mean a pointless one) of 'communion' with God. (W. Brueggemann, 1995, pp. 113–23)

So he concludes:

> Notice in saying this, however, what a deep claim is made. To say that our quintessential human act is not production of anything but is only extravagant communion, is to define our character and purpose in a most eccentric way, a way that breaks with the production–consumption ideology all around us. To focus on this extravagant communion as the purpose of life is to assert an outrageous destiny of repentance and reconciliation in which we enact a radical vision of true self, true communion, true world, true creation; not escapism, but an arrival, for the length of the song, at true destiny. (W. Brueggemann, 1995, p. 122)

The essay goes on to examine Psalms 145, 146, 149 and 150, which he calls the extreme case of 'inutility' (the word behind the 'useless' of thesis 11), in the light of these theses and to conclude with a powerful 'application'. This list gives a flavour of Brueggemann's approach and style. You will either love it or hate it. It is not easy to grasp, and Brueggemann often does himself no favours with some of his language, as in the last of those 11 theses, for example. The strength of his approach, however, is that it is not detached. It has neither the alleged detachment of some academic scholarly analysis, nor the otherworldly detachment of some worship and prayer. It is about life and the living of it in engagement with, against and for God, which is, to my mind at least, exactly what Psalms is about. Chronologically, Walter Brueggemann is the last of my four 'towering figures' in twentieth-century Psalms study. You will find the other three (Gunkel (see Chapter 3), Mowinckel (see Chapter 1) and Westermann (see Chapter 4)) discussed in any and every academic book on Psalms for their specific contributions to Psalms study, but Brueggemann's contribution (and to Old Testament study in general) is both less specific and more controversial.[5]

Other psalms that voice praise

'Praise' is one of the major categories in most of the lists of psalm 'types' (which we look at in the extended note in Chapter 3). In Gunkel's list, for example, about 40 psalms are included under the 'praise' headings of 'Hymn' and 'Thanksgiving'. My list, which is indicative only and makes no claim to be definitive, is somewhat shorter. The psalms that 'voice praise' in the open and less-defined sense that I have been employing in this chapter are, in addition to Psalm 150, Psalms 9, 18, 22, 30, 33, 47, 56, 65, 66, 67, 76, 95, 100, 113, 116, 117, 118, 124, 134, 138, 145, 147, 148 and 149.

Hebrew poetry

To do

Read Psalm 100.1–2. Compare that reading with this famous version of it by William Kethe (d. 1594):

> All people that on earth do dwell,
> Sing to the Lord with cheerful voice;
> Him serve with mirth, his praise forth tell,
> Come ye before him and rejoice.

What differences can you see?

Let me start by stating the obvious. When we read psalms, we read Hebrew poetry in translation. It is a truism that no translation reproduces 100 per cent of the meaning, content or effect of the original; and there is debate about whether poetry can really be translated at all. In poetry, words matter, and what matters is not only what they mean or suggest, but how they sound, where and how they appear in relation to other words, how they are constructed and even, a poet friend insists, what they look like on paper. This means that none of the things that a Hebrew reader can see, hear or feel in a psalm can be reproduced in a translation. Commentaries will sometimes point out that a verse contains particularly striking features of this kind, but translations are rarely able to reproduce them.[6] What makes Hebrew poetry easier to 'translate' than some, however, is its binary feature of repeating or balancing ideas.

Hebrew poetry is one of those topics that can be explained either in a couple of sentences or in a long book. The couple-of-sentences explanation is that there is such a thing but that it works on different principles to any kind of English poetry. Some of those principles continue to elude us, but we can say that instead of rhyme, metre, stanzas and what we might call a 'generous' use of words, much Hebrew poetry works by repeating or balancing ideas, most commonly within a two-part verse, and with what is best described as a 'terse' or minimal use of words. Needless to say, although these two sentences represent today's broad consensus, almost every clause could be challenged, and if this was the long-book explanation much in those sentences would need to be elucidated, justified and qualified.[7]

Some technical terms in Hebrew poetry

You will find descriptions of 'parallelism' below, explanations of *inclusio*, parataxis and gapping/ellipsis in the Glossary, and of alliteration, assonance, onomatopoeia and paronomasia in the extended comment on translation issues in Chapter 5.

There is debate about what constitutes the basic unit of Hebrew poetry, but majority opinion agrees that it is the 'line' or sentence that often, though not always, coincides with the Bible verse. Most lines or sentences consist of two parts, and liturgical psalm books often mark the division with a grammatical colon (not to be confused with the 'colon' in the next paragraph) or a little red diamond. This division is called a 'caesura'.

Colon, bicolon and *tricolon*. The smallest part of a line or sentence is the colon (plural *cola*), *verset* or *stich/stichos* (plural *stichs/stichoi*). Two of these together, as in verses 2–6 of Psalm 150, make a *bicolon* (plural *bicola*), couplet, distich or 'dyadic line' (which I called a 'two-part verse' in the paragraph before this text box). Three cola added together, as in Psalm 150.1, make a *tricolon* (plural *tricola*), *tristich* or *'triadic line'* (which I called a 'three-part verse').

Verse, strophe and stanza. In English poetry, these three words refer to the same thing, a collection of lines that form an identifiable unit within a poem. In Hebrew poetry, definitions differ. Some commentators use 'strophe' and 'stanza' interchangeably for an identifiable unit within a poem. Others use 'strophe' for a smaller identifiable unit and 'stanza' for two or three strophes together within a longer poem. In Bible study, 'verse' obviously means the numbered Bible verse. Whether there are actually any formal strophes or stanzas in Hebrew poetry we consider below.

Stress, rhythm and metre. Every language has natural speech rhythms, which usually include stressing particular words or parts of words, and speakers fall into those rhythms and make those stresses automatically. Hebrew words and sentences use stress and rhythm, but not mechanically. 'Metre' is rhythm made rigid, and traditional English hymns depend heavily on it, measuring it by counting syllables. Whether we can talk about 'metre' in Hebrew poetry is a controversial question, as we shall see.

We can begin with an uncontroversial statement, that Hebrew poetry is 'terse'. Both Gillingham and Berlin use this term, taken from the seminal work of Robert Lowth in the eighteenth century, to point out that psalms and other readily accepted examples of Hebrew poetry do not use a number of features that are common in written Hebrew: the 'definite object indicator' (*'et*), the definite article, the conjunction 'and', the relative *'ăšer* ('who' or 'which') and the common verb feature called the '*waw* consecutive'. Add to this the fact that two short lines are usually butted together without conjunctions ('*parataxis*') and the result is a staccato effect that uses a minimum of words.[8]

The technical term for the common binary technique widely used in Hebrew poetry, which also originates with Lowth, is 'parallelism' and it is controversial. Psalm 150 provides clear and simple examples of it.

> **To do**
>
> Reread Psalm 150 and see if you can see any 'parallels' or 'repetitions'. Compare the way NRSV sets the psalm out with any other versions you have.

In Psalm 150 we can see that:

- 'Praise the LORD!' serves as an *inclusio*;
- verses 2–5 are each in two parts (that is, each verse is a *bicolon*);
- in verses 2–5 each part of the verse is grammatically identical;
- in verses 2–5 each part of the verse repeats a number of the same words;
- in verses 3–5 the second half of each verse changes the musical instruments to be employed in praising God;
- verse 2 is not so simple (as we saw in the exegesis). Do both parts of this verse (both cola) speak of God's greatness in terms of what he has done? Or does the first speak of that and the second speak of God's greatness in terms of his character, of what he is?
- verse 1 has 'in his sanctuary' in parallel with 'in his mighty firmament', a parallel that is unexpected, to say the least,
- verse 6 has only one line before the concluding 'Praise the LORD!'

So even in such a short and simple poem as this, in which the 'parallelism' is of the most basic kind, we can see the method creating opportunity for surprise, imagination and reflection.

> **To do**
>
> Read Psalm 148 and identify the parallelism in it.

Psalm 148 is obviously longer and more complex than Psalm 150 and you will have noticed that in it some verses are grouped together and so the psalm is divided up with extra line spaces between the groupings. There is, however, only one type of psalm that can be confidently divided into strophes or stanzas like this and that is the acrostic psalm, of which there are nine (really eight) in Psalms. These are psalms that begin each line or set of lines with the next letter of the alphabet. They are Psalms 9–10 (which should be considered as one psalm as in LXX), 25, 34, 37, 111, 112, 119 (each strophe here consists of eight lines each beginning with the same letter) and 145. This is obviously another feature of Hebrew poetry that cannot easily be reproduced in translation. A number of psalms have refrains, but they do not seem to function as one might expect, except in Psalm 136, which has a refrain at the end of every line! It could be that the Hebrew term *selāh* introduces a division between strophes or stanzas, and it does occur in conjunction with a refrain in some places, but that is far from agreed (see the box on *selāh* on page 113). Obviously there are 'movements' in many of the psalms, changes of mood, theme, image, speaker and so on. There are some sentences that are complex and go on for more than one verse. Whether these changes or longer sentences should be seen as marking strophes or stanzas is, however, open to question, and in Hebrew poetry neither stanza nor strophe are the clear and formal demarcations that they often are in English poetry.

So now back to Psalm 148. Did you notice that

- the pattern changes in verses 1–4 at verse 4b? This line contains an example of ellipsis (or 'gapping'). There is no verb to parallel the 'praise him' of all the other half-lines, and so the verb of the previous line needs to be carried over to make sense of this line.
- the second half of verse 5 does not simply repeat the first, but is doing something different? It is giving a reason for the praise which is commanded in the first half.
- verses 7–12 are a list of those who are called to 'praise yhwh' by the single imperative in verse 7? This makes the decision of NRSV to divide the list into three rather odd.
- verses 13 and 14 have three lines each? Verse 13 does something similar to verse 5, but has two lines of explanation. Verse 14 is different again, with each line taking the idea further on – though in this case not particularly clearly in NRSV.

What we find in both Psalm 148 and 150 is what Lowth called 'synonymous parallelism'. The term is widely accepted and the feature it describes is common.

Line one makes a point and line two repeats it in some way, sometimes by as little as changing the words. We have only looked at two psalms and one of them contains some of the simplest poetry in the collection, but we have already seen that this 'synonymous parallelism' is neither simplistic nor poetry-by-numbers.

To do

Read Proverbs 10. What do you notice?

Lowth's second and equally widely accepted category of parallelism is 'antithetical parallelism' and in the 32 proverbs in Proverbs 10 there are 26 clear examples of it. Here the second half-line repeats the idea of the first, but does so by making a contrast. Proverbs 10.1 is an ideal example:

> A wise child makes a glad father,
> But a foolish child is a mother's grief.

This proverb opens the central section of Proverbs by boldly stating the fundamental principle of the 'wisdom' approach to life, that wisdom leads to success and folly to failure. So we find 'wise' in the first line, and its opposite, 'foolish', in the second; and the gladness that is the result of wise living in the first line is contrasted with the grief that results from folly in the second. The contrast is emphasized by the 'but' with which the second line begins. Whether there was originally any gender politics at work in the use of 'father' and 'mother' here can be left aside!

There are no psalms that use this form of parallelism all the way through (though you might like to notice Ps. 131), but we find it within verses and between 'parallel verses' or groups of verses. Psalms opens with a similar kind of programme statement in Psalm 1 to that of Proverbs 10.1:

> 1. Happy are those who do not follow the advice of the wicked,
> or take the path that sinners tread,
> or sit in the seat of scoffers;
> 2. but their delight is in the law of the LORD,
> and on his law they meditate day and night.
> . . .

6. for the LORD watches over the way of the righteous,
but the way of the wicked will perish.

Note the antithetical parallelism between verses 1 and 2 and within verse 6. Psalm 30.5 is a particularly interesting example:

For his anger is but for a moment; his favour is for a lifetime.
Weeping may linger for the night, but joy comes with the morning.

This verse consists of four lines in two sentences. Each sentence contains antithetical parallelism (anger/favour and moment/lifetime in the first; weeping/joy and night/morning in the second): but, put together, the two sentences constitute synonymous parallelism. Or look at the contrast in Psalm 103.9–13: verses 9–10 say what God does not do with regard to our sin, and verses 11–13 say what he does do.

Lowth identified a third type of parallelism, which he called 'synthetic parallelism', but unlike his other two categories this one is widely seen as flawed. In effect he suggested that every verse that did not use synonymous or antithetical parallelism was using 'synthetic parallelism', a complex category containing many variations and subgroups, almost a catch-all to mop up everything that did not fit in the other two; and this is where the view that parallelism is the fundamental and characteristic feature of all Hebrew poetry begins to unravel. There is no question that Hebrew poetry makes extensive use of both synonymous and antithetical parallelism, but 'parallelism' doesn't describe everything.

To do

Read Psalm 149 and identify its use of parallelism.

You probably identified the synonymous parallelism used in verses 1–5: but what is happening in verses 6–9? This might be another 'list', this time of what God's people might do to their enemies, but the two parts of verse 6 don't parallel each other too easily to begin the list and the two parts of the last verse don't parallel each other at all. What these verses mean is clear, and they share an identifiable pattern or rhythm: but that's as much as can be said. Recently a number of scholars have identified issues like this and argued cogently that while parallelism is one characteristic of Hebrew poetry, it is not the only and all-determining one. The biggest challenge came from Kugel, who went beyond suggesting that Lowth's kinds of strict parallelism don't fit all the facts to questioning whether there is anything identifiable as Hebrew poetry at all.[9] His detailed case has not been widely accepted, but he has helped to shape our present view that defining Hebrew poetry and speaking of how it works is not as simple as using the word 'parallelism' and drawing up ever more complex lists of different types of it.[10]

My last word on 'parallelism' is a practical one about using psalms in worship. Their binary nature invites the use of two voices, but what is sadly often found is that when congregations are invited to say the psalms 'antiphonally' the worship leader reads the odd-numbered verses and the congregation the even-numbered ones. This often makes nonsense of the form of the verses themselves. If the psalms are to be read 'antiphonally', doing it by the half-verse is best most of the time (but not invariably).

Finally, 'metre'. Older commentaries talked confidently about 'metre' and fre-quently used it as a template to rearrange words or phrases that they thought were defective in the texts themselves. We are no longer so confident:

> Scholars have long sought metrical regularity in biblical poetry, but no system
> – be it syllable counting, stress counting, thought-rhythm or syntactic con-
> straints – has met with unanimous acceptance. If there is such a metric form,
> it continues to elude us. It is more likely that the Hebrew poets embraced
> a looser system – one in which many lines of a poem are more or less the
> same length and partake of the rhythm of their parallelisms, but without the
> requirement of precise measurement. (Berlin, 1985, p. 599)

The concluding word must come from the opening of Susan Gillingham's important and accessible book on Hebrew poetry and the psalms, *The Poems and Psalms of the Hebrew Bible*. The first of its three parts discusses the issues we have been looking at in depth, but it opens with a reminder that reading poems involves both understanding and appreciation. Understanding and analysis by itself can be sterile, appreciation and enjoyment by itself can be facile, the two together complement each other to produce 'a more profound discernment' (Gillingham, 1994, p. 4). An important part of both understanding and appre-ciating psalms, she reminds us, is to recognize that they were originally, and have been almost continually since, 'performance poetry'. Hebrew poetry was 'heard as much as it was read' (Gillingham, 1994, p. 44). Psalms were 'sung speech' (Gillingham, 1994, pp. 45, 52). The musicality of psalms and their spoken, oral, character, she argues, 'raises significant questions about the limits of an exclusively literary approach to Hebrew verse' (Gillingham, 1994, p. 83).

Reflection

Has anything in this chapter excited you? What? Why? Has anything in it challenged you? What? How? Has anything in it worried you? What? Why? Has anything in it influenced the way you will read the Old Testament in future?

Suggestions for further reading

Exegesis

*Evans, R. (1999), *Using the Bible*, London: Darton, Longman and Todd.
*Fee, G. D. and Stuart, D. (2003), *How to Read the Bible for All Its Worth*, new edn, Grand Rapids MI: Zondervan.
Gorman, M. J. (2008), *Elements of Biblical Exegesis*, new edn, London: Hendrickson.
Hayes, J. H. and Holladay, C. R. (2007), *Biblical Exegesis: A Beginner's Handbook*, 3rd edn, Louisville KY: Westminster John Knox Press.
Stuart, D. (2002), *Old Testament Exegesis*, 3rd rev. edn, Louisville KY: Westminster John Knox Press.

Futato, M. D. (2007), *Interpreting the Psalms: An Exegetical Handbook*, Grand Rapids MI: Kregel, looks as if it should be ideal reading here, but it isn't. It is an introduction to Psalms that requires Hebrew, has a strong agenda to Christianize the book, and declares its final aim as to 'proclaim' the psalms, which is going considerably beyond exegesis.

Hebrew poetry

*Alter, R. (1985), *The Art of Biblical Poetry*, New York: Basic Books.
*Berlin, A. (1993–2002), 'Introduction to Hebrew Poetry', in *NIB*, vol. 4, pp. 301–15.
*Berlin, A. (1993), 'Poetry', in *OCB*, pp. 597–9.

*Berlin, A. (2004), 'Reading Biblical Poetry', in Berlin and Brettler (eds), *The Jewish Study Bible*, pp. 2097–104.

*'Characteristics of Hebrew Poetry' (1991) (unattributed), in *The New Oxford Annotated Bible*, pp. 392–7.

*Fokkelman, J. P. (2001), *Reading Biblical Poetry: An Introductory Guide*, Louisville KY: Westminster John Knox Press.

*Gillingham, S. E. (1994), *The Poems and Psalms of the Hebrew Bible*, Oxford: Oxford University Press.

Kugel, J. L. (1981), *The Idea of Biblical Poetry*, New Haven CT: Yale University Press.

*Lucas, E. (2003), *Exploring the Old Testament, vol. 3: The Psalms and Wisdom Literature*, London: SPCK, ch.2.

*Lucas, E. (2008), 'Poetics: Terminology of', in *DOTWPW*, pp. 520–5.

Miller, P. D. (1986), *Interpreting the Psalms*, Philadelphia: Fortress Press, ch. 3.

Schökel, L. A. (1988), *A Manual of Hebrew Poetics*, Rome: Pontifical Biblical Institute.

Vos, C. J. A. (2005), *Theopoetry of the Psalms*, London: T&T Clark.

Watson, W. G. E. (1984), *Classical Hebrew Poetry: A Guide to its Techniques*, Sheffield: JSOT Press.

Praise

Brueggemann, W. (1988), *Israel's Praise: Doxology against Idolatory and Ideology*, Philadelphia: Fortress Press.

Brueggemann, W. (1995), *The Psalms and the Life of Faith*, Philadelphia: Fortress Press, part 1.

Futato, M. D. (2008), 'Hymns', in *DOTWPW*, pp. 300–5.

*Hutchinson, J. H. (2005), 'The Psalms and Praise', in Johnston and Firth, *Interpreting the Psalms*, pp. 85–100.

*Miller, P. D. (1986), *Interpreting the Psalms*, Philadelphia: Fortress Press, ch. 5.

Westermann, C. (1981), *Praise and Lament in the Psalms*, Edinburgh: T&T Clark, book 1.

3

Voicing Shalom

What is this chapter about?

There is much in Psalms that is dramatic as psalms voice exuberant praise (as in the last chapter) or anguished lament (as in the next); their praise arising out of special and significant experiences beyond the ordinary and their lament from times of crisis. In the exegesis in this chapter, we read a familiar psalm that doesn't arise out of anything particularly special but expresses the psalmist's sense of well-being, of being blessed by God, 'through all the changing scenes of life'; a psalm that voices 'shalom'. The central part of the chapter explores metaphor and imagery in Psalms, and the comment is on Hermann Gunkel, the first of the four towering figures in Psalms study in the twentieth century, and psalm 'types'.

How is it organized?

- The psalm for exegesis is Psalm 23 and the exegesis includes a section on 'voicing shalom'.
- In 'Image and metaphor in Psalms', we define the terms and begin to explore what it means to do theology by image and metaphor.
- All introductions to psalms attempt to put them into categories or list them by 'types'. In the extended comment we shall see where this practice comes from and note its value and its shortcomings.
- There are boxes on the 'I' of the psalms, death in the Old Testament, life after death in the Old Testament, and images other than verbal ones.

- There are a number of 'To do' boxes.
- The chapter ends with suggestions for further reading on three Hebrew words (*ṣedeq*, *ḥesed* and shalom), metaphor and image, and death and life after death in the Old Testament.

What should I be able to do by the end of it?

- Understand what is meant by 'shalom'.
- Appreciate the nature of metaphor and define the word 'trope'.
- Reflect on issues around using some of the metaphors in Psalms today.
- Recognize the contribution of Hermann Gunkel to Psalms study.
- Evaluate the issues involved in assigning 'types' or categories to particular psalms.

Psalm 23

To do

Without looking anything up, jot down the points you would want to make in your exegesis.

---

1. Psalm 23, probably the most read psalm in Christian piety, is often called a psalm of confidence or 'trust', but it defies any of the repeated attempts to put it in a category, elicit its provenance or establish its purpose.

2. In it YHWH is very daringly celebrated as the worshipper's personal (note the repetitions of 'my' and 'me') caring 'shepherd' and generous 'host'. Both of these are rich images which work at various levels (see the fuller discussion below in 'Image and metaphor in Psalms'). Behind the first lies the widespread ancient Near Eastern understanding that the gods are the shepherds of their people and the kings are their under-shepherds, so there is more to the shepherd image than simply a rural idyll. Note the presence of those watching enemies in the second scene, which suggests that the host might also be rescuer and protec-

tor. Is this psalm, therefore, fundamentally celebrating that God is the king who cares, provides and protects?

The 'I' of the psalms

In its final form, Psalms is a published and public text. It is available to a multitude of users for a multiplicity of uses. One effect of this is that readers are able to appropriate the 'I' of any of the psalms for themselves and so make a psalm their own. Thus the 'I' of a psalm is everyone or anyone who chooses to be the 'I' of the text, just as the fictional anti-hero Jonah does in his praise psalm from the belly of the fish.[1]

In our discussion of the psalm titles we saw that we can say little about the 'authors' of psalms, but going back from post-publication usage to authorship it seems obvious at least to consider whether the 'I' of a psalm might not simply be a self-reference on the part of its author. This was what some editors of Psalms and many subsequent interpreters understood in the case of those David psalms that they ascribed to particular events in his life. Regardless of the unanswerable historical question, however, an original 'I' cannot survive liturgical usage, and in hymnody generally it is almost inconceivable that authors did not intend the 'I' of their hymns to be appropriated by their users. There is early evidence that 'individual' or 'I' form psalms were used corporately with the whole congregation and each individual within it identifying with its 'I' as Psalms 92 and 94 were sung by the Levites in the weekly Temple liturgy (together with the 'we' form Psalms, 24, 48, 81, 82 and 93) and the 'I' form Psalm 116 is numbered among the otherwise 'corporate' Hallel psalms (Pss 113—118) used at festivals. Ancient congregations, as modern ones, seem to have seen nothing odd in using the first person singular in their hymns and worship songs.

Details of Temple worship in ancient Israel are not as clear as we might like.[2] It is therefore no simple matter to identify 'original users' or the occasions on which 'I-form' psalms may have been used. What follows is therefore tentative, but we can imagine:

• the 'I' as an individual worshipper, who is offering the psalm personally (probably by employing a Temple singer to do it on their behalf) in a 'private' act of worship, at a family or personal sacrifice or on some other non-congregational occasion of thanksgiving (Pss 32 and 34), making a vow (Ps. 116), penitence (Pss 51 and 130), lament (Pss 6 and 26) or some possible legal examination or even trial by ordeal (Pss 17 and 26).

- the 'I' as an individual worshipper in the congregation in a service of 'public' worship.
- the 'I' as a worship leader voicing concern or thanksgiving on behalf of the congregation (e.g. Pss 5, 9/10, 28, 42, 43, 55, 92, 118).
- the 'I' as the Davidic king acting as worship leader on a major liturgical occasion, though without personally offering sacrifice (e.g. Pss 3, 5, 7, 9/10, 18, 22, 40, 55, 59).
- the 'I' as the king when some of the 'Royal Psalms' are being used (e.g. Pss 2, 61, 63, 89, 101). How many 'individual' psalms might be included here depends on how widely this category is stretched.

What emerges from this is that categorizing psalms as 'I' form/individual and 'we' form/corporate is of limited value. What evidence there is suggests that originally psalms were sung in corporate settings and that even 'private worship' took place in the corporate context of the Temple and its ongoing and busy liturgical life. And finally it must be observed that the 'I' of the psalms is never individualistic in our modern sense, because whoever speaks the 'I' of a psalm does so in a context that includes them among the people of YHWH, to whom and with whom they are bonded in covenant. Even if we are praying by ourselves we are never praying alone.

3. There is no obvious subdivision in this short psalm, other than the change of metaphor in verse 5.

4. 'A psalm of David', probably means that this psalm belongs to the Royal Collection.

In verse 3, 'life' (NJPS) or 'spirit' (NJB, REB) is better than 'soul' (NRSV, AV, NIV, NKJV, TNIV) because that traditional translation of *nepeš* now gives the wrong impression. In Old Testament thought we do not 'have' souls but we 'are' souls (see Gen. 2.7 where God breathes the breath of life into the clay form he has shaped and it becomes a 'living being', in most recent translations, or a 'living soul' in AV). When Psalm 103 opens with 'Bless the LORD, O my soul', the parallel 'all that is within me' indicates that the psalmist is intending the singers to bless YHWH with their whole being. The sense here is that YHWH has restored 'me' or 'my vitality', which may be nearest the original sense of *nepeš*.

To do

We have just seen how words can change their meaning over time and in different cultures. So before we go on to verse 3, what do you think 'righteousness' means?

In verse 3 the traditional 'paths of righteousness' becomes 'right paths' in most modern versions and that preserves the sense and nuance of the original. Within the metaphor of a shepherd and flock of sheep a 'right path' is a good path, safe to take sheep along, one which goes to good pastures and safe drinking places. But there is also the moral nuance of 'right' because paths, ways and walking is also a metaphor in Psalms for faith, spirituality, lifestyle and morality (see Ps. 1). NJB's 'paths of saving justice' picks up another sense of the Hebrew term, but it fits badly with the metaphor of sheep and shepherds, as do Eaton's 'ways of salvation' and Alter's 'pathways of justice'.

'Righteousness' and 'right' (*ṣedeq/ṣedāqāh*) are important words in the Old Testament, but like 'soul' have taken on a rather different life in much Christian theology and finding English translations that convey the sense of the Hebrew is difficult. It is all to do with being right or putting right. Weights and measures must be 'right'. Human beings must be 'right' if they are to function properly, and that 'rightness' includes health, attitudes, relationships, morals and finances. Society must be 'right' if it is to function properly. 'Laws, statutes and ordinances' exist so that everything can be kept right or put right again if things go wrong. When everything and everybody is 'right' that is 'shalom'. The facts of life, of course, are that things are not always 'right' like this, and 'sin', 'iniquity' and 'evil' are real. But according to the Old Testament, God is concerned above everything else to try to make things right, to keep things right when they are right and to put things right when they go wrong. That is what it means when it insists that God is 'righteous', which is one of its important ideas about God. This righteousness is a facet of his love (the *ḥesed* – 'love' or 'mercy' of verse 6). The plural of the word (*ṣidĕqōt*) can be translated as YHWH's 'triumphs' (Judg.

5.11, about a victory in battle), 'saving acts' (Micah 6.5, about events surrounding the Exodus) and 'saving deeds' (1 Sam. 12.7, also about the Exodus). In the Old Testament 'righteousness' vocabulary speaks powerfully about God's loving and generous kindness to his people, his benevolence which acts to save them. This is the positive context for God punishing individuals or nations, for laws intended to curb human selfishness and sin, and for the strong message of preachers and teachers (for example Amos 5.24; Prov. 12.28; Isa. 5.7). At the human level to be right and do right is to be blessed and be a blessing to others, to enjoy and share in God's fullness of life, and to experience salvation and shalom. Sadly, for many reasons, the old words 'righteous' and 'righteousness' convey little of this to us.

Finally in verse 3 there is the problematic expression translated literally as 'for his name's sake'. Elsewhere in the Old Testament much is said about God's name. Disclosed to Moses at the burning bush, it reveals his character (Ex. 3.13–15; 6.3–8). It is a top ten commandment that it must not be 'taken in vain' or 'misused' (Ex. 20.7). Psalms of lament appeal to God to act to defend his name (e.g. Ps. 74). So what might the phrase mean? NJPS offers a translation that goes beyond the literal with 'as befits his name', as does GNB, which has 'as he has promised'. Is it about God defending his reputation and demonstrating his character, not least in the context of flocks and journeying, his 'God of Exodus' reputation (cf. Ps. 106.8)?

Translations of verse 4 fall into two groups, those that contain some reference to death ('the valley of the shadow of death' (AV, BCP, NIV, NKJV), 'death's dark vale' (Crimond[3]), 'a ravine as dark as death' (NJB)), and those that don't ('the darkest valley' (NRSV, TNIV), 'deepest darkness' (GNB), 'a valley of deepest darkness' (NJPS, REB)). The Hebrew phrase is a construct[4] made up of two parts, a word for valley plus the compound word $ṣalmāwet$ (shadow/death), and so 'the death-shadow valley' would be a literal translation in which the adjectival phrase serves to emphasize how fearsomely dark the ravine is through which we pass and in which we can be sure of God's protection. Thus NRSV's omission of any adjectival use of 'death' makes its wording too feeble. In their turn, AV, BCP, NIV, NKJV and Crimond are plainly misleading because they turn the phrase into a reference to death itself by making 'death' the key noun, a mistake that has led directly to the popularity of this psalm as a hymn or reading at funerals.

Death in the Old Testament

The Old Testament views death in different ways. One portrayal sees death as 'friend'. It comes at its proper time, in old age at 70 or 80. The dead are 'gathered to their people'. Their relatives, though grieving, can rejoice for a life 'faithfully lived and peacefully died'. There is no fear in or of this death. The deceased leaves a good memory and their 'name' continues, so 'Abraham breathed his last and died in a good old age, an old man and full of years, and was gathered to his people' (Gen. 25.8). His sons bury him and life goes on (cf. Gen. 25.17; 35.29; 49.33; Deut. 32.50; 1 Kings 2.10; Job 5.26). So, in his turn, dies Job: content, his trials long forgotten (Job 42.16–17). A different portrayal sees death as 'enemy'. Psalm 103.4 blesses YHWH because he has 'redeemed' the singer's life 'from the Pit'. Here death is vicious, terrifying and completely negative; the great enemy. It leads those forces of evil which are always trying to destroy, hurt and deface what is beautiful, good and healthy. The universality of death as the common lot of all humanity is cheerfully accepted by the dying King David (1 Kings 2.1) and regarded with equanimity as 'one of those things' in Ecclesiastes 3.2 and by Job (amazingly) in 1.21 (by 14.1–2 he has changed his mind). This death is neither to be befriended nor feared: it just is, a universal experience, though in Ecclesiastes 6.2–6 it is the great leveller that casts a shadow of pointlessness, 'vanity', over everything.

Ancient Israel practised capital punishment and the portrayal of untimely death as 'punishment' pervades the Old Testament. Death is God's way of inflicting punishment (directly or indirectly) on a sinful people and on sinners. This is the standard approach of Deuteronomic or Yahwistic orthodoxy and is found in the recurrent theme of the Deuteronomic History that righteousness is rewarded and sin is punished, and in the preaching of the prophets. Though the vocabulary is different, the same idea is found in orthodox Wisdom, as seen in Proverbs, for example at 1.8–19 and 2.16–19, and heard in the argument of Job's three friends. The dire pastoral effect of this constant linking of 'death' and 'punishment' in the Old Testament cannot be overestimated.

Verse 6 ends on a note of celebration that we can dwell in the Temple our 'whole life long' (NRSV), 'for ever' (BCP, AV, NIV, NKJV, TNIV), 'as long as I live' (GNB), 'for all time to come' (NJB), 'for many long years' (NJPS), 'throughout the years to come' (REB) or 'for evermore' (Crimond). The Hebrew phrase (literally 'to/for length of days') is a common one, which NRSV translates elsewhere in Psalms as 'a long life' (Ps. 21.5), 'with long life' (Ps. 91.16) and 'forevermore' (Ps. 93.5). The duration of one's life is clearly intended, and NRSV differs from that in Psalm 93.5 only because the timescale reference there is to the hoped-for life of the Temple rather than that of any human being, and so 'forevermore' is an appropriate translation at that point. What is not appropriate in Psalm 23 is any translation that suggests that this psalm is talking about 'eternal life'.

Life after death in the Old Testament

Death is the return of dust to dust (Gen. 3.19; Ps. 104.29) or the emptying of a jar of water (2 Sam. 14.14): but the question of the finality of death in the Old Testament is not as easy to answer as is sometimes suggested.

It is often stated that:

- for the bulk of the Old Testament, death is indeed the end of a person's being, though not an immediate end;
- physical death is followed by the gradual dissolution and disappearance of the person in Sheol which is so feeble a state that it cannot be called 'life after death' or anything like it;
- for the beginnings of any hope of life after death we have to wait until the Maccabean text of Daniel 12.2 (though there might be glimmerings of the possibility in Isaiah 26.19 and Psalms 16.8–11, 49.15 and 73.24);
- the Old Testament is not really interested in this question at all.

The first and last of these statements are accurate enough but the second is risky because not every verse that speaks of Sheol understands it in the same way. In the majority of references Sheol is, without doubt, the dreary destination of all the dead: high and low, good and bad, faithful and faithless. Some texts grumble at the fairness of this (for example, Ps. 88.3–5, 10–12), while others accept that this is the way it is (but grudgingly, Eccles. 6.6). In Sheol, the remains of their human strength sap away as these 'shades' (Job 26.5; Isa. 14.9) of their former selves dissolve. There are other texts, however, in which hope is expressed that Sheol will not be the psalmist's destiny (Pss 16.9–10; 49.13–15), or even if it is that God will be there too (Ps. 139.7–8). These may be poetic expressions that express the hope that God will rescue them from Sheol's grip in this life and so give them a long and happy life, but they may be expressing a richer hope than that.

The third statement is difficult because the meaning of Daniel 12.2 is not as clear as is often assumed. To what does its 'resurrection' language refer? There is a clear hope in later Old Testament books for the rebirth of the nation, its 'return from exile', and Ezekiel 37 is a well-known picture of that hope. Another strand of this hope for national rebirth that uses 'resurrection' language can be traced from Hosea 13.14, through Isaiah 24—27 (especially 26.19) to Isaiah 52—53 to Daniel 12, which then speaks of a national rebirth. Of how much more it might speak is an open question.

Perhaps the perspective of Psalm 103.15–18 is a good last word on this question. It sets the transience of human life within the parameters of the eternity of God's steadfast love (*hesed*) and in so doing leaves the question of the finality of death tantalizingly open. Given the nature of YHWH, might we not expect some kind of eternal blessing?

5. The image of YHWH as shepherd is found in Isaiah 40.11, reinforced by Handel in his oratorio *Messiah*, Jeremiah 23.2–4 and 31.10 and Psalms 78.52–54 and 80.1, and lies behind the accusation that the kings and leaders of Judah have shepherded God's flock so badly in Ezekiel 34. The metaphor of Israel as God's 'flock' is also found in Isaiah 63.11, Jeremiah 13.17, Ezekiel 36.38, Micah 7.14f., Zechariah 10.3 and Psalm 77.20, with allusions to the Exodus wanderings in three of these passages. There are no explicit instances of the 'God as host at a banquet' metaphor in the Old Testament, though the image of a 'banquet in the last days' (Isa. 25.6, cf. 55.1) has been much used in later theology. That God provides food and drink for his people is a theme in the Exodus stories with quails supplied occasionally and manna daily (Ex. 16.9–36; Deut. 8.16; Pss 78.24, 105.40) and water obtained from the rock (Num. 20.2–13), and also a promise

of how things will be in Canaan, the land 'flowing with milk and honey' (Num. 13.27).

The word *ḥesed*, translated in verse 6 as 'mercy' (NRSV, AV, Crimond, NKJV), 'love' (GNB, NIV, TNIV), 'steadfast love' (NJPS), 'faithful love' (NJB) or 'love unfailing' (REB), is another rich technical term from the theological vocabulary of the Old Testament. The wealth of meaning in this evocative word can be seen in the variety of ways it has been translated: 'mercy', 'kindness', 'loving-kindness', 'steadfast love', 'covenant devotion', 'loyalty', 'tenderness', 'faithful love', 'constant love' or just that overworked but basic, 'love'. NRSV usually translates it as 'steadfast love', and that translation reflects an important aspect of God's love in the Old Testament, where his love is seen in terms of his covenant with Israel. God calls Israel to be his people, and pledges his loyalty and love to them in the covenant with Moses on Mount Sinai (Ex. 20—24; Deut. 5). In response the people are obliged to honour God and obey him in all they do. The Old Testament story then tells of God's reliability: he keeps his promises and honours his covenant. His love is reliable, and this reliability is emphasized in the phrase '*steadfast* love'. In Psalm 23.6 the psalmist affirms that because YHWH is shepherd and host he will continue to experience for himself the same continually faithful and loyal kindness, care and love that God has consistently shown towards the people of Israel. What the verb 'follow' does not make clear, however, is how energetically and forcefully God's *ḥesed* pursues or chases the psalmist!

Although the word is not used in this psalm, the picture painted is one of the Old Testament's best pictures of shalom as personal well-being, not least well-being that has known times of the opposite. What the good times, the shalom times, looked like in wider terms is seen in Micah 4.4 – 'they shall all sit under their own vines and under their own fig trees, and no one shall make them afraid', and in 1 Kings 4.25, which looks back to the reign of Solomon and says, 'During Solomon's lifetime Judah and Israel lived in safety, from Dan even to Beer-sheba, all of them under their own vines and fig-trees.'

Shalom, inadequately translated as 'peace', is one of the great themes and dreams of the Old Testament, though, human beings being what they are, the consistent storyline is of how shalom is so often spoiled and the vision but a distant dream, as we see in the verses preceding Micah 4.4 and which are also found in Isaiah 2.2–4:

In days to come the mountain of the LORD's house shall be established as the highest of the mountains, and shall be raised up above the hills. Peoples shall stream to it, and many nations shall come and say: 'Come, let us go up to the mountain of the Lord, to the house of the God of Jacob; that he may teach us his ways and that we may walk in his paths.' For out of Zion shall go forth instruction, and the word of the Lord from Jerusalem. He shall judge between many peoples, and shall arbitrate between strong nations far away; they shall beat their swords into ploughshares, and their spears into pruning-hooks; nation shall not lift up sword against nation, neither shall they learn war any more; but they shall all sit under their own vines . . .

Everyone sitting under their own vines and fig trees with no one to make them afraid is rather different from the refrain in Judges that 'everyone does what is right in their own eyes' with disorder and chaos as the result (Judg. 17.6; 21.25). Shalom is when everyone can live to a ripe old age and die 'full of years', sur-rounded by their family's love; where children are born and reared in security and hope; where vulnerable ones like orphans and widows are cared for; when the strong help the weak and the rich help the poor; when justice for all and kindness reign; where there is harmony and happiness for all; where the earth yields its increase and where the struggles against and within a hostile world are over; and where 'nation does not lift up sword against nation'. This is shalom. Such peace was frequently far off, and it took faith to cling to the vision that, in another picture, one day the wolf would lie down with the lamb in a 'peace-able kingdom' (Isa. 11.1–9). This is the sense of well-being reflected in Walter Brueggemann's 'psalms of orientation':

Human life consists in satisfied *seasons of well-being* (his italics) that evoke gratitude for the consistency of blessing. Matching this [are the] 'psalms of orientation' which in a variety of ways articulate the joy, delight, goodness, coherence, and reliability of God, God's creation, God's governing law. (W. Brueggemann, 1984, p. 19)

6. There is nothing to add here as much of the exegesis has involved demon-strating the place of Psalm 23's vocabulary in the Old Testament.

Other psalms that voice shalom

Psalm 23 is called a 'Confidence Psalm' in most of the category lists, and 'psalms of shalom' don't feature at all. Many of the psalms that I include in my indicative and definitely-not-definitive list of psalms that express shalom appear as 'praise' psalms in the usual lists. In addition to Psalm 23 my list would be: Psalms 4, 5, 16, 27, 40, 41, 52, 63, 73, 84, 87, 91, 92, 121, 126, 131, 133 and 144, though only Psalm 131 of these features in Walter Brueggemann's sample set of psalms of orientation.

Image and metaphor in Psalms

Psalm 23 works with two images: YHWH is 'shepherd' and 'host'. Each metaphor is carried through with appropriate detail.[5] Some commentators, however, see 'shepherd' and 'host' as secondary images behind which is the principal metaphor of YHWH as king (for example, Eaton, Kraus, Mays). Be that as it may, it is probably the richness of the imagery in this psalm that has contributed most to its ongoing popularity and to the many attempts to copy it. I am not a sheep in need of shepherding, but I do know what it is to experience danger and to receive care. I have never been to a banquet or had my head anointed with oil, and the times my cup has overflowed have usually been followed by a command to mop up the mess and put the tablecloth in the wash, but I do know what it means to be treated with unbelievable generosity. I don't think I have any enemies, but I do know how good smugness can feel and what relief after being in danger feels like. I wince at the spirituality industry's favourite metaphor of 'journey', but, however reluctantly, I have to admit that I know what it means. Psalm 23 is full of crafted metaphor evoking common experiences, and that is how it does its work. Thus Brown says that imagery is 'the most basic building block of poetry' (W. P. Brown, 2002, p. 2), Ryken that 'poetry is the language of images' (Ryken, 1984, p. 890) and Schökel that 'images are the glory, perhaps the essence, of poetry' (Schökel, p. 95).

Mary Mills points out that, 'Much biblical language is metaphorical; God is described through word pictures rather than defined by a tightly controlled selection of words' (Mills, p. vii). Others might say that it is not straining the meaning of 'metaphor' too hard to change her 'much' to 'all'.[6] There are important biblical adjectives which describe God, none more so than in the 'core creed' of Exodus 34.6–7 and there are rich verbs which speak of what he 'does', but all of them strain normal usage when they speak of God.[7] And it is a fact that nowhere in the Bible do we find the kind of 'tightly controlled selection of words' that emerges in the Christian creeds and preoccupies many systems of Christian doctrine. The Bible does not do theology that way, and whatever words one might choose to describe the Bible and its theological methods, 'textbook' is unlikely to be one of them. Both Testaments do much of their teaching by telling stories, and it would not be going too far to claim that the natural medium of theology in the Bible is 'poetry' rather than 'prose', narrative rather than dogma, and testimony in address or letter rather than ecclesial definition by rabbi or creed. All that comes later. It is not going too far to say that metaphor is the Bible's medium, and metaphor is certainly the most common of the tropes used in Psalms. Here are two definitions of 'metaphor' from literary theorists:

> Metaphor is the general term for the figure of resemblance, whereby one thing is likened to another. (Bennett and Royle, p. 80)

> Traditionally the most important figure (of speech) has been metaphor. Metaphor treats something as something else. Metaphor is thus a version of a basic way of knowing; we know something by seeing it as something. Theorists speak of 'metaphors we live by', basic metaphorical schemes like 'life is a journey'. Such themes structure our ways of thinking about the world. (Culler, p. 68)

Metaphors work, therefore, by bringing two things together. One way of putting it is to say that a metaphor takes a word from one place (its 'source domain') and applies it to another (its 'target domain') (Futato, 2007, p. 44). Another is to say that there are two parts to a metaphor: what it says or the word it uses (its 'vehicle' or 'image') and what it means, or the idea it conveys (its 'tenor' or 'theme') (W. P. Brown, 2002, p. 5). The classic example is Robbie Burns' 'My love is like a red, red rose'. In this metaphor (though purists point out that this is actually a simile and not a metaphor) the source domain is horticulture and the target domain romance. Its 'vehicle' or 'image' is a red rose and the 'tenor' or 'theme' is my love's beauty. In Psalm 23 the source domains are agriculture and banquets and the target domain is YHWH's blessing of the psalmist. The vehicle or image of the first metaphor is 'shepherd' and its tenor or theme is God's care, protection and provision; in the second, the vehicle or image is 'host' and its tenor or theme is God's generosity, protection and hospitality. The durability of Psalm 23 testifies that its metaphors are still 'live' rather than 'tired, inactive or dead', themselves neat metaphors describing the effectiveness of metaphors themselves. It is a truism that psalms are full of metaphors: for God, for faith and spirituality, for Israel and Jerusalem, for life's joys and its sorrows, but, as Brown points out, few commentators and little scholarly exegesis currently engage with what he calls 'the iconic dimensions of the psalms' or 'the poet's evocative use of imagery' or what we have simply called 'metaphor and image' (W. P. Brown, 2002, p. 14). In his book he first focuses on what he calls the two embedded or 'root' metaphors in Psalms, the metaphors of refuge and pathway, before exploring its images of the 'transplanted tree' (Ps. 1), the 'sun of righteousness' (Ps. 19), water and animals and concluding with two chapters on metaphors for God, one on the personal ones and one on the impersonal or inanimate ones.

Like all language, metaphors are not neutral. They have been chosen by speakers or writers to perform a task, which is to make hearers and readers think, believe or do something or another. Therefore they have a 'rhetoric' (a way of performing that task) and an 'ideology' (a position or point of view to promote). Both of these invite analysis, and so 'rhetorical analysis' of a metaphor asks how it works and 'ideological analysis' asks what its agenda is. We could say that the metaphor of God as shepherd 'works' at a number of levels. At its most obvious level it works by evoking the positive image of shepherds (even though as an occupation it developed a bad name). Shepherds care for sheep, they help struggling ewes give birth and they carry weakling lambs, they lead the flock to green pasture and good water, but they also have to be tough enough to defend their flocks from lions and wolves, and Psalm 23 explicitly utilizes these secondary images which were culturally familiar. While people are not sheep, they are aware of vulnerability, and this metaphor fuses the picture of God as shepherd with this sense of vulnerability and produces a sense of confidence and well-being. The use of the first person 'my' and 'me' intensifies and personalizes the sense of God's care, allowing the singer to further express needs and wants, as well as testify to previous experiences of care, thus reinforcing the new experience generated by the metaphor. At another level, the image of YHWH as shepherd guiding his flock through 'desert places' and to 'still water', accompanying and protecting it, draws on Exodus imagery with its themes of covenant, chosenness, liberation, safety, blessing and privilege, thus reinforcing the individual's sense of security among the covenant people. And possibly the stress that 'YHWH is my shepherd' works because it numbers the speaker among the faithful, chosen covenant group. At another level the psalm uses conventional and widespread images of gods as shepherds, and YHWH as the 'Shepherd of Israel' (Ps. 80.1). All of these, and more, are possibilities when it comes to reflecting on the 'performative value' of this metaphor.

To do

Try your own rhetorical analysis of the God-as-host metaphor in Psalm 23. How does that one work, do you think?

An ideological analysis of YHWH as shepherd might conclude, quite simply, that the metaphor aims to promote YHWH, that its agenda is to assert the superiority of YHWH over all other potential providers. A less suspicious analysis would be to see its agenda as encouraging faith in YHWH. The ideology of these metaphors is part of the systematic ideological programme of the Old Testament, and we will explore that further in Chapter 8.

Metaphors can be risky. There is, for example, the harmless risk that if you don't know the culture you might not understand the metaphor. Did Palestinian shepherds really 'lead' their sheep rather than drive them like British shepherds do (Ps. 23.2–3)? And what is that business of anointing guest's heads with oil about (Ps. 23.5)? Or what about the 'grass' of Psalm 103.15–16? The metaphor of grass here is intended to convey the sense of the transience of human life; we are here today and gone tomorrow. Human life is, the psalmist says, just like the grass which appears suddenly after the rains in a semi-arid climate like Palestine, but in a few weeks all is dead and brown again. In Britain, however, there is nothing more permanent than grass! One of the helpful things about *DBI*, and also the work of Otto Keel, is that it illustrates the 'source domains' of the Bible's metaphors and images so that potential misunderstandings can be avoided.

Other risks are more dangerous. Even the metaphor of YHWH as 'shepherd', for example, is not risk-free. Shepherds produce sheep for meat, and so a vegetarian reading of Scripture is not going to tolerate that image for God. In his criticism of the corrupt leaders of the nation, Ezekiel makes powerful use of 'shepherd' imagery, which risks making it unusable again (Ezek. 34). Here we encounter the complication that words have denotations and connotations. The word 'toad' denotes a species of reptile, but its connotations, except for toad-lovers, are 'slimy', 'greedy', 'untrustworthy' and 'unpleasant'. Denotations remain constant, a toad will always be a reptile (or, for a particular subculture, a type of railway wagon), but connotations can change with time and context. The metaphor of 'father' for God is not common in the Old Testament, but it is found and it is positive (Deut. 32.6; Isa. 1.2–3; 63.16; 64.8; Jer. 3.19; Hos. 11.1–4; Pss 68.5, 103.13). Christianity took it further and invested heavily in it, but in some Christian circles it is now a liability and its use is actively discouraged. What once spoke of care or authority or both now for many speaks only of misused power, abuse, violence and oppression. Brian Wren's *What Language Shall I Borrow?* highlights such issues. He questions how many of the Bible's 'KINGAFAP' metaphors (King, God, Almighty, Father, Protector) we can still use, given that they are rooted in patriarchal language, and suggests that it is time we found less damaging ways of talking about God. Sally McFague asks the same questions in *Metaphorical Theology*.

To do

Do your own SWOT analysis (Strengths? Weaknesses? Opportunities? Threats?) of the metaphor of 'Father' for God.

Metaphors, therefore, require vigilance and a hermeneutic of suspicion as well as a hermeneutic of trust.

Other images?

Our discussion of 'images' has focused, as discussions of imagery in the Old Testament usually do, on how words are used to create images. This is mainly because there are no pictures in the Old Testament and its prohibitions about making any other kinds of 'images' except verbal ones were taken seriously (Ex. 20.4–6). There is, however, no shortage of iconography from Israel's surrounding cultures, and growing evidence that more was produced in ancient Israel itself than we might think. See the article by Klingbeil, which explores the pictorial element of Israel's metaphors and images.

Hermann Gunkel and psalm 'types'

Almost all commentaries on Psalms attempt to classify each psalm. It is the done thing, and in the doing of it homage will be made, even by those who do it differently, to Hermann Gunkel.

Hermann Gunkel (1862–1932) is a giant among the pioneers of Psalms study. Like many of his contemporaries he was primarily interested in the history of Israelite religion. His particular contribution was to pioneer the method of 'form criticism', believing that behind the diverse types of written material in the Old Testament lay older oral traditions, formed and developed in different contexts. If one could identify these different forms and trace their oral development back, he argued, one could arrive at their original 'situations in life'. Thus he gave us the technical term *Sitz-im-Leben* for the 'setting in life' in which particular types of biblical material first took shape. Identifying and classifying the different 'forms' or 'types' (*Gattungen*) in the psalms was therefore, for him, a means to a bigger end. That end was to understand the religion out of which the psalms came, and in attempting to classify the different types of psalms he was doing something more than offering literary or theological classifications. It is the attempt at classification, however, that has tended to preoccupy Psalms study, rather than his wider task, and Hunter suggests that the association of his name almost exclusively with defining and analysing 'psalm types' is a legacy with which he would probably not be best pleased (Hunter, 2008, pp. 8–11, 34–5, 43–54).[8]

Appendix 1 in Johnston and Firth (pp. 295–300) is a useful 'Index of Form-Critical Categorizations', which lists each psalm and gives the category in which it is placed by Gunkel and six more recent scholars. Lucas offers the following 'classification of most of the psalms that would be fairly widely accepted' (Lucas, 2003, p. 11):

Hymns:	General Praises
	Celebrations of Yahweh's kingship
	Songs of Zion
Laments:	Individual and Communal
Songs of Thanksgiving:	Individual and Communal
Royal Psalms	
Psalms of Confidence:	Individual and Communal
Wisdom Psalms	
Torah Psalms	

Other classifications obtained by using other criteria, asking other questions, and for other purposes are also possible. Westermann argues cogently for only two 'categories' of psalms (Westermann, 1981, pp. 15–35). As there are only two modes of speaking to God, praise and petition, so there are only two types of psalms, praises and laments (Westermann, p. 35), though there are subgroups within each class. The best known modern classification, however, is probably Walter Brueggemann's threefold division of Psalms into psalms of orientation, disorientation and reorientation (W. Brueggemann, 1980, 1984, 2002), which he calls a 'typology of function' (W. Brueggemann, 1995, p. 3). A more modest one is the way this *Studyguide* identifies psalms with different 'voices'. And in Psalms itself, the psalm titles might supply us with different categories, if only they weren't so problematic.

To do

First: if you had to classify Psalm 23, how would you classify it? Now, having made the attempt, how helpful was the exercise?[9]

Readers read Psalms and psalms for different purposes, and that is no less the case with academic readers than with any others. Gunkel's reading was primarily historical, Brueggemann's is passionately theological. The listings that arise out of and then further facilitate these different interests will therefore be different. Each will have its own agenda and serve particular purposes. But all listing carries a health warning. Listing is not the same as reading; and putting a psalm in a category is almost certainly not the most important or interesting thing to do with it.

> ## To do
>
> Has anything in this chapter excited you? What? Why? Has anything in it challenged you? What? How? Has anything in it worried you? What? Why? Has anything in it influenced the way you will read the Old Testament in future?

Suggestions for further reading

Death and life after death in the Old Testament

*'Death', in *DBI*, p. 198, and 'Rebirth', pp. 696–7.

*Jacob, E. (1962), 'Death', in *IDB*, vol. 1, pp. 802–3.

Johnston, P. S. (2002), *Shades of Sheol: Death and Afterlife in the Old Testament*, Leicester: Apollos.

*Johnston, P. S. (2008), 'Afterlife', in *DOTWPW*, pp. 5–8.

*Martin-Achard, R. (1992), 'Resurrection – Old Testament', in *ABD*, vol. 5, pp. 680–4.

*Richards, K. H. (1992), 'Death – Old Testament', in *ABD*, vol. 2, pp. 108–10.

Gunkel and psalm types

Buss, M. J. (2007), 'Gunkel', in *DMBI*, pp. 499–503.

*Crenshaw, J. L. (2001), *The Psalms: An Introduction*, Grand Rapids MI: Eerdmans, pp. 80–6.

Hunter, A. G. (2008), *An Introduction to the Psalms*, London: T&T Clark, pp. 8–11, 34–5, 43–54.

*Johnston, P. S. (2005), 'Appendix 1: Index of Form-Critical Categorizations' in Johnston and Firth (eds), *Interpreting the Psalms*, pp. 295–300.

Seybold, K. (1990), *Introducing the Psalms*, Edinburgh: T&T Clark.

Metaphor and image

Brown, W. P. (2002), *Seeing the Psalms: A Theology of Metaphor*, Louisville KY: Westminster John Knox Press.

DBI is devoted entirely to this.

Keel, O. (1978), *The World of Biblical Symbolism*, London: SPCK.

Keel, O. (1997), *The Symbolism of the Biblical World: Ancient Near Eastern Iconography and the Book of Psalms*, Winona Lake: Eisenbrauns.

Klingbeil, M. G. (2008), 'Iconography', in *DOTWPW*, pp. 621–31.

McFague, S. (1982), *Metaphorical Theology*, Philadelphia: Fortress Press.

*Mills, M. (1998), *Images of God in the Old Testament*, London: Cassell.

Soskice, J. M. (1985), *Metaphor and Religious Language*, Oxford: Clarendon Press.

*Wren, B. (1989), *What Language Shall I Borrow? God-talk in Worship: A Male Response to Feminist Theology*, New York: Crossroad Books.

Ḥesed

Baer, D. A. and Gordon, R. P. (1996), '2874 הסד', in *NIDOTTE*, vol. 2, pp. 211–18.

*McCann, J. C. (1993–2002), in *NIB*, vol. 6, pp. 670–2.

Sakenfield, K. D. (1992), 'Hesed', in 'Love – Old Testament', in *ABD*, vol. 4, pp. 377–80.

Snaith, N. H. (1994), *The Distinctive Ideas of the Old Testament*, London: Epworth Press, pp. 94–130.

Zobel, H.-J. (1974–2006), 'הסד', in *TDOT*, vol. 5, pp. 44–64.

Ṣedeq

*Achtemeier, E. R. (1962), 'Righteousness in the OT', in *IDB*, vol. 4, pp. 80–5.

Johnson, B. (1974–2006), 'צדק etc.', in *TDOT*, vol. 12, pp. 239–64.

*Kwakkel, G. (2008), 'Righteousness', in *DOTWPW*, pp. 663–8.

Reimer, D. J. (1996), '7405 צדק', in *NIDOTTE*, vol. 3, pp. 744–69.

Scullion, J. J. (1992), 'Righteousness – Old Testament', in *ABD*, vol. 5, pp. 724–36.

Shalom

Good, E. M. (1962), 'Peace in the OT', in *IDB*, vol. 3, pp. 704–6.

*Healey, J. P. (1992), 'Peace – Old Testament', in *ABD*, vol. 5.

Nel, P. J. (1996), '8966 שלם', in *NIDOTTE*, vol. 4, pp. 130–4.

Stendebach, F. J. (1974–2006), 'שלום šhalōm', in *TDOT*, vol. 15, pp. 13–49.

4

Voicing Dissonance

What is this chapter about?

So far we have looked at psalms that express a sense of gratitude that all is well. In this chapter we encounter a unique kind of religious song or prayer, traditionally in Psalms study called a 'lament'. Here all is definitely not well. The lament demands to know why all is not well, urgently appeals to God for help and, sometimes, accuses God of doing nothing when he should be doing something. Over a third of the psalms express this sense of dissonance in one way or another, and we consider one of the sharpest of them. In 'Voicing dissonance' we widen the discussion of the Old Testament's treatment of 'dissonance' and the final comment is a reflection on 'theodicy' in the Old Testament.

How is it organized?

- The psalm for exegesis is Psalm 74.
- In 'Voicing dissonance' we consider responses to 'dissonance', including that of cursing those who cause it and demanding vengeance on them.
- The extended comment invites you to get to know four acquaintances whose different explanations of that perennial experience of bad things happening to good people, to borrow from the title of Rabbi Kushner's excellent little book, represent the different approaches to theodicy in the Old Testament.
- There are boxes on lament, the four creation 'pictures' in the Old Testament, the frequently occurring contrast in Psalms between 'the righteous' and 'the wicked', theodicy, and 'enemies' in Psalms, plus an extended quote from the

classic *The Courage to Doubt* by Robert Davidson.
- There are a number of 'To do' boxes.
- The chapter ends with suggestions for further reading on lament, vengeance and theodicy.

What should I be able to do by the end of it?

- Understand what is meant by 'dissonance', 'lament' and 'theodicy'.
- Recognize the key features of 'psalms of lament'.
- Appreciate the contribution of Claus Westermann to Psalms study.
- Reflect on the issues about using some of the psalms of lament today.
- Begin to appreciate the variety of approaches to the question of theodicy in the Old Testament.

Psalm 74

To do

Jot down your exegesis points.

1. Psalm 74 is usually listed as a 'community lament'. It is the second in the 'collection' of 11 Asaph psalms in Psalms 73—83. It builds on the urgent questions raised in Psalm 73 and is similar in tone and content to Psalm 79.

Lament

In English, a lament is a mourning song, such as David sang when he heard of the deaths of Saul and Jonathan (2 Sam. 1.17) or the famous 'Flowers of the Forest', which laments the fallen Scots dead at Flodden in 1513. About a third of the psalms are usually put in the lament category but none of them is a mourning song in this sense. Some express individual pain and suffering, but none voice the grief and loss of personal bereavement. Others express the nation's grief at invasion, defeat and calamity, exactly as Lamentations does over the fall of Jerusalem in 586 BC. In Psalms study the technical term 'lament' refers to a style of urgent prayer to God which often accuses God of neglect and almost invariably demands God's help in trouble.[1]

2. In it the psalmist voices an urgent plea to God to act to save his Temple and his people from attack.

3. The psalm divides into three parts, each of which addresses God directly. Verses 1–11 focus on the acute suffering of his people and ask pointed questions about it, beginning with one that uses the 'shepherd' metaphor: why has the shepherd deserted his flock? Verses 12–19 remind God of his power and ask why he is not using that power now. Verses 18–23 complete the appeal for him to act.

4. The NRSV footnotes indicate three translation difficulties. In verses 5 and 9b the footnote says that the Hebrew is 'obscure', but all the recent translations opt for similar readings. The third is in verse 14b where REB has a dramatically different translation in which the carcase of Leviathan, the dead sea monster, becomes food for 'sharks'. The other modern translations say that it feeds desert animals. Alter has 'desert folk' and the footnote in NJPS offers 'seafaring men'. (See the extended comment at the end of Chapter 5.)

5. The title: tradition regards Asaph as the original head of the Temple singers appointed by David (1 Chron. 6.39; 16.5; Ezra 2.40). 'Of Asaph' occurs in the title of 12 psalms and it probably indicates that they 'originate from this continuing guild of temple musicians' (Lucas, 2003, p. 21). The meaning of 'maskil' is unknown.

Verses 1–2 take us to the heart of the dynamics of lament. The acutely felt problem is that YHWH seems to have forgotten his covenant commitment. 'Covenants' in the ancient Near East were agreements or contracts ranging from marriage to trade agreements and international treaties. These agreements might be between two equal parties, like the kings Solomon of Israel and Hiram of Tyre (1 Kings 5.12), or they might be between two unequal ones, like gods and people. In some covenants there might be few, if any, conditions and the covenant might look like an unconditional promise; in others the list of terms and conditions might be long. The 'covenant' framework is seen here in the terms 'congregation' and 'redeemed' and the particular covenant in mind is the Sinai one. God had led the Israelites out of Egypt and in the covenant on Mount Sinai he had committed himself to them and they to him in a unique way. But, shouts this lament, why hasn't God kept his side of this agreement? He had 'acquired' Israel on that holy mountain years before, but what is happening on another holy mountain now calls that into question. Mount Zion, the Temple mount in Jerusalem, is God's special place. It is the place where he 'dwells', the place that symbolizes his power, and where he is experienced in worship. But not any more!

Verses 3–11 give a graphic description of devastation in the Temple. The usual suggestion is that this refers to the destruction of the Temple by the Babyloni-ans in 586 BC (for example Alter (2007), A. A. Anderson (1972, vol. 2), Broyles (1999), Curtis, Eaton (2003), Hossfeld and Zenger, Limburg (2000), and Tate). On this count the serious lack of prophets mentioned in verse 9 would indicate a possible time of writing a few years after that event when Jeremiah and Ezek-iel were no longer on the scene. Other suggestions are that it reflects the havoc in the Temple caused by Antiochus Epiphanes in 167 BC, or on an otherwise unknown occasion, or that this psalm is the libretto of a cultic drama performed regularly or occasionally with no actual historical reference at all.

Verses 12–17 work with a second powerful theological theme. Verses 1–11 challenge the Covenant God who brought Israel out of Egypt but who now is nowhere in sight. Verses 12–17, which might be spoken by another voice – did you notice that a first person singular voice has now appeared? – address God in a different way. Angry challenge is replaced by insistent reminder, reminding God that he is the King of Creation, using images derived from an old crea-tion story that Israel adapted from a widespread ancient Near Eastern picture of creation as the outcome of a battle between the gods and the monsters of watery chaos. In the Israelite version, before the earth was formed there was God and his great enemy, a sea monster with various names, including Rahab and Leviathan, the monster of chaos and evil. They had fought. God had won. So God made the heavens and the earth: life triumphed over death, order over chaos, good over evil. This image of the defeat of watery chaos lent itself to reuse with reference to the Exodus (for example in Isa. 51.9–11) and such is the rich potential of image and metaphor that exodus motifs can be read here too. In the middle of this psalm, which is lamenting the destruction of the Temple and what seems to be God's helplessness or reluctance to do anything about it, the psalmist remembers his power. God is the King of Creation who has defeated his enemies before and who can be expected to do it again.

The four creation 'pictures' in the Old Testament

Contrary to much popular misunderstanding there are neither two, nor one, but four creation 'pictures', 'parables' or threads in the Old Testament:

1 *Designer World*: Genesis 1.1—2.4a. This, the so-called 'P' account, is the majestic and familiar picture in which God speaks creation into being in an ordered seven-day plan.
2 *Gardeners' World*: Genesis 2.4b—3.24. This equally familiar, horticultural, picture focuses on the ambiguities and alienations of life in the real world.
3 *Chaoskampf* ('Conflict/War with Chaos'): Psalms 74.12–17; 89.5–18; and Isaiah 51.9–11 (see also Job 7.12; 26.12; 38.8–11). Here are snippets of that older and wider ancient Near Eastern creation myth of the King of Creation's battle with the Chaos Monster.
4 *Wisdom's Playground*: Proverbs 8.22–31 and Job 28.20–28 (see also Job 38—41). This picture shows the role of 'Wisdom' in creation, and includes careful observation of the realities of nature and human experience.

To do

You have been asked to read Genesis 1.1—2.4 in your church or synagogue next Sunday or Sabbath. You are expected to provide a very brief introduction to the reading. So how would you introduce this reading?[2]

All these feature in one way or another in the creation hymn, Psalm 104. These creation threads can also be seen elsewhere in the Old Testament:

- in the Wisdom literature generally. Note the reference to 'Creator' in Ecclesiastes 12.1.
- in Isaiah of Babylon, especially Isaiah 40.12–26 and the word 'Creator' at 40.28 and 43.15.

> • in Psalms, for example Psalms 8, 19, 24, 29, 33, 93, 95, 96, 98, 136
>   and 148.
> • in the ancient hymn quoted by Amos in 4.13; 5.8–9; 9.5–6.

In verses 18–23 the psalm ends as it began, by reminding God, this time by name, of his covenant obligations in the hope that this reminder will shame him into action. Note the designation of God's people as the 'poor and needy', a frequent designation in Psalms (which is where Matthew gets his 'poor in spirit' from in the first of the Beatitudes at Matt. 5.3).

6. Psalm 74 voices the key theological question of the lament – where is God when his people are in distress? It also provides examples of many of the key features of the vocabulary and grammar of the sub-genre:

- Urgent, even accusatory, questions are addressed directly to God, for example 'Why?' in verses 1 and 11 (only once in the Hebrew in each case) and 'How long?' in verse 10 (compare also verse 9b).
- Imperative verbs tell God to 'remember!' (verses 2 – only once in the Hebrew – 18 and 22) and instruct him 'Do not forget!' (verses 19 and 23).
- Other verbs tell God the specific actions that must be taken, for example 'Come and see' (verse 3), 'Save your people' (verse 19), 'Honour your covenant' (verse 20), 'Do not let the downtrodden be shamed' (verse 21), 'Do something' (verse 22).
- The people's distress is painted in vivid colours (verses 3–9).
- Second-person possessive pronouns are used to identify the suffering people or devastated buildings as belonging to God. They are, for example, 'the sheep of your pasture' (verse 1), 'your congregation' (verse 2), 'your holy place' (verse 4), 'your sanctuary' (verse 7), 'the dwelling place of your name' (verse 7), 'your dove' (verse 19), 'your poor' (verse 19).[3]
- God is reminded in direct address that his reputation is at stake when his people suffer and that he is being insulted by his enemies in this process (verses 10, 18, 22). See also the 'your foes/enemies' phrases in verses 4 and 23a and b.
- Appeal is made to God's past deeds (verses 2, 12–17, 20).
- God is blamed for allowing the enemy to hurt his people (verses 1 and 11).

Voicing dissonance

It is not easy for twenty-first-century westerners to imagine life in ancient Israel, but it is none the less probably true to say that the wars, famines, brutality, poverty, genocide, terror and sheer slow grinding misery that make up life for so much of the world's population today was a reality for many people in many places in the ancient Near East then. Likewise, it is also true to say that the crises, bereavements, illnesses, anxieties and traumas that hit us all from time to time now, also hit people from time to time then. Equally, however, there would have been the good times, the shalom times (see Chapter 3). The shalom vision of how things ought to be, and indeed of how sometimes things actually were, forms the background to the phenomenon of 'lament'. At the heart of lamentation is the experience of dissonance, that things are not as they ought to be. The world is not as it ought to be. Society is not as it ought to be. Human life is not as it ought to be. Laments shout that 'It shouldn't be like this!' This powerful feature of ancient Israel's spirituality and worship arises out of the experience of dissonance, and that experience has two components. One is the hurt and pain that is experienced when things are not as they ought to be. The second is theological, the confusion and anger directed at God's failure to put this right and his perceived absence when he is needed most.[4] This is felt so strongly because fundamental to the Old Testament is the conviction that YHWH is an active and powerful God of blessing who intends shalom for his people and his creation.

The Old Testament accepts that it is a fact of life that shalom can be and is easily and often destroyed. It can be damaged by

- the weakness and failure, individually or corporately, of God's chosen people;
- the sin, wickedness and evil-doing, individually or corporately, of God's chosen people;
- the action of foreign enemies and their gods;
- evil spirits or lesser divinities;
- the evil power of resurgent chaos; and
- Israel's own God in punishment, testing or caprice.

We met Westermann's important *Praise and Lament in the Psalms* in Chapter 2.[5] At the beginning of his discussion of lament, Westermann points out that biblical 'laments of distress', such as we find in psalms and in the 'laments of Moses, Samson, Elijah, Jeremiah and Job', are quite different from the common ancient Near Eastern 'laments for the dead' (Westermann, pp. 167–8). These complaints, which are central to Psalms, involve three subjects: God, the one who laments, and the 'enemy'. So each lament has a 'history', it arises in and out of a situation (Westermann, 1981, p. 170). As such, laments work on the assumption that bad things are happening to good people. They are written, said, sung or used by people who, quite properly, think that they are innocent victims. They are not psalms of 'confession'. There are penitential psalms in Psalms (see Chapter 5), but 'confession' is quite a different sub-genre to 'lament'. Laments are sung by 'the righteous' who are suffering because of 'the wicked'. Those two terms are not employed in Psalm 74, but this is a crucial distinction to grasp in Psalms.

The 'righteous' and the 'wicked'

Christians are used to thinking of themselves as 'sinners'. Almost every act of worship in a Christian church requires the congregation to confess their sins in the early minutes of the service. We are not encouraged to think of ourselves as 'righteous' and we tend to associate the word 'righteous' with the phrase 'self-righteous'. Our role model in the parable of the Pharisee and the tax collector is the tax collector who knew he was a 'sinner' and not the Pharisee who knew he was 'righteous' (Luke 18.9–11). This puts Christians in a difficult position when reading psalms, because in Psalms the terms 'the righteous' and 'the wicked' or 'sinners' have quite different connotations. The congregation in Temple or synagogue would have been horrified to have been called 'sinners' and would have expected, without any hint of self-righteousness or pretence, to have been thought of as 'the righteous'. For Psalms and the Old Testament, 'the wicked' are that minority, albeit often a powerful one, who by intent and purpose ignore Torah. By contrast, 'the righteous' are those who try to live by Torah, as God intended all his people should and could. They are not super-holy nor even particularly good, and they are certainly not immune to mistakes, failings and 'committing sin', but when they do wrong and lapse from faithful living, Torah makes provision for restoring them. In other words, to be 'righteous' is the default position of God's ordinary people in the Old Testament, and to be among the 'wicked' is to make the lifestyle choice of consciously and deliberately denying Torah and acting against it and God.

The Old Testament recognizes that shalom may be restored in these cases, respectively, by

- the expression of repentance and the receipt of forgiveness in the liturgies of sacrifice for sin plus appropriate restitution;
- the punishment and extermination of those doing evil or, possibly, by their expression of repentance;
- God fighting back on behalf of his people;
- God demonstrating his power over the spirit world and the lesser gods;
- God defeating resurgent chaos; and
- God's decision that sufficient punishment has been inflicted or testing done, possibly in response to his people's pleas for mercy.

It was a fact of Israelite life, however, that shalom was not always restored and it is at that point that dissonance is experienced at its most acute. The theology of lamentation in the psalms is built on the conviction that YHWH is a God who acts, saves and blesses, restores and puts right; and that when that does not happen he can be and should be called to account. As Abraham argued with God over Sodom – 'Shall not the judge of all the earth do justice?' (Gen. 18.25) – so, even more strongly at times, did Abraham's descendants. This experience of dissonance, the key feature in Walter Brueggemann's 'psalms of disorientation', leads straight into the question of theodicy.

Theodicy

'Theodicy' – from the Greek words *thēos* (God) and *dikē* (justice/rightness) – is the shorthand term for the discussion of 'the problem of evil'. Can the idea that 'God is good' be reconciled with the obvious facts of suffering and evil? How is the world as it is, given that God is its good creator? If God is supreme, good and 'in control', why is there pain, suffering and evil?

There are a number of 'theodicies' in the Old Testament, but it is probably fair to say that lamentation is the one that best characterizes the Old Testament approach as a whole. Not only is lament found in the psalms of lament, but it is also the style and theme of Habakkuk, Lamentations and Job. It is equally clear from any reading of Job that the Old Testament puts forward no conclusive and final answer to this universal question. The psalms of lament, however, insist on sharply raising the issue, and directing the questions straight at God, as we saw in Psalm 74. Robert Davidson's *The Courage to Doubt* is a classic on the Old Testament's approach to dissonance. He does not use the term much if at all, but the book faces squarely up to the experience as we have named it. Writing of Psalm 74 he says:

> It is important to grasp the tensions within this psalm: the tension between what the past affirms to be true and what the present seems to deny; the tension between believing that the key to God's nature is to be found in the idea of love and facing a situation in which there are no evident signs of such love. If you have been brought up to affirm that God is a powerful, active, living God and live through an experience which seems to speak only of the triumph of ruthless and arrogant evil, how do you explain it? Is God asleep?
>
> Such community laments . . . are never content merely to note the meaninglessness of the present crisis, nor do they show any passive acceptance of it. They are characterized by protest and they have nowhere to take their protest except to God. The harsh reality of life has forced the community to ask probing questions about its faith – and to these questions there are not immediate or easy answers. (Davidson, 1983, pp. 6–8).[6]

The psalms of lament do not react to dissonance with a resigned, 'The LORD gave and the LORD has taken away, blessed be the name of the LORD' (Job 1.21), if indeed that verse is to be read in a resigned and accepting kind of way, as it traditionally has been in Christian circles. It sounds rather different if you read it as a piece of sharp sarcasm! They respond to dissonance with pointed questions directed at God.

To do

Can you think of any Christian hymns or worship songs that are 'laments' or in any way equivalent to these psalms of lament?[7]

There is, however, another kind of reaction in the laments which we find particularly difficult. Psalm 74 demands that God should take vengeance on his enemy and the enemy of his Chosen People, though it does not go into detail. Other laments are not so reticent. The sharpest example is Psalm 137.9, 'Happy shall they be who take your little ones and dash them against the rock!' This lament almost certainly had its origin in response to real crisis and trauma, in the destruction of Jerusalem in 586 BC and the exiling of Judah's leading citizens to Babylon. Given the horror of that, the feelings this psalm vents about the Babylonians and their Edomite allies are at the very least understandable. This cursing psalm, however, and others like it (sometimes called 'imprecatory psalms' in older textbooks) is not simply a historical text, of its time and place, understandable in its original context and possibly interesting as an ancient text from a long dead culture. Its place in the Jewish and Christian Scriptures also makes it a contemporary text, and one that carries the approval of those faiths as part of their 'Holy Scripture' read in synagogue and church and used in private prayer. Should you be unfortunate enough, you could even find yourself surrounded by people saying 'Thanks be to God' after someone had concluded the reading of this psalm in church with the words, 'This is the Word of the Lord'.

One response to verses of this kind is simply to reject them, to censor them as Holladay puts it (1993, ch. 16), to be upfront about doing this and to say that Psalm 137.9 and verses like it are absolutely dreadful and should be edited out of any edition of Psalms for public use. So out also would go Psalm 58.6–8, which Hunter says takes some beating for 'sheer imaginative nastiness' (Hunter, 2008, p. 6). This response was heard in some Parochial Church Councils in the early 1980s, when the Church of England produced its Alternative Service Book, which put psalm verses of this kind in square brackets and let local churches decide whether they would say or sing such verses. Other versions of psalms for use in worship give congregations no choice and simply edit out such offensive verses that wish real vengeance, violence and viciousness on equally real people. For many readers these kinds of verses render the psalms in which they are found, or Psalms itself, or even the whole Old Testament, unusable, dangerous and best avoided. Officially, however, that option is not open to churches or synagogues.

Enemy and enemies in Psalms

'Enemies' appear frequently in the psalms. Sometimes they are the psalmist's enemies, sometimes God's and sometimes both. Occasionally God is the enemy behind the enemies (Pss 44.9–16; 89.38–45; 106.40–42). Psalms of praise celebrate their defeat. Laments plead for God's help against them as they attack, oppress and destroy, hate, scorn and taunt. In some psalms these 'enemies' are foreign nations that have attacked or threatened Israel or its king (Pss 60.10; 74.3–8; 83.2–8). In others they are the 'wicked', 'evil-doers', 'sinners' or 'fools', the criminal and anti-social elements in Israel who don't observe the covenant and oppress and exploit those who do (Pss 3.1; 6.10; 7.1), scorning God in the process (Pss 74.18; 89.49–51; 139.19–22). In others they are malicious people telling lies against and falsely accusing the psalmist in court (Pss 27.12; 69.4; 127.5) or just rather nasty neighbours (Pss 13.2; 40.4–7; 102.8). They are Leviathan (Ps. 74.14) and Rahab (Ps. 89.10), the old forces of chaos, once defeated, but always ready to take on new guises and inflict new damage. In Ps. 18 the identity of the enemies whose defeat it celebrates mutates. In verses 3–4 and 16–17a they are the forces of chaos and death: but verse 17b begins to personalize them as those who 'hate' the psalmist and who are routed in battle by him (verses 37–42). Finally in verses 47–48 they are defeated nations. This gives a clue to the use of the term. 'Enemy' is a metaphor, a versatile and lively image. It may be that real people, forces or situations were intended by the term when some of the psalms were composed, but the term has become a trope, a figure of speech, part of the stock in trade of the psalmists when they want to talk about 'dissonance'.

There are, sad to say, those who see no problem in such verses at all in either historical or contemporary terms, though they are probably unlikely to be reading this book. Those who see the problem but wish to retain these verses use, broadly speaking, two different but often intertwining and mutually reinforcing approaches:

1 'Psychological' approaches

'Psychological' approaches begin by accepting that the feelings these verses express are real, and that real people have them, including people of faith today. When people are threatened, hurt, humiliated or distressed, particularly in a situation of powerlessness, they can and do respond with anger. At the very least, the argument runs, there is a human honesty about these sharp verses. In addition, as C. S. Lewis suggested in *Reflections on the Psalms*, letting that feeling out is healthier than keeping it in and verbalizing your violence is better than actualizing it (Lewis, pp. 23–33, as Hunter, 2008, p. 116). And any psychologist will confirm that verbalizing our anger is better than denying that we feel it. Denying what we feel will do us no good. Speaking what we feel may be healing. H. N. Wallace sums it up like this:

> If we are honest with ourselves, there are times when we feel angry, threat-ened, vulnerable, or anxious, and we might want to utter words as dark as in these psalms … In such situations the psalms offer us words to express our feelings. We may feel as though our prayers are not the place for such words or feelings. But the psalms suggest otherwise … Prayer is the place where those experiences are voiced … in conversation with God … about our 'enemies' and our feelings of oppression, anxiety, anger and even hatred. (Wallace, p. 46)

2 'Justice' approaches

David Firth's discussion in *Surrendering Retribution* focuses on the laments as a whole rather than the specific cursing psalms and argues that the laments 'reject all forms of human violence' and teach that 'only the violence that may be enacted by Yahweh is acceptable' (p. 3). He suggests, therefore, that the laments recognize that the desire for vengeance is real, and deal with it by providing a mechanism whereby this desire is handed over to YHWH in the knowledge that vengeance is indeed his and that he will definitely repay (Rom. 12.19).

Walter Brueggemann is probably the best-known advocate of justice approaches, however. He starts from the fact that laments deal with real life, do so honestly, and do so in dialogue with God. He acknowledges that voicing lament is therapeutic, both for individuals and communities, in that it enables them to move 'from hurt to joy, from death to life' (W. Brueggemann, 1995, ch. 3). It does this, not least, by giving a form, in prayer and liturgy, for 'grief' (W. Brueggemann, 1995, ch. 4). He then argues that if we take away the lament, faith becomes skewed into a docile submissiveness which will include submission to 'the politico-economic monopoly of the status quo' as well as submission to God (W. Brueggemann, 1995, p. 102):

> In the absence of lament, we may be engaged in uncritical history-stifling praise. Both *psychological inauthenticity* and *social immobility* may be derived from the loss of these texts. If we care about authenticity and justice, the recovery of these texts is urgent. (W. Brueggemann, 1995, p. 111 – original italics)

These vengeful texts keep real justice for real people in the real world on the agenda, and do so in the name of God!

Erich Zenger shares Brueggemann's concern for social justice in the real world but takes in some ways an even more robust approach to these texts. He acknowledges that there is a major discussion about 'enemy images' in anthropology and social analysis (Zenger, p. viii) and that the 'psalms of enmity' arise out of a basic model of human life as one of 'daily, ongoing, struggle' (Zenger, p. 9) which produces 'much shrieking for violence and the hope that there is a God of retaliation, vengeance and destruction' (Zenger, p. 11). For him these psalms speak of God's vengeance, which is thoroughly deserved. In the real world full of violence, terror, injustice and anguish those who perpetrate such things need to know that there is an accounting by the God of justice (Zenger, p. 69). This is not vigilante vengeance or retribution, but the restoration of true law and order for the sake of the victims of injustice. The cry for vengeance in these psalms is a cry for justice, and it will not go unheard. Victims need to hear that and take heart! Oppressors need to hear it and stop!

Other psalms that voice dissonance

'Lament' is the most distinctive of the psalm 'types' and in Gunkel's list about 40 psalms are listed as 'laments'. My list of psalms that voice dissonance includes most of them. In addition to Psalm 74 there are Psalms 6, 7, 10, 11, 12, 13, 17, 20, 22, 28, 31, 35, 42, 43, 44, 54, 55, 57, 59, 60, 64, 69, 70, 71, 79, 80, 83, 86, 88, 102, 109, 120, 123, 137, 140, 142 and 143.

> **To do**
>
> You worship in a synagogue or church that expects everyone to get involved, and you find yourself on the Worship Committee. The committee has been given the task of editing the version of Psalms to be used in the services. There is a heated debate about whether Psalm 137 should be included. The committee chair turns to you and asks what you think. What do you say?

Theodicy in the Old Testament: a reflection[8]

Let me introduce you to three well-known Bible characters – Shadrach, Meshach and Abednego – and tell you a bit more about each of them than you already know, which is that they were thrown into the burning, fiery furnace and lived to tell the tale (Dan. 3.8–30).

Shadrach, or to give him his full name, Shadrach ben Levi of Jerusalem, was, as his name suggests, a Levite. He was a member of the Temple staff in Jerusalem and worked in the Theology School there as Professor of Systematic Theology. He had immersed himself from boyhood in study of the Torah, and in order to obtain that post he had gladly and wholeheartedly given his assent to the 613 Articles after being vetted for his Absolute Orthodoxy of Life and Faith. Shadrach ben Levi of Jerusalem was kosher indeed. Old Testament scholars of the third Christian millennium would call him a 'Yahwist' or a 'Deuteronomist', meaning that he represented the orthodox, official line in the Jewish thought of his day, and that he was one of those members of the Deuteronomic school who were largely responsible for editing and shaping the Hebrew Bible, deciding what was in and what was out. He was very proud of the fact that among his own teachers were the three heroes who had gone to support and correct that old saint, Job, when he had temporarily gone off the rails and started to say all those heretical things that he had. Shadrach still shuddered at the thought. Thank goodness for those three great old theologians, he thought, Eliphaz the Temanite, Bildad the Shuhite (the smallest man in the Bible) and Zophar the Naamathite who had put Job right (Job 4.7–9; 8.1–7; 11.6b). It is quite straightforward, Shadrach mused: 'the soul that sinneth, it shall die'. Righteousness is rewarded, sin is punished. Moral evil is a lifestyle choice and it has real consequences; no one suffers without a cause, and that cause is their sin, their moral choice to do evil, or the sin and choice of their family or their community. That is all that needs to be said. If anyone suffers, they should ask themselves what they have done to deserve it, and when they find the answer, repent of that sin and be healed. God has created us as moral, responsible, beings (Gen. 1.26f.) and given us the gift of free will and choice (Deut. 30.11–20), and so suffering is retribution, deserved, and if that is recognized it can even be redemptive. There is no 'problem of suffering' or of moral evil, insisted Shadrach, suffering is the result of sin, moral evil, and if people choose to sin, for they have the choice, then they must bear the consequences (Gen. 3.14–19; Deut. 30.15–20; the cycles in Judges e.g. 3.7–11; Ps. 37; Isa. 1.1–8; Lam. 1.4–5).

Meshach, or to give him his full name, Meshach ben Solomon the Wise, was a very different kind of person, urbane, travelled, cultured. He had retired to the new suburbs to the north of the Temple after a lifetime as a diplomat, serving his nation in numerous foreign embassies and heading various diplomatic missions before ending up as Ambassador to the Court of Pharaoh. He had enjoyed the life, and still enjoyed entertaining his foreign friends who hadn't yet retired when they found themselves in Judah's capital. He liked to keep his language skills alive, and, to be frank, the wine they brought was usually better than the local and the conversation almost always was. His fellow Jews were, though he sometimes felt disloyal for thinking it, really a bit parochial. He would sometimes, reading the latest book review from Babylon, look back over his life and reflect – for the wise are much given to theological reflection – that his schooling in the Wisdom Academy had opened up all kinds of avenues for him. It had been good of Uncle Job to give him that scholarship, though he was glad that few knew that Job was his uncle, that would be an embarrassment too far. He could never make out, no matter how much he thought about it, quite what had happened to Uncle Job's otherwise fine mind: how could such a learned and wise man deny or forget all that basic knowledge, that suffering is a result of folly, of choices wrongly made, of false paths unwisely followed? That moral evil is in essence human wrong choice. How could he deny that most ancient of Wisdom's tenets that Wisdom leads to life, to integration and wholeness, achievement and success, but that Folly leads to death, to ruin and disintegration, to poverty and failure? Sad, he thought, but that's what Uncle

Job had so nearly forgotten. There is no 'problem of suffering' or of moral evil, reflected Meshach, suffering is the result of folly, and if people choose the way of folly rather than the way of wisdom, they will reap the inevitable reward of their foolish decision, their evil morality, though of course he preferred not to use such a crude term as 'evil', moral or otherwise, himself (Ps. 1; Prov. 1.20–33; 5.1–6; 8:32–36; 10.27).

Abednego ben Enoch, to give him his full name, was odd company for the other two to keep. He was from a long line of rebels and prophets. He saw the sufferings and misfortunes of Israel's poor as the result of the wickedness of Israel's rich, their acute and vicious moral evil, and he had little time for the Temple and its official religion and even less for the so-called Wise Men who had sold their souls to international culture and Global Wisdom, as they called it. No, he liked the look of that new group hoping to set themselves up as Alternative Israel if they could get hold of that land by the Dead Sea. Then he would join the struggle to set Israel free, wage the War of the Children of Light against the Sons of Darkness; and it wouldn't just be a spiritual warfare either, though it was that too. There were times when he felt the demons gathering even round his own soul, and they were getting more powerful all the time: the devil and his angels playing havoc with people's lives, causing famines, bringing epidemics and encouraging enemy attacks on villages and towns, bringing illness, suffering and death to men and women. The old dragon of chaos and evil was not dead; it and its cohort spirits still brought suffering and destruction wherever they could. Victims, that's what these poor suffering souls were, he would mutter to himself when the other two would blame them for their own blindness or leprosy or hunger, sneering at their sin or folly. They were victims of the forces of evil, the principalities and dark powers in the heavenly places. That's what moral evil was, being gripped by the evil forces in the heavenly places. Look at old Job, he would say to the other two, look what happened to him, attacked by Satan, suffering that devil's onslaught just because he was such a good and upright man! He couldn't understand Shadrach, especially, who never seemed to have asked himself the question why the Temple's own psalmists cried out in such agonized urgency to God to do something, to defend them, to rescue them from their enemies spiritual and earthly. Life was a battle, suffering was enemy action, Evil's doing! What other explanation could there possibly be, thought Abednego (Isa. 51.4–23; Ezek. 34.1–6; Dan. 7.1–14; Joel 2.26–33, but especially in non-canonical texts and clearly accessible in Rev. 12.7–17).

None of these three had met Reuben the Scribe, who was even then at work on his theological biography of Job. It would have been a lively meeting. Shadrach the Levite would have accused him of being outrageously hard on the three friends, who were only doing their best to defend orthodox Yahwism. Meshach the Wise would have argued that it was completely unfair of him to have sensationalized a sad episode in the life of such an otherwise wise and upright man as Job. Abednego, from his apocalyptic stance, would have damned him for portraying the Satan so weakly – he wasn't one of the sons of God, he was the Arch-Enemy himself. And they would all have agreed that God doesn't gamble with human lives just to win a bet (Job 1.8–12). They would have debated among themselves and with Reuben about whether or not God tested people through suffering, and Abednego especially would resist the idea that God really did send these things to try us. He knew all about the hard trials of faith and the sufferings of the righteous; had not two of his brothers been among the Maccabean martyrs? And he knew, too, how such trials could refine discipleship and faithfulness, but that was different; God had not sent that suffering, that was the Enemy's work from start to finish. But, to be fair, had Reuben himself realized how much pastoral damage that little literary touch would do, he would never have put it in. He was, after all, only trying to open up a much bigger discussion, about the suffering of the righteous, the problem of evil and the presence or absence of God in his world. He knew full well what Shadrach, Meshach and Abednego all stood for, and that there was some truth in what each of them believed, but he also knew that none of them had a final explanation. That's what his hero Job would argue and argue and then come to accept, that there was no final explanation to the problems of moral evil and suffering. Or at least there was no final answer other than the one he had learned from the old prophet Habakkuk, who had just asked that pointed question over and over again, 'Why do the wicked prosper and the righteous suffer? O Lord, why?' (Hab. 1.1–3; 2.1). He'd got an answer, actually, but not the one he wanted; it was all about hanging in there, in confidence and the sure and certain hope, that the last word lay with Israel's God and not with evil, suffering and death (Hab. 2.2–3; 3.16–19; Job 38.1—42.5). What else could you say, thought Reuben? Believing in heaven helps; he agreed with those new-fangled Pharisees to that extent at least and had slipped a hint about that into his book (Job 19.23–27), and of course some suffering was sometimes inevitable in fighting for a good cause, that was obvious too, especially the way the world is. Think of all those prophets who had suffered and died, not least Jeremiah, though he would have got more sympathy if he hadn't been such a whinger, Reuben thought (Jer. 15.10–18; 17.9–18; 18.18–23; 20.7–18). And he knew too that that kind of suffering especially could bring blessings to others, like that anonymous prophet they called the 'Suffering Servant' (Isa. 42.1–4; 49.1–6; 50.4–9; 52.13—53.12): but all that was different, that was suffering voluntarily embraced in opposition to evil. There was something else, of course, but he concluded he couldn't write that into his biography: that was the question that had bugged him for years, why couldn't the theologians just say that suffering was random, chance, accidental, that 'stuff just happens'? No, that was too big to tackle. Perhaps he'd better end his book with a happy ending after all? It would be neat and tidy and it's what people liked and expected, even needed (Job 42.7–17).

Oh, you want to know what happened to Shadrach, Meshach and Abednego? Well, after they got pulled out of the burning, fiery furnace they fell to discussing this question of suffering again. They still couldn't agree. But they remembered what they had said to Nebuchadnezzar when he gave them the opportunity to escape the flames by denying their God and worshipping his. They chuckled at how cussed they must have sounded: 'Even if our God does not deliver us, we are staying with him and we aren't going to worship yours! So there!' (Dan. 3.16–18). But then, they concluded in strangely sombre tones, when you think about it, that is perhaps the last word to be said about this whole question of suffering after all. Hadn't Habakkuk said as much?

To do

Has anything in this chapter excited you? What? Why? Has anything in it challenged you? What? How? Has anything in it worried you? What? Why? Has anything in it influenced the way you will read the Old Testament in future?

Suggestions for further reading

Lament

*Broyles, C. C. (2008), 'Lament: Psalms of', in *DOTWPW*, pp. 384–99.

Broyles, C. C. (1988), *The Conflict of Faith and Experience in the Psalms*, Sheffield: JSOT Press.

Brueggemann, W. (1995), *The Psalms and the Life of Faith*, ed. Miller, P. D., Minneapolis MN: Fortress Press, part 1.

Johnston, P. S. (2005), 'The Psalms and Distress' in Johnston and Firth, pp. 63–84.

*Miller, P. D. (1986), *Interpreting the Psalms*, Philadelphia: Fortress Press, ch. 4.

Westermann, C. (1981), *Praise and Lament in the Psalms*, Edinburgh: T&T Clark, book 2.

Theodicy

Brueggemann, W. (2002), *The Spirituality of the Psalms*, pp. 58–74, which is a revision of *The Message of the Psalms*, pp. 168–176.

Crenshaw, J. L. (2005), *Defending God: Biblical Responses to the Problem of Evil*, Oxford: Oxford University Press.

*Davidson, R. (1983), *The Courage to Doubt*, London: SCM Press.

Davies, J. (2008), 'Theodicy', in *DOTWPW*, pp. 808–17.

*Kushner, H. S. (2002), *When Bad Things Happen to Good People*, new edn, London: Pan.

Phillips, A. (2005), *Standing up to God*, London: SPCK.

*Yancey, P. (1997) *Where is God When it Hurts?* Grand Rapids MI: Zondervan.

Vengeance

*Bullock, C. N. (2001), *Encountering the Book of Psalms*, Grand Rapids MI: Baker Academic, pp. 227–38.

Brueggemann, W. (1986), 'The Costly Loss of Lament', in *JSOT* 36, pp. 57–71, reprinted in Brueggeman, *The Psalms and the Life of Faith*, pp. 98–111.

Firth, D. G. (2005), *Surrendering Retribution in the Psalms*, Milton Keynes: Paternoster Press.

*Lewis, C. S. (1961), *Reflections on the Psalms*, London: Collins Fontana, ch. 3.

Strawn, B. A. (2008), 'Imprecation', in *DOTWPW*, pp. 314–20.

*Wallace, H. N. (2005), *Words to God, Word from God*, Aldershot: Ashgate, pp. 36–49.

Zenger, E. (1996), *A God of Vengeance? Understanding the Psalms of Divine Wrath*, Louisville KY: Westminster John Knox Press.

5

Voicing Penitence

What is this chapter about?

Dissonance has many facets and causes, but the default position in Psalms is that the psalmists and their congregations ('the righteous') are its innocent victims. There was provision in ancient Israel's liturgies, however, for those occasions when 'the righteous' failed in one way or another, and in this chapter we will note the main element of that liturgical provision (the 'sacrifices for sin') and look at those psalms that voice penitence. The final comment will be on issues in translating psalms.

How is it organized?

- The psalm for exegesis is Psalm 51.
- In 'Voicing penitence' we look at failure, penitence and sacrifice.
- The extended comment is on translating the psalms.
- There are boxes on the names for God used in the Old Testament and 'Deuteronomic orthodoxy'.
- There are a number of 'To do' boxes.
- The chapter ends with suggestions for further reading on sacrifice, sin, worship in ancient Israel, the names for God and translation issues.

What should I be able to do by the end of it?

- Understand that the 'penitential psalms' are not laments and why.
- Compare different approaches to human failure in Psalms.
- Identify the contours of 'Deuteronomic orthodoxy'.
- Appreciate the key theological features of sacrifice.
- Distinguish between the different names for God in the Old Testament.

Psalm 51

To do

Make your exegesis notes on Psalm 51.

---

1. Psalm 51 is the best known of the seven 'penitential psalms'.[1] As usual, we know nothing of its author or date of composition. The editor of Psalms, however, puts it on the lips of David 'when the prophet Nathan came to him, after he had gone in to Bathsheba'. For that sordid episode, which began with rape and ended with murder, see 2 Samuel 11.1—12.13.

2. It is a genuinely penitential psalm which voices a direct appeal to a compassionate God for 'mercy' (verse 1). Its 'I' form makes it available for both personal and communal use.

3. The main part of the psalm begins with an appeal for forgiveness and 'cleansing' (verses 1–2) and moves seamlessly through 'confession' (verses 3–5) and repeated appeal (verses 6–12) to vows to live differently if forgiveness is granted (verses 13–17). Verses 18–19 appear to be a later addition in a new and wider context.

4. The psalm opens with three of the major words for God's compassion: the verb 'to have mercy' (ḥānan) and the nouns 'steadfast love' (ḥesed as explained in the exegesis of Ps. 23 in Chapter 3) and 'compassion' (rāḥûm). The translations employ a confusing variety of synonyms for these three, but why NRSV follows its predecessor and uses 'mercy' twice is as unclear as it is unnecessary. Here are clear echoes of the 'core creed' of Exodus 34.6–7, which we consider in Chapter 8.

In a parallelism of six lines that extends over two verses, the three expressions of God's compassion are balanced by three words for the psalmist's wrongdoing: 'transgressions' (*pĕšā îm*), 'iniquity' (*'awōn*) and 'sin' (*ḥēt*). It is common to distinguish between these three synonyms by understanding transgression as rebellion against God, iniquity as going astray and sin as 'missing the mark': but this might be a touch too neat. These suggestions come from considering the derivation and etymology of the Hebrew words, but how much of their derivation and etymology words retain (in any language) in their ordinary usage is a big question.

'Purge me with hyssop' is a metaphor for personal 'cleansing' (literally 'de-sinning') taken from rites such as that for purifying people who have touched dead bodies (Num. 19.14–17), where water is sprinkled on them using a sprig of hyssop.

5. In verses 3–5 the psalmist acknowledges the past, but we should not be misled here. This is urgent and vivid language expressing abhorrence of what he has done. It is the language of remorse rather than repentance (that comes later) and it is dramatically overstated in the way the Bible does. It should not be used to create doctrines of 'original sin' or 'total depravity', for that is making the mistake of taking metaphorical language literally and hardening poetry into prose.

In metaphor piled on metaphor the psalmist pleads for a new start: to be 'washed' (verse 7, picking up from verse 2), made new (verse 10) and 'delivered' (verse 14); for the past to be put behind him (verse 9), to learn better ways (verses 6 and 12) and to 'make a life of praise' (verses 14–15). The pleas climax in verse 17, which unfortunately contains a translation difficulty (see the extended comment at the end of the chapter). All that is necessary to receive God's forgiveness and its renewing and transforming vitality is repentance – 'a broken and contrite heart', which is not about feelings or emotions, crying and despairing, but about admitting that wrong has been done and having a serious intention to turn away from it and set off in a new direction.

Note the lower case initial letters on 'holy spirit' in verse 11 in NRSV but 'Holy Spirit' in NIV, NKJV and TNIV, and 'holy Spirit' in RSV. Hebrew does not have upper- and lower-case forms and so these decisions are editorial ones. Using upper-case forms here (as many do with *rûaḥ*, 'spirit', in Gen. 1.2) is anachronistic, reading back Christian and trinitarian understandings into these older texts which know nothing of such notions.

On the theology and practice of sacrifice (verses 16–17), see the following section of this chapter.

Verse 16 appears to be a condemnation of sacrifice and with it the whole religious system that it represented. Similar statements are found in Isaiah 1.11–15, Amos 5.21–24, Hosea 6.6, Micah 6.6–8 and Psalm 40.6. They may be an attack on Temple worship which an editor found necessary to correct by inserting verses 18–19. Or, more likely, they are part of the condemnation frequently made by prophets against worship that is divorced from committed and faithful living.

The psalm ends oddly. Up to verse 17 it has been an individual penitential psalm but the last two verses go off at a tangent into an appeal for the rebuilding of the walls of Jerusalem. This could simply be bad editing, but it makes the valid point that wrongdoing has consequences that can go beyond the original wrongdoer. In these two last two verses the psalm makes the same point as the Deuteronomic history as a whole, that the catastrophe of the destruction of Jerusalem in 597 and 586 BC can ultimately be explained as a consequence of David's act of rape and murder. That having been faced and acknowledged, it is now possible to offer hope for the future.

6. Psalm 51 is a psalm of repentance and renewal after serious sin and crime. It can be used both by individuals and communities, but it is surely not for everyday use. Indeed, verses 10–12 assume that normally the average Israelite has a clean heart and a right, holy and willing spirit, as we saw in the box in the last chapter.

Names for God in the Old Testament

1 *'ĕlôhîm* is the Hebrew word translated as 'God', 'god' or 'gods' in the Old Testament. It is the plural form of *'ēl*, the usual semitic word for a god and the name of the Canaanite High God, El. Despite its plural form it can be used of a singular god, as it is of Chemosh, the god of Moab in 1 Kings 11.33 and of the God of Israel throughout the Old Testament.

2 Variations on *'ĕlôhîm* include:
el šaddai' (El Shaddai), which is usually translated as 'God Almighty' as in Exodus 6.3;
'el 'elyôn (El Elyon), which is usually translated as 'God Most High'. Often this name just appears as *'elyôn*, 'the Most High' as in Psalm 82.6;

'elohê 'abraham, the God of Abraham (. . . Isaac . . . Jacob etc.);
'elohê sĕbā'ôt, God of Hosts (though NIV and TNIV usually translate this as 'God Almighty') – see below;
'ĕlāh – the Aramaic word for God used in Ezra 5—7 and Daniel 2—6;
'ĕlôah – a form particularly common in Job where it occurs 43 times out of the total of 58 occurrences in the Old Testament.

3 *šaddai'* (Shaddai), 'The Almighty', again particularly common in Job.

4 YHWH – LORD. This is the name which is not to be spoken. It was disclosed to Moses at the Burning Bush with a riddle about its meaning (Exodus 3.13–15) and again in Exodus 6.2–3, although in another tradition it has been used since Genesis 2.4.

5 Variations on YHWH include:
yhwh sĕbā'ôt – LORD of Hosts (but usually 'the LORD Almighty' in NIV and TNIV). The 'Hosts' in the title might be the 'Heavenly Host' of sun, moon and stars and so on – in which case this title is firmly putting them in their place as subordinate to YHWH (they are gods in their own right in some ancient Near Eastern systems). Or they might be the 'Heavenly Host' of angels and archangels and 'all the company of heaven', including the lesser gods of Psalms 82 and 58.1. Or they might be the armies of Israel. The meaning is uncertain. What is not in question, however, is that this ancient title should be reproduced in translation as accurately as possible, even if it means refusing to translate it at all as NJB opts to do. NIV and TNIV are misleading when they translate *'el šaddai'* and *yhwh/'elohê-sĕbā'ôt* in the same way as 'God Almighty'.
yāh – LORD, especially common in Psalms, for example *hallĕlû – yāh.*

6 *'ădônay* – '(my) Lord/lord', a common term of respect (wife for husband, servant for master, subject for king), also sometimes used in address to God, as in Psalm 51.15.

7 *'ĕlôhîm* and YHWH are occasionally used in combination, for example, in the second creation parable in Genesis 2—3, *'ĕlôhîm* YHWH, 'the LORD God'.

8 *'ădônay* and YHWH together is common in Ezekiel but is also found in Isaiah, Jeremiah and Amos and occasionally elsewhere – *'ădônay YHWH* – 'the Lord GOD'.

9 More complex combinations are also found occasionally, for example Amos 9.5 *'ădônay yhwh sĕbā'ôt* – 'the Lord GOD of Hosts' – and Psalm 89.8, *yhwh 'elohê-sĕbā'ôt* – 'the LORD God of Hosts'.

Voicing penitence

'David and Bathsheba' is a sordid story of rape and murder, the opening chapter in a tragedy that lasts for centuries. 'Naboth's vineyard' is another, quite different, murder story.

To do

Read 1 Kings 21.

Naboth's vineyard is next door to King Ahab's palace in Samaria. The king wants to extend the royal gardens. Naboth refuses to give up his ancestral inheritance. Calling her husband a weak fool, Queen Jezebel arranges for Naboth to be accused of blasphemy and treason and has him stoned. Ahab, knowing nothing of his wife's plans until it is all over, takes possession of the vacant vineyard. The issues are injustice, oppression and the rights of the poor in relation to the state. Here too the consequences are more than at first appear. In both stories we see the terrifying power of wickedness to destroy and mar. This failure is more than David's scheming lust or Ahab's greed. It is woven into the fabric of society and life itself, and in one sense David and Ahab are just two more victims. These two stories give specific examples of failure; and failure forms a key part of the story line of the Old Testament as a whole. God creates the world, and it is good. He creates men and women and entrusts them with power and responsibility (Gen. 1). Soon they are estranged from each other, from God and from the natural world (Gen. 2—3). The original shalom is gone. Things get worse and violence spirals (Gen. 4—6). God regrets what he has done, wipes almost everything out and tries to start again, but no sooner has the floodwater subsided than things start going wrong again (Gen. 9—11). This time God takes a different line and decides on a long-term attempt to put matters right through one man and his descendants (Gen. 12). But the sorry story of failure repeats itself in Abraham's descendants: arrogant Joseph and his brothers who try to get rid of him (Gen. 29—50), their numerous descendants freed from Egypt by God who complain against Moses and turn to other gods (Exodus and Numbers), the tribes settling in Canaan and deserting the God who has given them their new land (Joshua and Judges), and then all through the history of the united kingdom and the divided states until first the one and then the other is destroyed and its people exiled (Samuel and Kings). Why? According to the storyteller, it was because the kings 'did what was evil in the sight of the LORD' (for example, 2 Kings 23.37). The long story points out that this is how it was from beginning to end, from creation to exile, a story of failure on the part of those who ought to have known better.

The English word used most in religious circles for this failure is, of course, 'sin', and the list of English words associated with it in a thesaurus includes: wickedness, evil, wrongdoing, transgression, iniquity, error, vice, trespass and offence. Closely related are words like guilt, crime, immorality and impurity. Hebrew has a similarly wide range of terms for this condition, and in the exegesis we noted three of the prominent ones, 'transgression', 'iniquity' and 'sin'. Each language can also make long lists of actions or attitudes it calls 'sins'. A word of caution is needed here, however. At this point Christians are only a step away from quoting Romans 3.23, that 'all have sinned and fall short of the glory of God', and Christian preachers down the ages have been adept at illustrating how badly their hearers have sinned: but as we saw, psalmists do not often consider themselves or their congregations to be 'sinners'. According to the Old Testament, sin, however it is defined, is a real part of the human story; but despite that, the words 'sin' and 'sinner' are not allowed to define the human condition in the Old Testament in the way they have done in much Christian discourse.

In the Old Testament the prophets come nearest to doing that. Whether the canonical prophets are 'announcers of doom' insisting that people will soon reap what they have sown or whether they are offering a last chance to those hearers to 'turn and live', there is a powerful severity about much of their message. Sin is to be punished. This prophetic attitude is seen especially clearly in Amos, despite the 'happy ending' that the editors added, and in the almost identical Psalms 14 and 53. These psalms look as if they are the perfect Old Testament match for Romans 3.23, but that looks less certain if they are read alongside Elijah's despairing, but mistaken, cry in 1 Kings 19.10. The prophetic attitude to failure

- is essentially Deuteronomic and works with a set of opposites: good and evil, life and death, righteousness and sin, blessing and curse. Humanity faces a simple choice (for example, Deut. 30.15–20);
- is strongly negative in tone and depicts human failure, identified particularly in the rich and powerful, in terms of 'evil' (*ra*'), 'wickedness' (*reša*') and 'sin' (*ḥaṭṭā't/ḥēṭ*');
- offers no remedy other than the destruction of 'sinners' and their replacement with the 'righteous'.

'Deuteronomic orthodoxy'

'Deuteronomic orthodoxy' (also called 'Yahwism' or 'Yahwistic orthodoxy') is the term given to the dominant theology in the Old Testament that YHWH alone is to be God in Israel. Those who live by YHWH's teaching are blessed. Those who do not are cursed. It is called 'Deuteronomic' because it is found particularly plainly in Deuteronomy (30.15–20 is especially clear) and it forms the pattern underlying the Deuteronomic History as a whole. The stories in Judges provide good examples of the theory: Israel does 'what is evil in the sight of the LORD', God delivers them into the hands of an enemy, they cry for help, God sends them help, the enemy is defeated and the land 'has rest' for a period, then the cycle begins again (for example Judg. 3.7–11). The formula is simple: righteousness is rewarded and sin is punished. So one psalmist can assert, 'I have been young, and now am old, yet I have never seen the righteous forsaken or their children begging bread' (Ps. 37.25).' As we saw in the last chapter, the psalmist who wrote Ps. 74, the author of Job and the prophet Habakkuk might ask rather sharply where this psalmist had been all his life: but the Deuteronomists were not alone in their view. Using different vocabulary and approaching the question from another angle, orthodox Wisdom made the same observation: wise living leads to prosperity and success, folly to poverty and failure (as in Ps. 1 or Prov. 2.20–22). Shadrach ben Levi of Jerusalem and Meshach ben Solomon the Wise had much in common.[2]

Another model, which we might call the 'pastoral' one, operates alongside this one. It undergirds the liturgical provisions for dealing with human failure in Leviticus and is perhaps seen at its clearest in Psalm 103.8–14. This model

- operates with the image of a parentally forgiving God;
- is much more generous and much less stringent than the prophetic one;
- depicts human failure in terms of 'weakness, frailty and need';
- offers a remedy for failure through various liturgies of confession and absolution.

These two models are, however, not as different as they might look. The pastoral model makes provision for sin to be dealt with provided it is named and acknowledged. There is no remedy for those who sin 'high-handedly' other than the destruction of which the prophets speak (Num. 15.27–31[3]). For those who are prepared to name and so acknowledge their failure, there is both practical and liturgical provision for handling it and restoring the individual to their normal and proper place among the 'righteous'. The practical provision is that offenders make restitution wherever appropriate (Lev. 6.1–5; Num. 5.5–8). The liturgical provision is the sacrifices for sin.

Squeamish modern westerners should not try to imagine the scene in the Temple, especially at a major celebration. It would have been noisy, smelly and gruesome. For this reason alone it is difficult to enter the mindset of ancient Israel and understand the rich and complex theology involved. Add to that the complexities of the sacrificial system itself and of its development, the immense difficulties in reconstructing it from the texts about it, and our own tendencies to read our own presuppositions and assumptions into it all, and the task becomes almost impossible. But there are two simple points that can be grasped: first, that sacrifice was the normal way of worship in the Temple, all Temple worship of whatever kind, for whatever purpose and on whatever occasion was done by sacrifice; second, that the sacrificial system was seen as part of God's gift of the Tabernacle to Moses in the desert and part of his blessing of Torah (Ex.

25—30), it was not a 'human' system designed to influence, persuade, flatter or appease God.

The details of the different sacrifices are not recoverable from the descriptions of sacrifice or the instructions for them given mainly in Leviticus, and the fact that different Bible translations give them different titles makes a complex situation even more confusing. What is important is to recognize that there were different sacrifices, each serving a different purpose. The Sacrifice of Well-being was quite distinct from the Burnt Offering and neither these nor any of their variations had anything to do with the two sacrifices that were specifically designed to deal with sin, the Sin Offering (the *ḥaṭṭā't*, Lev. 4.27–31) and the Guilt Offering (the *'āšām*, Lev. 7.1–10). Whatever the precise differences between those two, they form the Temple's liturgical provision for confession and absolution. In addition, with a national focus and the purpose of 'cleansing' the Temple and nation, there were the rituals that made up *Yom Kippur*, the Day of Atonement (Lev. 16). Atonement, or 'expiation' (REB) is the 'covering up' (the literal sense of the Hebrew verb *kippēr*) of sin, its removal and disarming. The gift of liturgies for that purpose suggests that it is God's will that the scourge or contamination of sin should be removed. The instructions spell out what should be done, but they do not say how these actions bring about forgiveness. What they do say is that the person who does these things is forgiven (Lev. 4.20, 26, 31, 35 etc.), and that through the Day of Atonement services the nation is 'cleansed' from its sin (Lev. 16.30). These liturgies of forgiveness presuppose that the worshippers are 'repentant' (Lev. 26.40–41). So for the people who know that they have done wrong and fallen short of what God expects of them, God provides a liturgy in which to express their repentance, receive forgiveness and be restored to the community of the righteous.

Other psalms that voice penitence

Seven psalms are traditionally designated as the 'penitential psalms' (Pss 6, 32, 38, 51, 102, 130 and 143). Three of those are not in my shorter list of psalms that voice penitence (Pss 6, 102 and 143) because there is nothing penitential in them. As I read them they are voicing dissonance and contain no sense that the psalmist is responsible for the misfortune that has befallen him. To those that remain I would add Ps. 90.

Translating the psalms

Reading modern Bible translations it is easy to forget that we are reading translations of an ancient and foreign text; the English is fluent, the cover is often colourful and the print style is contemporary. Most Bibles are no longer bound in black leather, printed on rice paper and full of archaic language; and most of us are grateful for that development. Today's Bibles also demonstrate over a century's experience of growing translation expertise since the Revised Version was produced in 1884 and are almost always based on the standard Hebrew text published in *BHS*.[4] Nevertheless, unresolved translation problems remain.

It is customary to distinguish between 'translations' and 'paraphrases', but that distinction can be elusive. 'The LORD is my shepherd, I shall not want' (NRSV) is a translation. It reproduces the four words of the Hebrew original as succinctly and accurately as possible. 'Dear God, you sustain me and feed me, like a shepherd you guide me' is not a translation.[5] It puts the words in a different order and changes the style to a direct address. It is a paraphrase. But what about the 'Crimond version'? This changes the style, divides the psalm into five 'common metre' verses and ends lines 2 and 4 of each verse with rhyming English: but is it so 'free' as to be called a paraphrase? A further complication comes with GNB, a translation about which it is fashionable to be rude. GNB is, however, properly called a translation, though it differs from the other recognized translations (NRSV, REB, NIV, NJPS etc.) in its translation method. To risk oversimplifying it, the others use a traditional method loosely called 'verbal equivalence', which aims to translate, as far as possible, 'word for word'. GNB uses the 'dynamic equivalence' method, again the term is rather a loose one, which aims to give 'sense for sense' or 'meaning for meaning'.

Translation is widely seen as more art than science, though there are times when I wish my Japanese motor scooter manual was a bit less art and a bit more science. In Chapter 2 we noted how important the 'balancing of ideas' was in Hebrew poetry, and that translators of Hebrew psalms do not have to find English words that rhyme in order to match rhyming words in Hebrew because there aren't any. So there are no rhyming endings in Jim Cotter's psalms, though there are good ones in the Crimond version. 'Parallelism' offers translators another help too. If there is an uncertain Hebrew word or phrase in line 1, then line 2 can provide some sort of a clue. It's not foolproof, but it helps.

We met one stark translation issue when we looked at the psalm titles. We saw there not only differences between contemporary translations but also differences among the ancient versions and observed that we simply do not know what some Hebrew words mean. The particular difficulty in the psalm titles is that unknown Hebrew words stand there alone, without the benefit of company, and it is always more difficult to deal with an unknown stand-alone word than it is when such a word is nestling in a sentence or a paragraph with neighbours we recognize and a general sense we can pick up. We saw a similar kind of thing in Psalm 150. It is clear from the context that the cluster of unknown words in that psalm are names of musical instruments, but we can't identify what those instruments were. At this point it is worth noting that by 'we' I do not mean contemporary Christian or secularist Old Testament scholars, but the whole, multinational scholarly community, which includes practising Jews and modern Hebrew speakers. That is why I deliberately drew attention to the frequency with which NJPS, the New Jewish Publication Society translation, uses the 'Hebrew obscure' footnote in the psalm titles.

When we looked at Hebrew poetry in Chapter 2 we noted that although much of the 'meaning' of poems like the psalms can be reproduced in a translation, few of the things that a Hebrew reader can see, hear or feel in a psalm can be replicated. This issue is wider than that of translating poetry, so here are some examples, none from Psalms:

- 'A formless void' (NRSV) and 'formless and empty' (TNIV) convey the sense of *tohû wā* (and) *bohû* in Genesis 1.2. Now say that out loud. These translations don't capture much else about the expression, do they? This repetition of vowel sound (the technical term for it is 'assonance') is fairly common in Hebrew poetry, mainly because Hebrew uses suffixes for personal pronouns and many of these end with vowel sounds. In Isaiah 53.4–5, for example, the Hebrew suffix for 'our' occurs twice in each verse: 'infirmities-our' and 'diseases-our' in verse 4, and 'transgressions-our' and 'iniquities-our' in verse 5. It hardly qualifies as good rhyming.
- The vision description in Amos 8.1f. depends on a play on words. Amos says that he sees a 'basket of summer fruit (*qayiṣ*)', so YHWH says to him, 'The end (*qēṣ*) has come . . .'. Translations cannot reproduce this, so they usually explain this play on words (the technical term for which is 'paranomasia') in a footnote. A really good example of this is Isaiah's short, sharp and snappy retort to the king in Isaiah 7.9b, 'If not *ta'ămînû* then not *tĕ'ămēnû*'. This play

on words plays on both their meaning and their sound, the word being the Hebrew verb related to 'Amen', which is to do with believing, trusting, having faith and being secure. Many translations attempt to reproduce this one, for example, 'If you do not stand firm in faith, you will not stand at all' (NRSV and TNIV), 'Have firm faith, or you will fail to stand firm' (REB), and 'If your faith is not enduring, you will not endure' (GNB), but you can see the problem the translators have.

- Onomatopoeia (the use of words that sound like what they describe) is found in Hebrew as in many languages, and so can sometimes be reproduced. A good example is the sound of the thudding hooves of galloping horses in the Song of Deborah in Judges 5.22, which some English versions capture because 'gallop' is itself onomatopoeic. An example that cannot be reproduced is the sound of roaring waters conveyed by the Hebrew words in Isaiah 17.12–13.
- 'Alliteration' is the technical term for the repetition of the sound of letters, and this cannot be reproduced in translation. Isaiah 1.18–20, with its six 'k' sounds, three 's' sounds in verse 18 and five 't' sounds in verses 19–20, is often cited as a good example here. 'Pray for the peace of Jerusalem, "May they prosper who love you"' (Ps. 122.6) conveys the sense of the verse well, but cannot capture the effect of the four 'sh' sounds and four 'l' sounds in its four consecutive words.

Three different and common translation and interpretation issues came up when we looked at Psalm 23 and we reserved one of them to this point. Psalm 23.3 speaks of YHWH leading us in 'right paths' (NRSV) and we looked at the problem of that 'righteousness vocabulary' changing its meaning over time. NKJV and NIV, however, retain the older 'paths of righteousness'. The translation issue here is minor but very common. It concerns a feature of Hebrew grammar called the 'construct' where two nouns are placed side by side and the result gives a range of meaning possibilities. AV, however, often translated construct phrases as 'the x of y' and so gives us 'the paths of righteousness' here. Not so, however, with its translation of the two constructs in verse 2 where 'pastures/grass' becomes 'green pastures' and 'waters/rest' becomes 'still waters'. BCP has 'green pasture' for the first and 'waters of comfort' for the second. If the two nouns are the same, the result is usually 'the lord of lords' ('king of kings', 'song of songs' etc.). Given the influence of the AV on the English language this has become an accepted idiom, even though 'right paths' is a better English translation than 'paths of righteousness', as 'The Best Song' would be a better translation of the opening phrase and title of the Song of Songs.

We reserved another good example of the problem in translating constructs earlier in this chapter, not least because it illustrates another problem too. AV, NIV and NKJV translate the opening of Psalm 51.17 literally as 'The sacrifices of God are . . .', which doesn't make much sense. NRSV interprets this as 'The sacrifice acceptable to God is . . .', and NJPS follows suit with 'True sacrifice to God is . . .' as they try to bring out the meaning of the phrase. 'The best sacrifice is . . .' or 'The best sacrifice of all is . . .' are also possible translations, given that occasionally in Hebrew the word 'God' can function as a superlative (as in NEB's translation of *rûaḥ ʾĕlôhîm* in Gen. 1.2 as 'mighty wind'). But at Psalm 51.9 there is another possibility as well, which is given in the NRSV footnote. This suggests that the phrase could be translated by 'My sacrifice, O God, is . . .', and this is the translation preferred in GNB, REB and TNIV. This involves the change of a tiny vowel point changing the Hebrew word from the construct form *zibĕhê* ('the sacrifices of') to *zibĕhî* ('my sacrifices'). Sometimes, the translators argue, the Jewish textual scholars who finalized the text of the Hebrew Bible in the first Christian millennium (the Masoretes) might have got it wrong.

Then there are those 'sharks' in the REB translation of Psalm 74.14. The other translations have 'desert creatures' or 'desert people' and that is matched in the 'jackals' of the Targum and the 'Ethiopians' of LXX. NJPS is nicely ambiguous with 'denizens of the desert' and it adds a footnote giving 'seafaring men' as another possibility and noting that the meaning of the Hebrew is uncertain. What is going on here? First, there is an odd bit of Hebrew grammar. Second, there is a difficult and unique word. It might be related to a similar Hebrew word for 'dry', which explains where the translations get their 'desert' idea from. Or it might possibly be related to the word for 'ship', which is where the NJPS footnote comes from. But neither of those possibilities have any connection with 'sharks'. *BHS* has a footnote which suggests that the Masoretes made a mistake by dividing up the original consonants wrongly and so creating the wrong two words out of the eight consonants involved. It should be 'creatures of the sea': but only REB and Kraus among recent commentators agree.

Entry-level commentaries rarely mention such things as these and there are, needless to say, many more issues that could have been touched on. This is another reason to gather as many translations as possible and to be vigilant about footnotes in them. They might not explain the problem but at least they will make you aware of translation difficulties. Despite appearances, our English Bibles are translations of ancient texts and we need to remember what that word 'translation' implies.

To do

Has anything in this chapter excited you? What? Why? Has anything in it challenged you? What? How? Has anything in it worried you? What? Why? Has anything in it influenced the way you will read the Old Testament in future?

Suggestions for further reading

Sacrifice

*'Sacrifices' and related entries in *DBI*.
*Anderson, G. A. (1992), 'Sacrifice: Old Testament' in *ABD*, vol. 5, pp. 870–86.
Ashby, G. (1988), *Sacrifice*, London: SCM Press.
Bradley, I. (1995), *The Power of Sacrifice*, London: Darton, Longman and Todd.
*de Vaux, R. (1961), *Ancient Israel: Its Life and Institution*, London: Darton, Longman and Todd, chs 10 and 13.
*Gaster, T. H. (1962), 'Sacrifices and Offerings', in *IDB*, vol. 4, pp. 147–59.

Sin

The entry for 'Sin etc.' in the Index of Semantic Fields on p. 175 of vol. 5 will give you the specific words to follow up and their location in *NIDOTTE*.

*Cover, R. C. (1992), 'Sin: Old Testament', in *ABD*, vol. 6, pp. 31–40.
*de Vries, S. (1962), 'Sin, Sinners', in *IDB*, vol. 4, pp. 361–7.
Koch, K. (1974–2006), חטא *chāṭā*", in *TDOT*, vol. 4, pp. 309–19.
Koch, K. (1974–2006), עון *'āwōn*', in *TDOT*, vol. 10, pp. 546–62.
Seebass, H. (1974–2006), פשע *pāša*ʿ, in *TDOT*, vol. 12, pp. 133–51.

*A shortcut into all this can also be found by reading the Old Testament sections on the key words in *NIDNTT*, in this case by looking under 'Sin' in vol. 3 (pp. 574–5 and 577–9).

The names for God

*Anderson, B. W. (1962), 'God, names of', in *IDB*, vol. 2, pp. 407–17.

*Emerton, J. A. (1993), 'Names of God in the Hebrew Bible', in *OCB*, pp. 548–49.

*'Name', in *DBI*, pp. 582–6.

Mettinger, T. N. D. (1987), *In Search of God: The Meaning and Message of the Everlasting Names*, Philadelphia: Fortress Press.

Rose, M. 'Names of God in the OT' in ABD vol. 4, pp. 1001–11.

Worship in ancient Israel

Albertz, R. (1994), *A History of Israelite Religion in the Old Testament Period*, 2 vols, London: SCM Press.

*de Vaux, R. *Ancient Israel*, part 4.

Kraus, H.–J. (1966), *Worship in Israel*, Oxford: Blackwell.

Rowley, H. H. (1967), *Worship in Ancient Israel*, London: SPCK.

Translating and translations

*'English Versions of the Bible' (1991) (unattributed), in *The New Oxford Annotated Bible*, pp. 400–6.

*Greenspoon, L. J. (2004), 'Jewish Translations of the Bible', in Berlin and Brettler (eds), *The Jewish Study Bible*, pp. 2005–20.

*Nida, E. A. (1992), 'Theories of Translation', in *ABD*, vol. 6, pp. 512–15.

OCB contains a series of fascinating articles under the heading 'Translations', among which 'Theory and Practice' is treated by E. A. Nida (pp. 750–2), 'Ancient Languages', which includes discussion of LXX and the Latin versions, by S. P. Brock (pp. 752–4), 'The Targums' by R. P. Gordon (pp. 754–5), and 'English Language Versions' by R. G. Bratcher (pp. 758–63).

6

Voicing Hope

What is this chapter about?

Psalms contains a set of psalms usually designated 'royal psalms' because, in one way or another, they feature the Davidic king in Jerusalem. In this chapter we look at these psalms but also go on to ask why they were included in a worship book for Temple use when there was no longer any king in Jerusalem. A number of other psalms focus on YHWH as King and we look at these too. The final comment looks at psalms outside Psalms.

How is it organized?

- The psalm for exegesis is Psalm 89.
- In 'Voicing hope' we look at the 'royal psalms', the 'YHWH is king' and the Zion songs and suggest that their primary purpose is to express 'hope'.
- The extended comment is entitled 'Psalms before and after Psalms' and looks at other 'songs' in the Old Testament and especially at the psalms from Qumran.
- There are boxes on Messiah, the 'end of book doxologies' such as Psalm 89.52, *selāh* and Pseudepigrapha.
- There are a number of 'To do' boxes.
- The chapter ends with suggestions for further reading on Messiah, royal psalms and the theology of kingship, God as king, the Psalms of Solomon and psalms at Qumran.

What should I be able to do by the end of it?

- Describe what is meant by 'royal psalms'.
- Understand the twentieth-century debate around the 'New Year Festival'.
- Reflect on the image of YHWH as 'King'.
- Understand the meaning(s) of 'Messiah' and 'messianic'.
- Compare Qumran psalms with biblical ones.

Messiah

Question What would you do if you were walking along a street in Jerusalem in 847 BC and heard someone shouting, 'The Messiah is coming! The Messiah is coming!'?

Answer Get out of the way because everyone knew that the king's charioteers did not take kindly to pedestrians obstructing the road.

'Messiah' is the English form of the Hebrew word *māšiaḥ*, which means 'anointed'. 'Christ' is the English form of the Greek word which means the same. It was the custom to anoint kings (1 Sam. 2.10; 1 Kings 1.39; Ps. 89.20) and chief priests (Ex. 30.30; Lev. 4.3, 5) and occasionally other persons of note. In Psalms, 'Anointed' with a capital 'A' (to use a figure of speech – Hebrew has no capital letters) means the king (as in Ps. 89.38, 51). Later on, when they had no kings and looked forward to better days, some Jewish groups expressed their hopes in terms of a 'new messiah'. At Qumran, for instance, they seem to have prayed for the coming of two messiahs, one of the royal line of David to be the new king and, to them more important, one of the priestly line of Aaron to be the new High Priest. Other groups at the time of Jesus had other 'messianic' hopes, but the extent of such expectations should not be exaggerated.

Psalm 89

> ## To do
>
> Make your own notes for an exegesis of Psalm 89.

1. Psalm 89, the final psalm in Book 3 of Psalms, is a 'lament' which most would call a 'royal psalm', though Gunkel didn't.

2. It is spoken by or on behalf of YHWH's 'Anointed One', the Davidic King, who is suffering acute distress, and it exhibits all the features of psalms that voice dissonance.

3. It begins brightly, however, with an affirmation of YHWH's *ḥesed* ('steadfast love' or 'commitment') and *'ĕmûnāh* ('faithfulness') in verses 1–2 (a pairing of words found seven times in the psalm), a reminder of his covenant with David in verses 3–4, a hymn celebrating YHWH as the incomparable 'King of Creation' in verses 5–18 and a detailed restatement of his promises to David in verses 19–37. This long build-up leads to the sharply accusatory 'But now' of verse 38, which introduces a description of the crisis (verses 38–45), angry questions (verses 46–49) and an appeal to YHWH to 'remember' (verses 50–51). At the end, editors have attached the doxology that concludes Book 3 of Psalms, and its tone is totally at variance with the concluding verses of the psalm.

> ## End-of-book doxologies
>
> 'Doxology' comes from two Greek words, *doxa* ('glory') and *logos* ('word'), and so a 'doxology' is an affirmation in which God is praised. These may be as short as those in Genesis 24.27 or 1 Chronicles 16.36 or as long as Psalm 150. Books 1–4 of Psalms end with doxologies (Pss 41.13; 72.18–20; 89.52; 106.48), of which Psalm 89.52 is the briefest. It consists of a base affirmation, 'Blessed be YHWH', a note that YHWH is to be so affirmed 'eternally' and a double concluding 'Amen' ('Yes' or 'So be it'). The others supplement this with the definition, 'the God of Israel'. The doxology to Book 2 adds more detail and that to Book 4 invites the congregation to say that double 'Amen'. Psalm 72.20 adds 'The prayers of David son of Jesse are ended'. Book 5 contains no such

ending, but it is widely held that Psalm 150 itself forms the concluding doxology of Book 5 and Psalms as a whole. We will look at the implications of these endings and the division of Psalms into five books which they mark in Chapter 9.

4. Verses 5–7 introduce us to the 'Heavenly Court' or 'Council' and its membership of 'holy ones' or 'heavenly beings'. See:

- Psalm 82, which pictures the God of Israel as the President of the Heavenly Council taking the chair in the assembly of the gods and calling the other gods to account for the way they have mishandled their responsibilities, especially towards the vulnerable and needy (cf. Ps. 58.1);
- Job 1.6–12 and 2.1–7 where this Heavenly Court is the scene of the conversations between YHWH and the Satan (his Chief Investigating Officer);
- 1 Kings 22.19–23 and the vision of Micaiah ben Imlah;
- Psalm 95.3, which speaks of the LORD as a 'great God, and a great king above all gods';
- Deuteronomy 32.43, 'Praise, O heavens, his people, worship him, all you gods!' and 32.8–9:

> When the Most High apportioned the nations, when he divided humankind, he fixed the boundaries of the peoples according to the number of the gods; the LORD's own portion was his people, Jacob his allotted share.

The Hebrew of Deuteronomy 32.8 and 32.43 has been censored, and now contains no reference to other gods. The official Hebrew version has 'according to the number of the sons of Israel', but NRSV and those other translations that recognize this find their reading in LXX, which has 'according to the number of the angels of God', and in a Hebrew manuscript from the Dead Sea Scrolls, which has 'according to the number of the sons of God' (4QDeut^j).

This is the gathering that lies behind the 'us' of Genesis 1.27 and whose vocal seraphim members are heard in Isaiah 6, which has its own 'us' in verse 8. These 'divine beings' ('holy ones', *qĕdošîm* in verses 5 and 7; *bĕnê-'ēlîm*, 'heavenly beings', literally 'sons of gods', in verse 6), who make up the membership of the Heavenly Court, morphed into the 'angels and archangels and all the company of heaven' of later Jewish and Christian vision.

The psalm uses a variety of names for God: YHWH predominates, with the variant 'Lord God of hosts' (*yhwh 'elohê-sĕbā'ôt*) in verse 8a and the short form *yāh* in verse 8b. He is named as 'the Holy One of Israel' in verse 18 (*qĕdôš yiśrā'ēl*) and 'Lord' (*'ădônay*) in verses 49 and 50. Because of the covenant the king can call him 'my Father', 'my God' (*'ēlî*), and 'the Rock of my Salvation' (verse 26).

The historical setting of this psalm is beyond recovery, though suggestions like the death of Josiah or the fall of Jerusalem are made. Equally beyond recovery is any original liturgical setting, though suggestions like a National Day of Fasting or Mourning, or some kind of ritual humiliation of the king are made. The term 'festal shout' (the *tĕrû'â*) in verse 15 reminds us of how little we know about details of Temple liturgies. The term is used for a war-cry (1 Sam. 4.5) and the trumpet signal for starting to march or indicating the beginning of a festival (Lev. 23.24; 25.9). It is also used in the name of the last musical instrument in the list in Psalm 150. It is the term for the shout with which David and the people brought the 'ark of the covenant' up to the city (2 Sam. 6.15) and the 'shouts' of Psalms 33.3 and 47.5.

'Horn' is a symbol for strength, and the 'exalted horn' of verses 17 and 24 is an idiom for being raised proudly up or 'holding (one's) head high' (REB).

For Sheol (verse 48), see the box on 'Life after death in the Old Testament' in Chapter 3 (pp. 60–1).

---

selāh

The word *selāh* occurs 71 times in 39 psalms: once in 16 of them, twice in 15, three times in 7 and four times in Ps. 89. The distribution is uneven: 17 times in 9 of the 42 psalms in Book 1, 30 in 17 of the 30 psalms in Book 2, 20 in 11 of the 17 psalms in Book 3, in none of the 17 psalms in Book 4 and 4 times in 2 of the 44 psalms in Book 5. It is found at the end of four (Pss 3, 9, 24, 46). It occurs in all types or categories of psalms. At Psalm 9.16 it keeps company with the untranslated *Higgaion*. Only two major translations attempt to translate the term, and both are working from the equally unclear *diapsalma* in LXX: NJB has 'Pause', and *NETS* 'interlude with strings'. Commentaries offer numerous suggestions for what this rubric means, but beyond saying that it is probably a liturgical or musical direction of some kind there is 'no way of determining [its] meaning or etymology' (Alter, 2007, p. 8).

5. The principal theme of this psalm is God's covenant with David (verses 3, 28, 34, 39). The dissonance which the psalm voices is that YHWH has reneged on this covenant. It is one thing for the agreement to contain clauses that allow for the king to be punished (verses 30–32, as in the oracle of Nathan in 2 Sam. 7.4–17, to which this psalm might be linked, and in Deut. 17.14–20), but what is happening now goes far beyond that (verses 38–45)! For covenants in general, see the exegesis of Psalm 74 in Chapter 4.

Psalm 89 is the fullest statement of the covenant with David in the Old Testament. Apart from the general terms mentioned in verses 30–31, the psalm says little about 'David's' obligations (verses 30–31 only) and much about God's promises and commitments to him. God promises to 'establish' and maintain the Davidic dynasty (verses 3, 21, 29, 33, 36, 37), protect David from enemies (verses 22–23), 'exalt' him (verse 24) and give him power over all the forces of danger and death (verse 25). David is God's 'chosen one' (verses 3, 19) and 'servant' (verses 3, 39, 50) who 'belongs' to God in a special way (verse 18). God has 'found' him (verse 20) and anointed him (verses 20, 38, 51). So David can call God 'Father' and acknowledge that special relationship (verse 26). He is 'the firstborn', the highest of all kings (verse 27). The psalm is full of words for God's covenant love and loyalty: 'steadfast love' (ḥesed) in verses 1, 2, 14, 24, 28, 33, 49; 'faithfulness' ('ĕmûnāh) in verses 1, 2, 5, 8, 24, 33, 49, and 'emet in verse 14; 'righteousness' (ṣedeq) in verse 14 and ṣĕdāqāh in verse 16 and 'justice' (mišpāṭ) in verse 14. This makes the change in verse 38 all the more shocking.

For the imagery in verses 9–11 and 25, see the box on the four creation pictures in Chapter 4 (pp. 77–8). It was God's victory over chaos that established him as King of Creation and supreme over other 'gods'.

6. Psalm 89 offers us a clear and unambiguous theology and ideology of the Davidic monarchy, but the Old Testament as a whole is ambivalent about monarchy, even the Davidic monarchy, as we shall see in the next section.

Voicing hope

Psalm 89 is a powerful lament; how then can it be used in a chapter headed 'Voicing *hope*'? Some might argue that all laments voice hope, in that they expect an answer to their urgent appeal to God: but that is not at all apparent, nor would it be widely agreed. This psalm voices hope, I suggest, not because it is a lament but because it is a 'royal psalm'.

Introductions to Psalms always include material on the 'royal psalms' and related matters. What is included in this category will vary. The long lists of such psalms and their characteristics found in Eaton's commentaries were always hypothetical and have become increasingly suspect, as have the attempts that go back to Mowinckel to reconstruct a New Year Festival in Jerusalem in which the king was alleged to play a major role. There is no doubt, however, that some psalms can be called 'royal psalms' in so far as they concern the person and role of the Davidic king, and that some psalms belong to royal rituals of one kind or another: but the preoccupation with recovering ancient royal rituals and seeing the role of the king as crucial to much of Psalms is now dated. But an obvious question remains. Given that there was no monarchy after the Exile and that Psalms is almost certainly a Second Temple collection, why were such psalms included in a Temple book when there were no longer any kings and no longer any royal liturgies? One answer is that these psalms developed an afterlife as expressions of hope, that they came to be seen as 'messianic' in the new and developing sense of that old word. They became, in effect, a way of voicing hope. So here we will look at the theology of the Davidic monarchy as found in the 'royal psalms' and, after that, at the related theme of the 'kingship of YHWH' and those psalms that celebrate it.

The Old Testament story of monarchy in ancient Israel can be quickly told. Saul was appointed, after some opposition from the prophet Samuel, to deal with the threat of the Philistines against which the old loose federation of the Tribes of Israel was helpless (1 Sam. 8—11), and if you read that story you can 'see the joins' where two different points of view are woven together.

To do

Read 1 Samuel 8—11. Can you 'see the joins'?

His successor David, neither the first, nor the holiest, nor the most powerful of the kings, was the one who made the lasting impact. His dynasty lasted for 400 years in Judah, and later, when some expressed their hopes for a better future, they did so by saying that God would raise up a new king like David

(Zech. 6.9–14; 9.9–10; Hag. 2.21–23; 2 Esdras 12.32). After the division of the kingdom on the death of Solomon, the story is downhill all the way to the Fall of Samaria and the end of Israel in 722 BC and that of Jerusalem and Judah in 586. The Deuteronomic Historian blames both on the failure of their kings to honour God (2 Kings 17.7–18; 24.9). Indeed, Deuteronomy 17.14–20 is perhaps the text on which the whole Deuteronomic History is the sermon. How this rich theological narrative relates to the 'real history' of Jerusalem and Judah, Samaria and Israel and the 'kings' of both 'kingdoms' is one of the most controversial areas of current Old Testament scholarship.[1]

Gunkel designated 11 psalms in whole or in part as 'royal' and a brief survey of these will identify the main features of the theology of the Davidic monarchy:

- Psalm 2 appears to have been composed for a coronation on Mount Zion. In it YHWH's 'anointed one' gives testimony and warning to his watching enemies that YHWH has decreed that he is his 'son', 'begotten' in this liturgy.
- Psalm 18 contains the kind of vivid, exaggerated language which is common in psalms that voice praise for deliverance and help received. It is only in verse 43 that there is anything to suggest that the 'I' who speaks is the king, giving testimony to 'his rock' and 'the God of his salvation' for delivering him from enemies in battle.
- Psalm 20 is a prayer for such help for the king.
- Psalm 21 is a testimony to how God has blessed the king and a warning to his enemies.
- Psalm 45 is a royal wedding psalm. Verse 6 possibly addresses the king as 'God' but other ways of translating the verse are possible. Verse 7 speaks of God's special anointing of the king.
- Psalm 72 is a prayer for the king, but one of those prayers that preaches as much as prays. It is a powerful statement of the king's responsibility towards the vulnerable and marginalized.
- Psalm 89 is a lament that asks why God has reneged on his covenant with 'David'.
- Psalm 101 contains none of the markers of a 'royal psalm'. It reads well as a declaration of royal intent to rule according to Torah (e.g. against the background of the requirements listed in Deut. 17.14–20), but that is as much as can be said.
- Psalm 110 possibly formed part of the coronation rituals, but it is a mystery

from beginning to end, with significant translation problems in verses 3 and 7.

To do

Compare any three translations of Psalm 110.

- Psalm 132 is a celebration of YHWH's choice of Zion and David, containing a promise of an eternal dynasty if David's sons keep his covenant (verse 12).
- Psalm 144 is a king's prayer.

From all this we can identify a 'theology of kingship'. The king, as YHWH's 'anointed' one and unique 'son', is privileged, blessed and assured of God's special care and protection (though Ps. 89 does rather indicate that this is not 100 per cent guaranteed). With this status and blessing come responsibilities, to live by Torah, to defend his people, to ensure justice, to witness and give testimony to God's grace and to care for the marginalized. Whether there were any liturgical responsibilities is now widely questioned. Above all, perhaps, is the symbolic importance of the king. Just as Jerusalem and its Temple are important symbols of the special relationship between YHWH and his people, so is 'David'.

What happens, then, when there is no longer any monarchy and these psalms are in the public domain? Do they become available to be used by or about any speaker, celebrating the 'special relationship' of blessing and support available to every member of God's covenant people as well as reminding them of the principle that blessings bring responsibilities? The principal early afterlife of the royal psalms, however, lies in their messianic interpretation in the newer sense of that word and seen clearly in the use of the psalms in the New Testament, though we must heed N. T. Wright's warning that 'messianism' is a many-faceted, complex and much smaller movement than is usually thought (N. T. Wright, 1993, pp. 307–8). When they had one, the king was a sign of this hope. When they didn't, the old psalms continued to be used. Some saw in them a hope for a new king, others 'democratized' them and saw the old 'special relationship' as now available to all. Either way these old psalms continued to voice hope.

Mowinckel, Johnson and Eaton made large claims for a 'royal theology' celebrated and promoted in the Jerusalem Temple, central to which was the 'Annual

New Year Festival'.[2] Eaton described this festival as the most prominent of the three main festivals and saw it as an extended holy season including New Year, the Day of Atonement and the week-long Feast of Tabernacles (Booths, *Sukkot*) at the start of the new agricultural cycle after the summer drought. Part of its purpose was to renew the covenant with YHWH and seek his gift of rain, and so of life. The festival was therefore a celebration of YHWH as King of Creation, 'victor, the most high God, the Creator-King' (Eaton, 2003, p. 23). Eaton then went further still and imagined ceremonies depicting YHWH's defeat of his chaos enemies and triumphal processions involving the king, maybe even a 'drama of atonement won for many by the suffering of a royal figure' which could have 'fed into the great prophetic vision of Isaiah 52—53' (Eaton, 2003, p. 24). This would also be a time of making personal vows, of people coming to the Temple for asylum, and of national thanksgivings and laments, quite conceivably spoken by the king as figurehead (Eaton, 2003, pp. 34–5). Much of this is now seen to be hypothetical and suspect, but the fact that there was a strong theology of YHWH as king associated with the Temple and seen in Psalms is uncontested.

'YHWH is king' or 'YHWH has become king' is the opening acclamation of Psalms 93, 97 and 99 and God is pictured as king in Psalms 95, 96 and 98, giving rise to the title 'Enthronement Psalms' for this group of psalms. Whatever liturgy they might or might not have been used in, these psalms are powerful in their imagery of God as a king.

To do

Read Psalms 93 and 95—99 and note how they use the image of YHWH as king. Now read Psalm 94, which does not use such imagery, and think about why it might have been included at this point and how it is affected by the company it keeps.

These psalms celebrate YHWH as King of Creation, King of the gods and of the nations and King of Israel; the king who defeats the forces of chaos and death, pictured as mighty floods and surging 'waters' (Ps. 93.3–4). YHWH has imposed his rule on this chaos so the earth has been made firm and secure so that 'it shall never be moved' (Ps. 96.10). He is God of the whole earth, even to the farthest coastlands (Ps. 97.1), and of all the nations (Ps. 96.10). He is king over all the gods (Pss 95.3; 97.9). 'All the earth' is called to worship him (Pss 96.1; 97.1; 98.4). His throne is set in heaven, surrounded by clouds, thick darkness, fire and lightning (Ps. 97.2–5). His royal will is to be obeyed (Ps. 93.5), and past disobedience is cited as a warning (Ps. 95.8–9). Like a true king he has been the saviour and helper of his people in the past (Pss 98.1–3; 99.4–9) and the psalmists rejoice because he is coming again 'to judge' (i.e. to save!) the earth and its people (Pss 96.10–13; 97.10–12; 98.7–9). Behind these images lies that old *Chaoskampf* creation story and in celebrating YHWH as king these psalms give voice to hope, the sure and certain hope of the fulfilment of YHWH's purposes, the establishment of his 'kingdom' or rule, and the victory of Life over Death.

To do

We noted in Chapter 3 that some images and metaphors can be unhelpful, and that there is unease about this one. What do you think about the image of God as king?

To do

Gunkel lists 'Songs of Zion' as a subset of the 'Hymns', and Psalm 74.2 pleads with God to 'remember Zion'. The image of 'Zion' is one of the most potent images in Psalms. Use your concordance to check out every reference to Zion in Psalms (there are 37 in 31 psalms). Note the evocative power of this image. Note also how often the image is used to convey a sense of blessing, security and hope.

Other psalms that voice hope

'Psalms of hope' is not a category in the usual lists. Many of those in my more general list would be called 'royal psalms' or 'Zion songs' or hymns of YHWH's 'Enthronement'. The psalms that seem to me in all their diversity to be united by the fact that they 'voice hope' are (in addition to Ps. 89): Psalms 2, 3, 21, 24, 29, 45, 72, 75, 82, 93, 94, 96, 97, 98, 99, 108, 110, 122, 129, 132 and 146.

Psalms before and after Psalms

Similar material to psalms is found elsewhere in the Old Testament, though never called 'psalms'. The Songs of Moses and of Deborah and Barak (Ex. 15.1–18 and Judg. 5. 2–31) and the snippet from Miriam (Ex. 15.21) are ancient victory songs. Personal laments can be found in Job 3.3–26, Jeremiah 18.19–23 and 20.7–18. The other Song of Moses (Deut. 32.1–43) and the Song of David (2 Sam. 22.2–51) are songs of testimony and praise, the latter reappearing as Psalm 18. Hezekiah's Song is a testimony to be accompanied by stringed instruments (Isa. 38.10–30). Jonah and Hannah's words (Jonah 2; 1 Sam. 2.1–10) are 'prayers'. The prayer in Habakkuk 3 even has a title with an untranslated word in it and a note at the end that it is 'To the leader: with stringed instruments'. 1 Chronicles 16.8–36 is a song of praise, either Asaph's first attempt or David's exemplar to him, and verse 34b reappears four times as the Chronicler's story unfolds (2 Chron. 5.13; 7.3; 20.21; Ezra 3.11). The five chapters of Lamentations, however they may be divided, voice their dissonance in classic lament style. All of these, with the possible exception of the two victory songs, can be paralleled in Psalms.[3]

From the Septuagint, and available therefore in the Apocrypha, we have two prayers and an act of praise which are embedded in Tobit (3.2–6; 3.11–15; 13.1–17) and a victory song resembling Deborah's sung by Judith (Judith 16.1–17). A thanksgiving to be sung with harp accompaniment appears at Ecclesiasticus 39.16–31 and another at 51.1–11, to which a Hebrew appendix adds 16 verses, 14 of which have the refrain 'for his mercy endures for ever', as in Psalm 136. In the Greek text of Daniel, Azariah sings a 22-verse 'hymn' amidst the flames of the furnace (at Dan. 3.23) and the three young men join in a longer one when the attendants had stoked it up even more (with the refrain of 'Sing praise to (the Lord) and highly exalt him for ever'). Orthodox apocryphas add a thanksgiving by King Manasseh at 2 Chronicles 33.19 and some Septuagint manuscripts add Psalm 151.

Psalms of Solomon is a collection of 18 psalms probably dating from the mid-first century BC and coming from Pharisaic circles. All but the first have titles that ascribe their authorship to Solomon and that are not dissimilar to the titles in Psalms. Two contain the term *diapsalma*, for which Gray prints *selah* and *NETS* 'interlude on strings' (Pss Sol. 17.10; 18.10). In style and in their diversity of voices these psalms are similar to those in Psalms, though there are changes in vocabulary and theology which reflect a later dating. There is, for instance, a rich theology of 'life after death' in these psalms (for example 3.16; 13.11; 14.6–7) as well as a pervasive 'wisdom' and didactic flavour (see Chapter 7). The first is a mild lament in the 'I' form and reads like the voice of Jerusalem under siege, a theme that is repeated in a number of the psalms against the background of the Roman invasion of Judah under Pompey from 63 BC. Others repeat the 'righteous' versus 'sinners' theme, though the terms 'pious' or 'devout' tend to replace the 'righteous' of Psalms. Psalms of Solomon 14 gives a feel for the similarities and the differences between these psalms and the canonical ones:

A hymn. Pertaining to Salomon.

1. Faithful is the Lord to those who love him in truth,
To those who endure his discipline,
2. To those who walk in the righteousness of his ordinances,
In the law which he commanded us that we might live.
3. The devout of the Lord shall live by it for ever,
The orchard of the Lord, the trees of life, are his devout ones.
4. Their planting is rooted for ever,
They shall not be pulled up all the days of heaven,
5. For the portion and the inheritance of God is Israel.
6. But not so are the sinners and transgressors of the law,
Who loved a day in the companionship of their sin.
7. Their desire was for the briefness of corruption,
And they have not remembered God.
8. For the ways of human beings are known before him at all times,
And he knows the storerooms of the heart before they come to pass.
9. Therefore their inheritance is Hades and darkness and destruction,
And they shall not be found in the day when the righteous obtain pity,
10. But the devout of the Lord shall inherit life with joy.[4]

Around 200 of the 900 or so fragments that constitute the Dead Sea Scrolls are of biblical books, and 39 of them are of Psalms, the single largest number of manuscripts of any biblical book, a fact that probably indicates the importance of Psalms and psalmody in the community there.[5] These discoveries have been important in a number of ways, one of which has been to indicate how flexible 'translation' and 'copying' were in the scriptorium at Qumran. The 'big ideas' are unaffected, but at that stage there is little sign of the textual uniformity that the Masoretes were later to establish and promote so efficiently. With regard to Psalms, Qumran has revealed what look like different 'collections' of the canonical psalms, or at least interesting differences in the order of psalms in some of the manuscripts. This has added another dimension to the question of the shape of Psalms, and the collections of material in it. Qumran has also given us some new psalms. In Chapter 1 we noted 'David's Compositions' in the Great Psalms Scroll (11QPsᵃ = 11Q5) and that scroll also gives us a Hebrew version of Psalm 151, the 'extra' psalm at the end of LXX. It divides it into two, making the reference to 'the Philistine' into a separate psalm (Ps. 151B) and ending Psalm 151A with a different verse, that '(God) sent and fetched me from behind the flock, and anointed me with holy oil, and he made me leader of his people and ruler over the children of his covenant' (*DSSB*, p. 585). There is also a badly fragmented apocryphal psalm dedicated to David (11QapPsᵃ = 11Q11), which is worth quoting because of its contents and because it illustrates the reconstruction that Scrolls scholars have to undertake:[6]

> To David. O[n words of incanta]tion. [Cry out al]l the time in the name of the Lor[d].
> Towards heave[n when] Beli[al] comes to you.
> [And sa]y to him:
> Who are you? [Be afraid of] man and of the seed of the ho[ly ones].
> Your face is a face of [nothin]g and your horns are horns of dr[eam].
> [You ar]e [d]arkness and not light; [injustic]e and not righteousness.
> [The prin]ce of the h[os]t [is against you]; the Lord [will cast] you [to] the nethermost [hell],
> [closed by] bronze ga[tes] through [which n]o light [shall pass];
> Nor [shall shine there the light of the] sun which [will rise] over the righteous to il[lumine his face.
> And] you will say:
> Is [there not an angel with the ri]ghteous when [judgement] comes [for] S[atan for] he caused him evil?
> [And the spirit of t]ruth [will save him] from dar[kness because right]eousness is for him.
> . . . for ever [all the] son of Bel[ial. Amen. Amen.] Selah.
> (Vermes, 1997, pp. 310–11)

The Great Psalms Scroll also contains five compositions not found in Psalms which are usually, and perhaps misleadingly, called 'Apocryphal Psalms' (Vermes, 1997, pp. 301–7). Psalm 154 is a call to glorify God, particularly for his gift of wisdom. Psalm 155 is a prayer for deliverance, not least 'from the evil plague', which ends with a prayer for God to 'redeem Israel, your pious one . . . and the house of Jacob, your elect'. Vermes entitles another composition simply 'Prayer for Deliverance'. There is also the Apostrophe to Zion (an 'Apostrophe' is a direct speech that addresses an absent person – *DOTWPW*, p. 589), which is a prayer for and celebration of Zion's deliverance. Finally there is a wisdom-focused Hymn to the Creator. That Apostrophe reappears in another scroll (4Q88), together with two other 'apocryphal psalms' (which Swanson calls 'Eschatological Hymn' and 'Apostrophe to Judah' (Johnston and Firth, 2005, p. 256)). The latter reads:

> Then heaven and earth shall exult together.
> Let all the stars of the evening twilight exult.
> Rejoice, Judah, rejoice!
> Rejoice, rejoice and be glad with gladness!
> Celebrate your feasts and pay your vows
>   for there is no Belial in your midst.
> Raise your hand and fortify your right hand!
> Behold the enemy shall perish
>   and all the workers of iniquity shall be dispersed.
> But, Thou, O Lord, art for eve[r].
> Thy glory shall be for eve[r and eve]r.
> [Ha]ll[eluiah].
> (Vermes, 1997, pp. 308–9).

One of the earliest of the scrolls to be published was the 'Hymns Scroll' found in Cave 1 (1QH). Because the scroll had deteriorated badly in places it was not always clear which columns fitted where, and Vermes reproduces an arrangement of it dividing the material into 24 hymns with a few fragments left over (Vermes, 1997, pp. 243–300). These are hymns of thanksgiving (*hodayot*, from the Hebrew verb for giving thanks) voiced by a singular voice which occasionally might be identified as the leader of the community (hymn 12, lines 23–9; hymn 14, lines 23–4; hymn 15, line 21, and especially 'the Master' in hymn 23, line 12). Suggestions are made about the community occasion when these might have been used, but the same question of the identity of this 'I' remains as in the biblical psalms. As in those psalms, much of this thanksgiving is set in the context of opposition, enemies and distress, but some of it also comes from forgiveness and renewal after failure. Other familiar themes and images reappear: the knowledge that God is merciful and compassionate, the Heavenly Council, God's 'holy spirit', the Pit, together with new ones like Adam, Hell, Belial, the Covenant of the Community and Vanity. There is a strong 'wisdom' thread, of secret and divine knowledge revealed. Here is the opening of hymn 12:

I thank Thee, O Lord,
    for Thou hast illumined my face by Thy Covenant,

. . .

I seek Thee,
    and sure as the dawn
    Thou appearest as [perfect Light] to me.
Teachers of lies [have smoothed] Thy people [with words],
    and [false prophets] have led them astray;
they perish without understanding
    for their works are in folly.
For I am despised by them
    and they have no esteem for me
    that Thou mayest manifest Thy might through me.
They have banished me from my land like a bird from its nest;
    all my friends and brethren are driven far from me
    and hold me for a broken vessel.

And they, teachers of lies and seers of falsehood,
    have schemed against me a devilish scheme,
to exchange the Law engraved on my heart by Thee
    for the smooth things (which they speak) to Thy people.
And they withhold from the thirsty the drink of Knowledge,
    and assuage their thirst with vinegar,
that they may gaze on their straying,
    on their folly concerning their feast-days,
    on their fall into their snares.

But Thou, O God,
  dost despise all Belial's designs;
it is Thy purpose that shall be done
  and the design of Thy heart
  that shall be established for ever.

Two poorly preserved manuscripts contain parts of nine psalms similar to biblical ones (4Q380 and 381) but they are in poor condition. Four have titles: 'Psalm of Obadiah', 'Psalm of the Man of God', 'Prayer of ... (k)ing of Judah' and another but different 'Prayer of Manasseh' (Vermes, 1997, pp. 312–18). Equally similar to the biblical material are the two laments from 4Q179 and 4Q501 (Vermes, 1997, pp. 319–20).

Quite distinct are 12 songs of praise to God, sung by the angels on named Sabbaths at the Sacrifice of the Whole Burned Offering, only one of which Vermes sets out in poetic form (Vermes, 1997, pp. 321–30). Here is the first half of the first one for a taster,

[To the Master, Song of the holocaust of the] first [Sabba]th, on the fourth of the first month.

Praise [the God of ...] the 'gods' (= *elohim*) of supreme holiness; in [his] divine [kingship, rejoice. For he has established] supreme holiness among the everlastingly holy, to be for him the priests of [the inner Temple in his royal sanctuary], ministers of the Presence in his glorious innermost Temple chamber. In the congregation of all the gods (= *elim*) of [knowledge, and in the councils of all the spirits of] God, he engraved his precepts for all the spiritual works, and [his glorious] judgements [for all who lay the foundations of] knowledge, the people (endowed with) his glorious understanding, the 'gods' who are close to knowledge ... of eternity and from the fountain of holiness to the sanctuary of supreme [holiness] ... prie[sts] of the inner Temple, ministers of the Presence of the [most] holy King ... his glory.

The remaining entry under 'Hymns and Poems' in Vermes is a Hallelujah psalm and prayer for Jerusalem and 'King Jonathan', which may be a psalm from Jerusalem that prays for the Hasmonean King, Alexander Jannaeus (103–76 BC), though this is disputed.

Finally from Qumran, and very significantly, 51 fragments of commentaries on 15 psalms were found in caves 1, 4 and 11, of which 27 are on Psalm 37 (Vermes, 1997, pp. 487–91). Some of these texts use the 'pesher' ('Interpreted this concerns . . .') method as in the more famous Habakkuk commentary. As in that commentary the 'wicked' is interpreted to mean the 'Wicked Priest' (the High Priest in Jerusalem) and the 'righteous' to mean the 'Teacher of Righteousness', the leader of the community. Two points are important here. First, that this use of commentary on Psalms indicates that at Qumran Psalms appears to have biblical status earlier rather than later. Second, that this use of pesher (or 'fulfilment interpretation') shows that at Qumran Psalms is read as a 'prophetic' text (see Chapter 9).

Two more 'David' psalms are found among the Pseudepigrapha. Both are of uncertain provenance and are extant only in Syriac. Psalm 152 (5ApocSyrPs4) is an appeal for help, 'spoken by David after fighting against the lion and the wolf which took sheep from his flocks'. Psalm 153 (5ApocSyrPs5) is a psalm of praise, 'spoken by David after receiving God's grace when he delivered him from the lion and the wolf and those two he killed by his hands' (Charlesworth, vol. 2, pp. 615–17).

Pseudepigrapha

'Pseudepigrapha' comes from two Greek words, *pseud* ('false') and *graphō* ('write'). 'The Pseudepigrapha' is the term for an indeterminate number of Jewish books occupying the next circle out, as it were, from the Apocrypha, many of which bear the 'false names' of ancient biblical heroes like Abraham, Adam and Enoch. Forty-seven such books are included in the two volumes of *The Old Testament Pseudepigrapha*, edited by Charlesworth.

This note has confined itself to psalms outside Psalms in the Old Testament, that is, to those in the Apocrypha, the Pseudepigrapha and at Qumran. Music and song have been part of religion from its earliest days. Seybold warns that comparisons of biblical psalms with the religious songs of the ancient Near East must be done very carefully in order to respect the integrity of the different examples and the contexts from which they come (Seybold, pp. 211–12[7]). To end this chapter, however, and without attempting any comparison, here is a lament or petition from Ugarit, in the north of Canaan, from perhaps the middle of the second millennium BC:

> O El! O sons of El!
> O assembly of the sons of El!
> O meeting of the sons of El!
> O Tkmn and Shnm!
> O El and Ashirat!
>
> Be gracious, O El!
> Be a support, O El!
> Be salvation, O El!
> O El, hasten, come swiftly!
> To the help of Zaphon,
> to the help of Ugarit.
> With the lance, O El,
> with the upraised (?), O El.
> With the battle-axe, O El,
> with the shattering, O El.
> Because of the burnt offering, O El,
> because of the appointed sacrifice (?), O El,
> because of the morning sacrifice, O El.
> (Beyerlin, p. 222)

To do

Has anything in this chapter excited you? What? Why? Has anything in it challenged you? What? How? Has anything in it worried you? What? Why? Has anything in it influenced the way you will read the Old Testament in future?

Suggestions for further reading

God as King

Brettler, M. Z. (1989), *God is King: Understanding an Israelite Metaphor*, Sheffield: Sheffield Academic Press.
*'King', in *DBI*, pp. 476–8.
Mills, M. (1998), *Images of God in the Old Testament*, London: Cassell, pp. 109–21.
*Whitelam, K. W. (1992), 'King and Kingship', in *ABD*, vol. 4, pp. 40–8.

Messiah

*'Anointing', in *DBI*, p. 33.
de Jonge, M. (1992), 'Messiah', in *ABD*, vol. 4, pp. 777–87.
Wright, N. T. (1993), *The New Testament and the People of God*, London: SPCK, pp. 307–20.

Psalms at Qumran

Abegg, M., Flint, P. and Ulrich, E. (1999), *The Dead Sea Scrolls Bible*, New York: Harper-SanFrancisco, pp. 505–11.
Brooke, G. J. (2004), 'The Psalms in Early Jewish Literature in the Light of the Dead Sea Scrolls' in Moyise and Menken, *The Psalms in the New Testament*, pp. 5–24.
*Eshel, E. (2004), 'The Bible in the Dead Sea Scrolls', in Berlin and Brettler (eds), *The Jewish Study Bible*, pp. 1920–8.
Flint, P. W. (2005), 'The Prophet David at Qumran', in Henze, *Biblical Interpretation*, pp. 158–67.
*Introduction to Psalms, in *DSSB*, pp. 505–11.
Henze, M. (ed.) (2005), *Biblical Interpretation at Qumran*, Grand Rapids MI: Eerdmans.
Swanson, D. D. (2005), 'Qumran and the Psalms', in Johnston and Firth, *Interpreting the Psalms*, pp. 247–61.
*Vermes, G. (1994), *An Introduction to the Complete Dead Sea Scrolls*, 3rd edn, London: SCM Press, pp. 45–58.
Vermes, G. (1997), *The Complete Dead Sea Scrolls*, complete edn, London: Allen Lane, Penguin.

Psalms in the ancient Near East

ANET – see the index.

Beyerlin, W. (1978), *Near Eastern Religious Texts relating to the Old Testament*, London: SCM Press.

Longman, T. (2008), 'Psalms 2: Ancient Near Eastern Background', in *DOTWPW*, pp. 593–605.

Longman, T. (2005), 'The Psalms and Ancient Near Eastern Prayer Genres', in Johnston and Firth, *Interpreting the Psalms*, pp. 41–59.

Seybold, K. (1990), *Introducing the Psalms*, Edinburgh: T&T Clark, pp. 191–212.

Royal psalms and the theology of kingship

*Atwell, E. A. (2004), *The Sources of the Old Testament*, London: T&T Clark, pp. 75–83.

*Birch, B. C., Brueggemann, W., Fretheim, T. E. and Petersen, D. L. (1999), *A Theological Introduction to the Old Testament*, Nashville TN: Abingdon Press, pp. 215–52.

Brueggemann, W. (1997), *Theology of the Old Testament*, Minneapolis MN: Fortress Press, pp. 600–21.

Day J. (1990), *Psalms: Old Testament Guides*, Sheffield: Sheffield Academic Press, pp. 88–108.

Eaton, J. H. (1976), *Kingship and the Psalms*, London: SCM Press.

*Eaton, J. H. (1990), 'Kingship', in *DBI-SCM*, pp. 379–82.

Grant, J. A. (2005), 'The Psalms and the King' in Johnston and Firth, *Interpreting the Psalms*, pp. 101–8.

*Halpern, B. (1993), 'Kingship and Monarchy', in *OCB*, pp. 413–16.

*Lucas, E. (2003), *Exploring the Old Testament, vol. 3: The Psalms and Wisdom Literature*, London: SPCK, pp. 13–19.

The Psalms of Solomon

*Nickelsburg, G. W. E. (1981), *Jewish Literature between the Bible and the Mishnah*, London: SCM Press, pp. 203–12.

Wright, R. B. (1985), 'Introduction to the Psalms of Solomon', in Charlesworth, *The Old Testament Pseudepigrapha*, vol. 2, pp. 639–70.

7

Voicing Spirituality

What is this chapter about?

We have, of course, already been listening to psalms voicing spirituality (and theology) in the last five chapters. What we will attempt to do here and in the next chapter, however, is identify some particular psalms that seem to address these concerns specifically and directly. Most introductions to Psalms include some kind of summary of the theological themes found in the anthology, and the next chapter will attempt to do that. Many also look at 'wisdom psalms' and 'torah psalms' and some others that don't quite fit the major categories, which is part of what this chapter attempts to do by including them in a wider discussion. 'Spirituality' is a slippery but important contemporary word and in this chapter we shall use two definitions of it to consider 'the spirituality of Psalms'. There is also an examination of the important word 'torah'.

How is it organized?

- The psalm for exegesis is Psalm 1.
- In 'Voicing spirituality' we begin with two definitions of the word, look at Walter Brueggemann's famous threesome and then explore Psalms 119, 19 and 49, which broadly belong together, and then the very different twin psalms, 14 and 53.
- The extended comment is on 'torah'.
- There are boxes on Wisdom literature, Haggadah and Halakah, and Simhat Torah.

- There are a number of 'To do' boxes.
- The chapter ends with suggestions for further reading on 'The spirituality of Psalms', Torah and Wisdom.

What should I be able to do by the end of it?

- Identify the ways in which psalms voice 'spirituality'.
- Appreciate Brueggemann's threesome of psalms of orientation, disorientation and reorientation.
- Recognize the features of the 'Wisdom' tradition in the Old Testament.
- Understand the various uses of torah, Torah and *tôrôt*.

Psalm 1

> ## To do
>
> Do the usual exegesis notes on Psalm 1.

1. There is no title to this opening psalm of the anthology, which is neither a worship song of any kind nor a prayer. Nor does it fit easily into any of the usually suggested classifications. There is currently a strong feeling that, whether or not this psalm was written specifically to introduce the anthology, that is its task. It may at one time have been joined with Psalm 2 in one psalm.[1]

2. It boldly points out that there are two ways of life, a good one and a bad one, and that those who choose God's way find their lives blessed and those who make the wrong choice find theirs blighted. Standing alone this statement could be dismissed as unrealistic and naive, but its setting counters that because it stands at the head of an anthology that as a whole cannot be accused of naivety or any lack of realism about the realities of life and faith (as we saw in Chapters 4 and 6). As such, Psalm 1 is a challenge to commitment, an act of defiance, an encouragement to faith and a promise of personal and corporate fulfilment. It also illustrates how torah spirituality, classic Wisdom and Deuteronomic

orthodoxy are each facets of one coherent system of beliefs, values and norms of behaviour.

3. It divides simply into two: verses 1–3 speak of the success of 'those who do not follow the advice of the wicked'; verses 4–6 point out that 'the way of the wicked will perish'.

4. The psalm begins with a translation problem. The Hebrew expression is *'ašĕrê-* . . ., which is a joyful exclamation about how rewarding is the life of those who do not follow the advice of the wicked. This is a common expression in psalms and in wisdom literature (for example, Pss 41.1; 94.12; 119.1–2; 127.5; 128.1; 137.8–9; 144.15; 146.5; Prov. 3.13; 8.34; 28.14 etc.). But are those who do this best described as 'happy' (GNB, NJPS, NRSV, REB and Alter) or 'blessed' (AV, KNJV, NIV, NJB, RSV, TNIV)? 'Happy' can sound trivial and 'blessed' can suggest something deeper. We can cope with unhappiness in our lives if we are sustained by a deeper blessing, but 'blessed' is hardly contemporary English. The same problem exists with the Greek equivalent, *makarios*, in the Beatitudes in Matthew 5.1–12, and a consistent translation will use the same English word in both places. NRSV and REB fail the test. What is intended here is a deep-rooted, serious and enduring happiness.

Some commentators (for example Cohen, Goldingay, Kraus) see significance in the sequence in the three verbs in verse 1 (walk, stand, sit). Start to walk in that wrong way and you eventually become habituated to it.

The verb translated 'meditate' in verse 2 is also used for lions growling (Isa. 31.4) and doves calling (Isa. 38.14), which indicates that ancient Israel was one of those cultures where reading was not done silently.

The central question here is: what is meant by '*tôrat yhwh*'? Is it to be translated as 'the teaching of YHWH' in a general sense, or is it a reference to '*The Torah*'? If so, it is the only such reference in Psalms. This verse, in the opening chapter of what eventually became the third part of the Hebrew Bible ('The Writings') points up the importance of reading torah with attention in the same way that Joshua 1.8 does about reading the Torah at the beginning of what eventually became the second part of it ('The Prophets'). Most translations have 'law' here, which is unfortunate because that word is a negative one for many, and particularly in Christian discourse (see the discussion on Torah at the end of the chapter).

5. The psalm calls those who make the wrong choice and choose the wrong path 'the wicked', 'sinners' and 'scoffers'. The first two are common words, as we

have seen, but the third is unusual: *lēṣ/lēṣîm* is virtually a technical term in 'wisdom' vocabulary for those who never listen and who talk big and freely, especially about things they know little about. Proverbs 21.24 almost gives a definition: 'The proud, haughty person, named "Scoffer", acts with arrogant pride.' Other translations therefore call these people 'the scornful' (AV, NKJV), 'the insolent' (NJPS), 'cynics' (NJB), 'mockers' (NIV, TNIV) or, pursuing the idea a bit further, 'those who have no use for God' (GNB). *The Message Bible*, not everyone's cup of tea as a modern translation, puts it superbly, 'You don't go to Smart-Mouth College'. The psalmist observes that they might make a lot of noise but their lives fail to blossom into usefulness. They make no contribution to society and in the end are like chaff blown away in the wind. Their lives will not stand up to God's 'judgement', which is his critical scrutiny in the here and now rather than, as later understandings developed the idea, in a post-death act of judgement.

By contrast, the 'righteous' who 'delight in YHWH's torah' are 'happy/blessed' because they have made the right choice and chosen the right path. Their prosperity and blessing is also a source of blessing for society. They produce fruit, like fruit trees planted in well-irrigated places (verse 3; see Jer. 17.5–8 where the same contrast is made under the headings of 'cursed/blessed', and also Ezek. 17.5–10, 19.10). In verse 6 the contrast is expressed differently: God 'knows' (AV, NKJV, RSV) the way of the righteous, but that of the wicked 'perishes'. Other translations interpret 'knows' in two ways: 'watches over' (NRSV, NIV, NJB, TNIV) and 'cherishes' (NJPS) or 'embraces' (Alter). The Hebrew verb for 'knowing' includes intellectual knowledge but goes much further, involving emotional ties and including the deepest intimacy of sex ('Adam knew Eve, his wife', as the AV translates Gen. 4.1). This happy state of one's 'way' being 'known' by God comes from taking proper notice of God's torah, his teaching and guidance.

The dominant metaphor in this psalm is that of two contrasting ways or paths. The same Hebrew word is translated by NRSV in verse 1 as 'path' and twice as 'way' in verse 6, which rather disguises the *inclusio* being used here. The idea of two contrasting paths or ways is a prominent metaphor in the 'instruction' in Proverbs 1—9 (for example 1.15; 3.17, 23; 4.10–27; 5.5–6 etc.).

To do

Read Proverbs 2 and see how the 'two ways/paths' metaphor is used there.

Wisdom invites you down one path, Folly another. They end up in very different places. Which path you chose to 'walk in' is a crucial choice. In Psalm 1, for 'wisdom' read 'torah', but the choice and its consequences are the same.

6. Psalm 1 makes its point in the clearest of terms. Torah is the way! In so doing, it sets the agenda and gives the theme for Psalms as well as providing a text that Psalms 19 and especially 119 will expound. The anthology it introduces contains material for those who 'walk' in and by torah to use to praise YHWH for his blessings on them. For those who do that but without the promised blessings, Psalms gives material in which to voice complaint to God because he is failing to go by the agenda. Psalm 1 insists, however, that in the end only one 'way' goes anywhere and only one 'lifestyle choice' satisfies.

Voicing spirituality

'Spirituality' is a slippery modern term, used widely in a variety of contexts and sometimes seeming to mean whatever its users want it to mean.

To do

Look up 'Spirituality' in Wikipedia.

Books on 'spirituality' will be found on the 'Mind, Body and Spirit' shelves in bookshops rather than the 'Religion' ones, and this reflects a distinction commonly made between 'religion' and 'spirituality', some going further and saying 'Spirituality good, Religion bad'. By any definition, Psalms is a religious book, the product of a particular religion, with its psalms produced for religious purposes (public worship, private prayer, teaching etc.) and voicing feelings and emotions at high and low points of religious experience, individual and corporate. Definitions of 'spirituality' vary and in *Spirituality for Dummies*, Sharon Janis devotes 16 pages to 'Defining Spirituality' and gives us this:

Spirituality is a personal approach to connecting with the divine and experiencing the realms that exist beyond the sensory world.

> Spirituality is the wellspring of divinity that pulsates, dances, and flows as the source and essence of every soul. Spirituality relates mainly to [our] personal search and connection with the divine, as [we] look beyond outer appearances to find deeper significance and meaning. (Janis, pp. 26, 29)

On that basis, Psalms offers its readers, hearers and users a spirituality. Marie McCarthy supplies this definition, widely used in theology:

> Spirituality is a fundamental component of our human beingness, rooted in the natural desires, longings and hungers of the human heart. It is concerned with the deepest desires of the human heart for meaning, purpose and connection, with the deep life lived intentionally in reference to something larger than oneself. (McCarthy, p. 196)

In this sense all psalms 'voice spirituality' in that they are 'concerned with the deepest desires of the human heart for meaning, purpose and connection', even if in the case of some of them we might wonder what contribution they can possibly make to satisfying such desires. Psalms that voice praise or shalom celebrate that their users have discovered the meaning and purpose of their lives and feel connected with their real selves, their environment and their God. Psalms that voice dissonance or penitence enable felt disconnections to be expressed and addressed. When it comes, however, to 'the deep life lived intentionally in reference to something larger than oneself', some psalms are clearly more focused than others. All are making, or attempting to make, connections with God. All are concerned with issues of faith and life, in one way or another, in a religion that knows no distinction between 'sacred' and 'secular' and in which all of life is lived under God. But there are some psalms that focus on that living of life under God intentionally and specifically, and it is these psalms that are the concern of this chapter. Some name these psalms as 'Torah psalms', 'Wisdom psalms' and 'Prophetic psalms'. Others, in my view rightly, query overidentifying psalms like this. Without assuming any specific categories of psalms here we will presently discuss four psalms as examples of those that 'voice spirituality', in the sense of informing, enabling, encouraging and sustaining the 'living of the whole of life towards God'.

First, however, we must consider the clearest contemporary presentation available on 'spirituality in the psalms', which is Walter Brueggemann's threesome of psalms of orientation, disorientation and reorientation. We have already mentioned this trio several times, and will do so again for a different purpose in Chapter 9, but this is the point to fill out his headings and explain his thinking. I have taken the following from Brueggemann 2002 (pp. 8–12), and added his samples from the fuller version in Brueggemann 1984 (which was itself a rewrite of Brueggemann 1980) in which he called the second set 'psalms of dislocation') in the order in which he discusses them there:

1 Human life consists in satisfied seasons of well-being that evoke gratitude for the constancy of blessing. Psalms of orientation (for example, Pss 145, 104, 33, 8, 1, 119, 15, 4, 37, 14, 112, 133, 131) articulate the joy, delight, goodness, coherence and reliability of God in such seasons.

2 Human life consists in anguished seasons of hurt, alienation, suffering and death, which evoke rage, resentment, self-pity and hatred. Psalms of disorientation (for example, Pss 13, 86, 35, 74, 79, 137, 88, 109, 50, 32, 51, 143, 130, 49, 90, 73), with their extravagance, hyperbole and abrasiveness, give the words needed for this season in its ragged, painful disarray.

3 Human life consists in turns of surprise when we are overwhelmed with new gifts of God, when joy and light break through despair and darkness. Psalms of reorientation (for example, Pss 30, 40, 138, 34, 65, 66, 124, 114, 29, 96, 93, 97, 98, 99, 47, 27, 23, 91, 117, 135, 103, 113, 146, 147, 148, 100, 149, 150) speak boldly about this new gift that makes all things new.

4 Human life is not static and the life of faith involves two decisive moves that are always underway, 'by which we are regularly surprised and which we regularly resist' (Brueggemann, 2002, p. 9).

5 One move is a dismantling move, which might be sudden or gradual and which may be brought about by a number of factors, out of a settled orientation into a season of disorientation.

6 The other move is the astonishing one from a context of disorientation to a new orientation, a new coherence when we thought all was lost.

7 Western society is committed to continuity and success and to the avoidance of pain, hurt and loss. It is also resistant to genuine newness and real surprise. Worship communities that practice either of these two moves are engaged in counter-cultural and genuinely transformational acts.

Some readers will identify immediately with the realities of these two 'moves' of personal and communal faith experience of which Brueggemann writes. Others, no less faithful and equally 'inside' Jewish or Christian faith communities, will not find themselves relating to this language of 'moves' much if at all. William James, the father of the psychology of religion at the dawn of the twentieth century, called his major book *The Varieties of Religious Experience* and his plural is a useful reminder that when it comes to spirituality one size, shape, form, vocabulary or experience does not fit all.

In Johnston's list of psalm classifications, Psalms 1, 19 and 119 are called 'Torah psalms' by one or more of the commentators cited (Johnston and Firth, pp. 296–300). Whatever the merits of this as a sub-genre of psalm types, and whatever the particular issues surrounding Psalm 1 (what category it is and how it relates to the rest of Psalms) and Psalm 19 (what category it is and whether it is one psalm or two), there is no doubt that torah is the theme of Psalm 119.

To do

Read Psalm 119 and note down what you observe.

You will probably have noticed some or all of these features:

- its great length;
- its repetitiveness;
- in certain versions its structure is made clear. It is an acrostic with a vengeance. It contains 22 stanzas of 8 lines each, in which all the lines of each stanza begin with the same letter of the Hebrew alphabet;
- it voices a variety of different feelings among which dissonance is prominent;
- it mentions 'paths', 'ways' or 'walking' in every stanza except stanzas 7, 10 and 18–20 (though it is not obvious in 11 and 12);
- 'steadfast love' (*ḥesed*) features in verses 41, 64, 76, 77, 88, 124, 149 and 159;
- the 8 synonyms for *tôrâ* ('law'), which are found in the first stanza, are repeated throughout the psalm: 'decrees' (*ʿēdōt*), 'ways' (*derākîm*), 'precepts' (*piqqûdîm*), 'statute(s)' (*ḥuqqîm*), 'commandments' (*miṣwōt*), 'ordinances' (*mišpāṭîm*) and 'word' (*dābār* as in verse 9, or *ʿimrāh* as in verse 11). These are the NRSV translations but as with the terms for sacrifices this is compli-

cated by the fact that different English versions assign the same English terms to different Hebrew words (e.g. NRSV uses 'decrees' for *'ēdōt* and 'statutes' for *ḥuqqîm* but NIV/TNIV do it the other way round, REB uses 'statutes' for *ḥuqqîm* but 'decrees' for *mišpāṭîm*, NJPS uses 'decrees' for *'ēdōt* while GNB and NJB use neither for either nor for any of the others).

Each of the 22 stanzas of Psalm 119 repeats the same ideas and rotates most of the vocabulary of the first stanza, and 'delight in torah' is clearly the dominant theme in this longest psalm of all. 'Torah' occurs 36 times in Psalms: 1.2 (twice), 19.8; 37.31; 40.9; 78.1, 5, 10; 89.31; 94.12; 105.45, and 25 times in Psalm 119. As each stanza contains synonyms for torah, each stanza also contains a variety of verbs that express the psalmist's 'delighting in' it. The psalm, however, voices dissonance as much as praise and ends with a prayer for help. The psalmist's 'way' is not an easy or uncontested one. There are enemies and challenges to be faced and opposition to be overcome, so the psalm appeals to YHWH for help. It does so urgently but in confidence that despite life's traumas torah offers a 'true faith and a sure hope' and the right path along which to 'journey'. The 'desires, longings and hungers of the human heart' that this psalm voices are for shalom, the blessing and fulfilment of life; and the psalm is unapologetic in naming this as the 'good' (*tôb*) or 'well-being' that the psalmist seeks (verse 122). What is at odds with much contemporary 'me-focused' spirituality, however, is the psalm's insistence that 'meaning' and 'purpose' are to be found in the fullest engagement with YHWH's 'instructions'. It is in keeping, observing and following these that 'connection' is made with that 'something larger than oneself' in which life is most fully lived. 'Journey' is one of the key metaphors in contemporary spirituality, Psalm 119 is clear about what constitutes the route, the signposts and the steps.

The opening verses of Psalm 19 voice praise for the natural world (verses 1–6). Verses 7–13 are a miniature of Psalm 119 celebrating torah and appealing for God's help. The psalm ends with a prayer. Three of the commentators in Johnston's list call this a 'Wisdom psalm' and two a 'Torah psalm' (Johnston and Firth, p. 296), a further example of the difficulties of applying category classifications. What is not in dispute is that this psalm contains a significant number of features of what is commonly called 'the wisdom literature' and its particular vocabulary and spirituality, as well as of what we have just discussed as Torah spirituality. Psalm 49 is unanimously designated a 'Wisdom psalm' in

Johnston's list. It certainly opens with a universal address which claims to 'speak wisdom' and then to offer a proverb and a riddle. What follows is less clear. Is the riddle that this wise man is suffering, a fact that goes against the theory? And that both the wise man and the fool die and 'leave their wealth to others'? Or is the proverb and riddle one that begins to raise a protest against the easy certainties of other proverbs about prosperity, rewards and success? Or is the riddle to do with the meaning of the strange and repeated 'Mortals cannot abide in their pomp' (verses 12 and 20)? Whatever its mysteries, and despite the fact that 'wisdom psalm', as with some others, is a disputed category, what is not in dispute is that this psalm contains a significant number of features of what is commonly called 'the wisdom literature'.

Wisdom Literature

Jeremiah 18.18 (cf. Ezek. 7.26) mentions three groups of key people: the priests, the wise and the prophets. In the literature that 'the wise' produced there are no visions of God and no statements of what God has said. The wise observe nature and human affairs and draw conclusions about the best way to live well. Their literature includes little about worship, prayer, sacrifice or any of the particular concerns of the priests. Neither the immediacy of prophetic religion nor the reality of God's sacramental presence features in Wisdom thought. Its basic conviction is that wise living leads to fullness of life and folly leads to death (see Prov. 3.13–18 for a very clear statement of the rewards of wisdom). This wise living is based on carefully reflecting on the way the world works. God is not left out of this ('The fear of the Lord is the beginning of wisdom' is a recurring statement – Prov. 1.7; 9.10; 15.33; Job 28.28; Ps. 111.10) but his will and his ways are to be seen in creation and in the life of nature and human beings. Israel shared this 'Wisdom' approach with other nations. It was an international heritage (for example, Prov. 22.17—24.22 are lifted straight out of an Egyptian collection of proverbs called the Instruction of Amen-em-opet). Although Proverbs, Job and Ecclesiastes read quite differently they are usually regarded as the Old Testament's sample of 'wisdom literature', containing its characteristic outlook, literary forms (the proverb as in Prov. 10.1—22.16 and the 'instruction' as in Prov. 1—9) and distinctive vocabulary (e.g. 'the wise', 'wisdom', 'understanding' and their opposites 'folly', 'the fool' and 'the scorner'). How and where else this 'wisdom tradition' may be found in the Old Testament is a matter of debate. For possible 'wisdom psalms', Johnston's list offers 'majority verdicts' for Psalms 1, 37, 49, 73, 112, 127, 128 and 133.

Given this delineation of the 'Wisdom' approach the following features of it can be seen in Psalms 19 and 49:

- the observation of nature in Psalm 19.1–6;
- 'wisdom' vocabulary in Psalm 19 at verse 2 ('knowledge'), verse 7 ('making wise' and 'the simple'), verse 9 ('the fear of the LORD'), verse 12 ('detect/discern'), and verse 13 ('the insolent' or 'proud thoughts'), and in Psalm 49 at verse 3 ('wisdom' and 'understanding'), verse 4 ('proverb' and 'riddle'), verse 10 (the antithesis of 'wise' and 'fool') and verse 13 ('fool');
- the general viewpoint in Psalm 19 that a successful life results from the awareness that this world is created and ordered by God and from that self-awareness which enables one to negotiate one's way carefully through it by paying attention to the accumulated wisdom of experience and avoiding the siren voice of hubris;
- the 'universal' appeal in Psalm 49.1;
- the use made of 'observation' in Psalm 49 (verses 10, 12 and 20, 13 and 17–20);
- the underlying critique of 'pride' in Psalm 49, which surfaces strongly in verse 6 and in the repetition in verses 12 and 20;
- the underlying preoccupation with prosperity and success in Psalm 49.

Psalm 19.7 points to the role of torah in 'making wise the simple' and verse 13 adds a plea that the psalmist might be helped to avoid either joining 'the insolent' or having 'proud thoughts'. It looks for meaning, purpose and connection in a life of integrity (verses 13b–14). Psalm 49 represents a form of wisdom spirituality that goes beyond the simple 'prosperity gospel' of Proverbs 3.13–18. Like Psalm 119, it lives in the real world where there are 'times of trouble', 'enemies' who persecute and the same death that awaits everyone. Observing this the psalm begins to murmur what will become a shout of protest in Job and Ecclesiastes. Unlike 'torah spirituality', this challenged wisdom spirituality cannot appeal to specific instructions for clear guidance, for it knows that the proverbs on which other forms of wisdom rely are not as reliable as they seem, as in the proverb that appears to be quoted in verse 18. Whether it is beginning to think its way in verse 15 to some sort of idea of 'life after death' that balances the equation is disputed, and much depends on the date of the psalm, which is impossible to ascertain. At the very least here is a spirituality that recognizes that one's 'deepest desires for meaning, purpose and connection' are not satisfied by prosperity, reputation and achievement, and that the attitudes and values that so often accompany these things (i.e. pride, arrogance, self-assertion) are to be deplored. What does provide that in wisdom spirituality is 'wisdom' itself, 'understanding' and 'discernment' and the attitudes and values of modesty and discretion. This comes out clearly in the translation of verse 20a in TNIV, which makes an excellent *inclusio* to verse 3 with 'Human beings who have wealth but lack understanding . . .', but the line is too unclear for us to be confident about its translation in this way or any other.

Psalm 14 and its twin Psalm 53 receive four blanks in the seven columns in Johnston's list (Johnston and Firth, pp. 296–7) despite the presence of obvious 'wisdom' vocabulary: 'fools' (verse 1), 'wise' (verse 2 – though this is not the more usual word) and 'knowledge' (verse 4).[2] Two of the columns call it a 'prophetic' psalm, meaning that it reflects the sharp preaching of the prophets. Here too there is an element of dissonance (verse 7). The first three verses are a profoundly pessimistic comment on all humanity, whereas the next three utilize the classic distinction in Psalms between the 'evildoers' and 'God's people' ('the righteous'). The saying of the fool (singular in the Hebrew) in verse 1 that 'There is no God' is translated as 'God does not care' in NJPS, a translation supported by the parallels in Psalm 10.4 (cf. Pss 73.11 and 94.7) and explained in a footnote in the *Jewish Study Bible*:

The translation of Heb. 'There is no God' as 'God does not care' is based on the assumption that atheism did not exist in antiquity. People could, however, believe in a deity who created the world, but then absented himself from running it.

Craigie adds further clarification:

That which gives rise to the entire psalm is the 'fool' and the nature of his folly. The fool is opposed to God, threatens the life of the righteous, and thus evokes both lament and prayer for deliverance from those whose lives he affects. But the fool is not simply one lacking in mental powers, indeed, the fool may be a highly intelligent person. The fool is one whose life is lived without the direction or acknowledgement of God. (Craigie, p. 147)

This psalm opens with an uncompromising, and obviously overstated, assertion that without God there is no morality, followed by a second one that 'there is no one, not even one, who does good'. Behind these assertions lie the Torah's insistence that 'Belief and Behaviour go together' and that God's concerns are for the whole of human life. Communal and personal wellbeing come from 'knowledge', which is paralleled with 'calling upon YHWH' (verse 4). Left to themselves, the psalm suggests, 'the natural desires, longings and hungers of the human heart' lead individuals 'astray' and result in destructive attitudes and behaviours. Acknowledging God is the only safeguard against living such disordered lives, the psalm insists, because it is only 'knowledge' of God that fulfils the 'deepest desires of the human heart for meaning, purpose and connection', because God alone is the only true 'something larger than oneself'. For this psalmist 'knowledge' is not simply 'knowing about' but also 'experience of', 'engagement with' and 'relationship to', and 'knowledge of God' is the way to wisdom, 'good' and human flourishing both personal and communal.[3]

When Psalms 119, 19 with 49, and 14/53 are read in the light of Marie McCarthy's definition of spirituality it is possible to identify common ground. Each identifies the essential 'something larger than oneself' with God, which rather invites the retort, 'Well they would, wouldn't they!' But here, as in other areas of biblical study, there is virtue in stating the obvious. Psalms is a religious text. 'God' is its presupposition and *raison d'être*. Whatever your question, 'God' will be part of its answer. So, with regard to spirituality, all these psalms assert that 'the desires, longings and hungers' of the human heart 'for meaning, purpose and connection' are satisfied only when reference is made to God, though each focuses its assertion in a slightly different way and approaches it from a different angle. Psalm 119 suggests that torah provides the 'place' where 'intentionally' we can 'make the journey'. For Psalms 19 and 49, 'wisdom' provides the vocabulary and framework. For Psalms 14 and 53, more explicit acknowledgement of God ('calling upon YHWH') is the way to personal and communal fulfilment.

> **Other psalms that voice spirituality**
>
> Using the more precise definition of spirituality we have been working with, my list would be Psalms 1, 19, 49, 119 and 14/53, plus 15, 25, 26, 34, 36, 39, 50, 61, 62, 85, 101, 111, 112, 128, 139 and 141, which are found in a variety of categories in most listings.

Torah

Psalm 119 is almost invariably called a 'Torah psalm'. It is never called a 'Law psalm' even in books that speak of 'the Law, the Prophets and the Writings'. This simple observation prompts this extended comment on 'torah', because it exposes the negative sense that 'Law' has in much Christian discourse, which leads to serious misunderstandings of both the Old Testament and Judaism, and invites reconsideration of this important Old Testament term.

The most obvious translation of the noun *tôrâ* is with words like 'teaching', 'guidance' or 'instruction'. The related verb is most naturally translated by 'teach', 'guide' or 'instruct'. Moses tells the Israelites that the skilled craftsmen Bezalel and Oholiab have also been inspired by God to 'teach' (Ex. 35.34). The speaker in the Instruction in Proverbs 1—9 tells his 'son' what his father had 'taught' him (Prov. 4.4). Job's friends, frustrated that he will not listen to them, tell him to ask the animals, birds, plants and fish to 'teach' him (Job 12.7–8). God tells Aaron to 'teach' the people everything Moses has told them (Lev. 10.11), and Moses reminds the people to observe carefully what the levitical priests have 'taught' them (Deut. 24.8). Ezekiel reminds the same priests about their 'teaching' role (Ezek. 44.23).

We saw that in Psalm 119 the noun is used for the sum total of God's instructions and as such is synonymous with his 'word' in making known God's 'ways'. In that psalm, NRSV and most others translate *tôrâ* by 'law' (NJB as 'Law'), but NJPS and Alter have 'teaching'. In the same way it is synonymous with the word 'covenant' in Psalm 78.10 and Hosea 8.1. Torah is also used in a general sense for parental 'teaching' (Prov. 1.8; 3.1; 4.2; 6.20; 7.2), the teaching of the wise (Prov. 13.14; 28.4, 7 – 'law' NRSV) and the 'kind teaching' of a capable wife

(Prov. 31.26). A psalmist requests a hearing for his 'teaching' (Ps. 78.1). Seers and prophets give God's teaching (Isa. 30.9, 'instruction' NRSV) or falsify it (Jer. 8.9). Isaiah uses the word for his own teaching and for the teaching that people receive when they consult 'ghosts and spirits' (Isa. 8.16, 20). Some passages see it as teaching particularly associated with priests (Jer. 2.8; 18.18; Ezek. 7.26; Mal. 2.6–9). It is teaching that some have appropriated (Pss 37.31; 40.8; Isa. 51.7) while others have not (Isa. 5.24; 42.24; Jer. 6.19; 16.11; Hos. 4.6; Hab. 1.4, and in the plural at Dan. 9.10). It is the teaching people will seek and find in 'the days to come' (Isa. 2.4; 42.4; 51.4; Jer. 31.33). In the large majority of verses where God's torah in this general sense is intended, though not elsewhere, NRSV translates the word by 'law' and NJPS usually 'teaching' or 'instruction(s)' but never 'law'.

The noun is also used for specific directions or instructions, especially those given by priests (Deut. 17.11; Hag. 2.11). Each ritual has its own torah (Lev. 7.1, 7, 11, 37 and frequently in Leviticus and Numbers). RSV translates the word here by 'law', NIV/TNIV by 'regulations' and NRSV, NJB and NJPS by 'rituals'. All the usages of the word so far have (with the exception of Dan. 9.10) been in the singular. In the plural it is used for all the *ḥuqqîm* and *tôrôt* which Moses has to explain to those whose disputes he is trying to settle (Ex. 18.16, 20 – NRSV 'statutes and instructions', NJPS 'laws and teachings'). Ditto in Psalm 105.45. Other examples of this plural use are Genesis 26.5, Exodus 16.28, Leviticus 26.46, Nehemiah 9.13 and Isaiah 24.5. Ezekiel 43.11–12 uses the word three times, first in the plural for all the particular regulations of the new Temple about which Ezekiel is being told, then twice in the singular, probably to stress that the regulation that really matters is that the Temple Mount is holy!

Another distinguishable and frequent use of the word, particularly with the definite article or in the expressions 'book of the law' (NRSV: Deut. 30.10; 31.26; Josh. 1.8; 8.34; NJPS 'Book of the Teaching') and 'law of Moses' (NRSV: 2 Chron. 23.18; 30.16; Ezra 3.2; 7.6 etc.; NJPS 'Teaching of Moses'), is for the collection of 'statutes and ordinances' given by God to Moses. It is this torah that Moses expounds in Deuteronomy (1.5; 4.8; 4.44 etc.) and a version of it that Hilkiah claims to have found 'in the house of the LORD' (2 Kings 22.8).

The best known use of 'torah', however, is not a biblical one. This is its use as the name of the first and most important of the three parts of the Hebrew Bible: Torah, Nevi'im and Kethuvim (as they are given in NJPS) or traditionally, The Law, The Prophets and The Writings. The earliest example of this use is in the Greek expression translated as 'the Law and the Prophets' in the Prologue to Ecclesiasticus, where the Greek term is *nomos*. This use is well established by the time of the New Testament (e.g. Matt. 5.17; 22.40; Luke 16.16; Acts 13.15), as is the expression 'the Law of Moses' (Luke 2.22; 24.44; John 7.23; Acts 13.39; 15.5). Judaism can refer to this as the 'Written Torah' to which it adds the 'Oral Torah', the rabbinic reflections, discussions, commentary and interpretations of it written down in the third century AD by Rabbi Judah haNasi in what we now know as the *Mishnah*.

From this data we can see that the word *tôrâ* has a number of meanings. 'The' Torah is the name of a five-part and hugely important 'book'. A 'torah' is an individual piece of teaching or instruction, which might be as specific as a regulation or a commandment. 'Torah' is a general term for teaching or instruction, and by extension for the content of what has been taught. And it is at this point that the question of what the term connotes comes in. There is no indication anywhere in the Old Testament that torah in any of its meanings or uses is perceived as anything other than a good thing. And that is the problem when it is translated as 'Law', especially with the capital letter, because in much influential Christian use 'Law' has a bad name. It is not going too far to say that in Judaism 'Torah' stands for the good news of God which is concentrated in the Torah book, and for which the English term 'gospel' would not be an inappropriate translation. This is why, presumably, Goldingay entitles volume 1 of his three-part *Old Testament Theology*, 'Israel's Gospel'. Christian discourse, on the other hand, habitually contrasts 'Law' and 'Gospel' with sinister results.

To do

What do you think about the suggestion that 'Torah' could, and probably should, be translated by 'Gospel'?

It is, of course, true that the Torah contains *tôrôt*; that the Teaching contains instructions, 613 of them in the traditional count: the decrees, precepts, statutes, commandments and ordinances mentioned so frequently in Psalm 119. And this raises the question of what these are and how they fit in. In the traditional Christian caricature of Judaism, and the traditional Protestant caricature of Roman Catholicism, the thinking is simple. These commandments or 'works' are exercises that earn merit marks by which people can gain salvation. Keep them, or enough of them, and you will be OK. Fail to keep them and you won't.

This legalistic religion of 'salvation by works' is in marked contrast, the argument goes, with the true evangelical message that salvation is by grace through faith, God's gift which we can never earn or merit. That this way of thinking is fundamentally mistaken can be seen in the introduction to the Ten Commandments, the Big Ten of the 613, in Exodus 20.1–2 (and Deut. 5.6): 'Then God spoke all these words: I am YHWH your God, who brought you out of the land of Egypt, out of the house of slavery; you . . .' The point is clear. God has already 'saved' his people from Egypt. These commandments are instructions about how to live their lives now that they are 'saved'. They are not about what must be done if God is to 'save' the doers.

It is also true that to many modern readers, Jew and Christian, the 613 *tôrôt* seem an odd mixture. Some are to do with how God is to be worshipped: what festivals are to be observed, when sacrifices are to be offered and how, or who are to be priests and what they have to do. Others are to do with crimes, not only with criminal acts like theft or murder, but with such things as slander or negligence. Others are rules to regulate social and economic practices like divorce, banking or slavery. There are rules to do with diet and cooking, what sort of animals can be eaten, and how they are to be prepared. The purpose of some of these is obvious, any civilized society needs laws about murder, and any religion needs rules about worship: but the Torah makes no distinction between criminal law, ritual rules, civil law or morals. God has given all the commandments, and they are all to be kept. God's covenant people are to be marked by the way they live and what they do, and in that living and doing the Torah does not distinguish between religion and the rest of life. The *tôrôt* cover all of life. Belief and behaviour go together. Faithfulness to God is to be seen just as much in the kitchen as in the Temple.

Haggadah and Halakah

The Torah contains a great variety of material, principally narrative and instruction. The technical terms for these are 'haggadah' and 'halakah'. Haggadah, with its plural 'haggadot' (from the verb 'to tell' or 'narrate'), is used for those stories, legends, parables, anecdotes and so on that provide examples of and inspiration for living in God's way. Halakah, with its plural 'halakot' (from the verb 'to walk'), is used for the rules, commandments and instructive guidance for living in God's way.

The implications of this understanding of torah for reading the New Testament (not least for appreciating Jesus' attitude to 'the Law' and Paul's wrestling with the question of gentiles and 'the Law') are considerable, as the work of E. P. Sanders and the 'New Perspective on Paul' show. Jesus and Paul were, after all, first-century Jews, not sixteenth-century Protestants.[4]

Simhat Torah

In the course of a year the Torah is read from beginning to end, and each Sabbath takes its name from its appointed reading. The cycle ends and immediately begins again in the autumn, at the festival of Simhat Torah or 'Rejoicing for the Torah'. This popular festival marks the end of a period of festivals whose dominant mood is solemn and earnest, and as if by way of relief after such solemnity the mood of Simhat Torah is one of unconfined joy. The scrolls are processed round the synagogue, at first with some semblance of dignity, but then with ever increasing joyfulness as they are passed from hand to hand amid songs and dances, while the children wave specially prepared flags. In some places it is still the custom to extend the procession out of the synagogue and into the streets. (de Lange, p. 53)

In Judaism and the Old Testament the word 'torah', in all its senses and uses, is entirely warm and wholesome. The 'Teaching of Moses' is a Good Thing. Its 613 commandments are good things too, God's guidance on how to live well and flourish. Psalm 119 expresses sheer delight in torah, as does the festival of Simhat Torah. The dynamic of 'good news' and 'instructions' is no different in Judaism than it is in Christianity (as Jesus, Paul and the writer of 1 John assert: Matt. 7.12–29; Rom. 12; 1 John 2.1–11). God has made himself known as a God who 'saves', and the scriptures of both faiths tell the story of 'salvation' and then follow that story with guidance about how to live out that salvation to the full.

> **To do**
>
> Has anything in this chapter excited you? What? Why? Has anything in it challenged you? What? How? Has anything in it worried you? What? Why? Has anything in it influenced the way you will read the Old Testament in future?

Suggestions for further reading

Spirituality in Psalms

Until recently books like some of these below would not have appeared as further reading suggestions in a book like this. They would have been seen as 'devotional' literature out of place in an 'academic' textbook. It is now increasingly recognized that 'devotional' readings of Scripture have their place alongside other 'readings' and that consideration of such readings has its place in academic studies. This makes all the more surprising the lack of any entry at all relating to 'Spirituality' in *DOTWPW*. The titles which follow explore the spirituality of Psalms in a variety of ways and from a variety of faith traditions.

Anderson, B. W. (2000), *Out of the Depths*, Louisville KY: Westminster John Knox Press.

Bartholomew, C. and West, A. (eds) (2001), *Praying by the Book*, Carlisle: Paternoster Press.

Bellinger, W. H. (1990), *Psalms: Reading and Studying the Book of Praises*, Peabody MA: Hendrickson.

Brueggemann, W. (2002), *Spirituality of the Psalms*, Minneapolis MN: Fortress Press. This is an abridged version of *The Message of the Psalms* and focuses the content of that important book well. It makes an excellent introduction to Brueggemann.

Cotter, J. (1989), *Through Desert Places: A Version of Psalms 1–50*, Sheffield: Cairns Publications.

Cotter, J. (1991), *By Stony Paths: A Version of Psalms 51–100*, Sheffield: Cairns Publications.

Cotter, J. (1993), *Towards the City: A Version of Psalms 101–150*, Sheffield: Cairns Publications.

Craven, T. (1992), *The Book of Psalms: Message of Biblical Spirituality 6*, Collegeville MN: The Liturgical Press.

Eaton, J. (2004), *Meditating on the Psalms*, London: Continuum.

Eaton, J. (2006), *Psalms for Life*, London: SPCK.

Magonet, J. (1994), *A Rabbi Reads the Psalms*, London: SCM Press.

Ryrie, A. (2004), *Deliver us from Evil*, London: Darton, Longman and Todd.

Stuhlmuller, C. D. (2002), *Spirituality of the Psalms*, Collegeville MN: The Liturgical Press.

Travers, M. E. (2003), *Encountering God in the Psalms*, Grand Rapids MI: Kregel.

Wallace, H. N. (2005), *Words to God, Word from God*, Aldershot: Ashgate.

White, R. E. O. (1984), *A Christian Handbook to the Psalms*, Grand Rapids MI: Eerdmans.

Torah

*Ehrlich, C. S. (1993), 'Israelite Law', in *OCB*, pp. 421–3.

Enns, P. (1996), 'Law of God', in *NIDOTTE*, vol. 4, pp. 893–900.

Harrelson, W. J. (1962), 'Law in the OT', in *IDB*, vol. 3, pp. 77–89.

LeFebvre, M. (2005), 'Torah–Meditation and the Psalms: the invitation of Psalm 1', in Johnston and Firth, *Interpreting the Psalms*, pp. 213–25.

*Sanders, E. P. (1992), 'Law in Judaism in the NT Period', in *ABD*, vol. 4, pp. 254–65.

*Sanders, J. A. (1976), 'Torah', in *IDBSupp*, pp. 909–11.

*Stern, P. (1993), 'Torah', in *OCB*, pp. 747–8.

Wisdom

*Crenshaw, J. L. (1993), 'Wisdom Literature', in *OCB*, pp. 801–3.

Dell, K. (2000), *Get Wisdom, Get Insight*, London: Darton, Longman and Todd.

*Lucas, E. (2003), *Exploring the Old Testament, vol. 3: The Psalms and Wisdom Literature*, London: SPCK, pp. 79–90.

*Lucas, E. (2008), 'Wisdom Theology', in *DOTWPW*, pp. 901–12.

Murphy, R. E. (1992), 'Wisdom in the OT', in *ABD*, vol. 6, pp. 920–31.

Wilson, G. H. (1993), 'Wisdom', in *NIDOTTE*, vol. 4, pp. 1276–85.

See also 'Walk, walking' and 'Path' in *DBI*.

8

Voicing Theology

What is this chapter about?

In this chapter we work with the simple definition that theology is 'talk about God'. It is therefore obvious that, as with spirituality, every psalm voices theology. Angry and accusatory questions and the shouts of praise that address God directly stand next to reflective meditations about God in a rich mix of styles, ages and approaches, as one would expect in a hymn book or an anthology of prayers or religious poetry. In this chapter we will focus on one psalm and see how it talks about God and then look at the treatment of theology in Psalms in some recent introductions and commentaries. The final comment will be on the development of 'monotheism' in ancient Israel.

How is it organized?

- The psalm for exegesis is Psalm 103 because, in the words of L. C. Allen, it 'takes the reader into the heart of Old Testament theology' (Allen, p. 23).
- In 'Voicing theology' we look at how some introductions and commentaries treat the theology of Psalms, including the so-called 'core creed' of Exodus 34.6–7.
- In 'Changing ideas about God' we look at the emergence of 'monotheism' in the Old Testament.
- There are boxes on intertextuality, Old Testament theology, 'Israel's core creed?' and the Shema.
- There are the last set of 'To do' boxes in the book!

- The chapter ends with suggestions for further reading on Asherah, *mišpāt*, Old Testament theology and the theology of Psalms.

What should I be able to do by the end of it?

- Appreciate the richness of Psalm 103.
- Describe what it means to 'bless YHWH'.
- Understand why Exodus 34.6–7 is sometimes called the Old Testament's 'core creed' and evaluate its central theological statements.
- Recognize that the development of ancient Israel's ideas about God was complex and understand the key terms in the debate.
- Begin to identify what is involved in talking about 'Old Testament theology' and the 'theology of Psalms'.

Psalm 103

> ### To do
>
> For the last time, jot down the points you would want to make in your exegesis of Psalm 103.

1. Psalm 103 has no title other than 'Of David' and no features that provide clear clues to its provenance. Majority opinion regards it as a late psalm, mainly for linguistic reasons.

2. It is a psalm that voices praise both for personal blessings received from YHWH (verses 2–5) and for his blessings on Israel (verses 6–18). The *inclusio*, 'Bless YHWH, my soul', with the repeated calls to 'bless YHWH' in verses 2 and 20–22, suggests that the purpose of the psalm is to 'bless YHWH', and so carefully considering what that might mean is important.

3. Different translations divide the psalm at slightly different points on the basis of movements in its thought. There is a move at verse 6 and another at

verses 19 or 20. The neatest division (and remember that these divisions are in the eye of the divider) is at verses 6 and 20, which then gives this structure:

- opening 'affirmation' of YHWH (using the expression 'bless YHWH') in which the psalmist gives his reasons why YHWH is to be 'affirmed' (verses 1–5);
- a depiction of YHWH using a number of traditional theological motifs (verses 6–19);
- closing 'affirmation' of YHWH (using the same expression) in which the psalmist calls on 'heaven and earth' to affirm YHWH too (verses 20–22).

4. There are no significant problem words or ideas in the psalm other than establishing the meaning of 'bless YHWH' (*bārăkî/bārăkû yhwh*), which occurs six times (in the *inclusio*, plus verses 2, 20, 21 and 22). Note that the second 'bless' in verse 1 is added in English translations; the Hebrew features an ellipsis at this point.

GNB, NIV, TNIV, BCP and Kraus translate *bārăkî/bārăkû yhwh* as 'praise the Lord', treating *hallĕlû – yāh/yhwh* and *bārăkû yhwh* as synonyms. NRSV, AV, NJB, NJPS, REB, CW, Alter, Eaton and Limburg, for example, translate them differently, but even commentaries that use 'bless the Lord' rarely stop to explain what this old-fashioned and rather curious expression means. We understand what is meant by God blessing someone or something, and for someone to pray that God might bless them or someone else, but in this phrase the Lord is the object of the verb. What, one therefore wonders, have we to give to God to enhance his life, which is what the verb means in normal liturgical use? Given that difficulty, it is easy to see why the phrase is translated by 'praise the Lord' or even 'thank the Lord', as when a congregation responds with 'Thanks be to God' to the liturgical invitation, 'Let us bless the Lord'. To praise and thank God, whether that is one activity or two, are recognizable components of worship, and it is apparent that for many to 'bless the Lord' is much the same thing. The question is whether, at least in the Old Testament, that is what it means to 'bless YHWH'.[1]

To do

1 Look up Psalm 100.4 in a variety of translations and compare the English verbs used.
2 Look up Psalms 100.4, 28.6–7 and 34.1 in NRSV and note the verbs used and the relationship between them.
3 Look up Psalms 100.3, 28.5 and 8, and 34.2–3 in NRSV and see if there is anything in these verses that are in close contact with the ones you have just looked up that adds anything extra.

At the end of the second exercise you might have concluded that 'praise', 'thank' and 'bless' are indeed synonyms, or at least are closely related. At the end of the third you might have noticed the emphasis on 'affirming YHWH'. This is also the emphasis in Psalm 103.1–5 where the psalm lists five ways in which YHWH has 'benefited' the psalmist, each one using the participle of a verb with the definite article, a most unusual feature in Hebrew poetry. The effect is dramatic, asserting powerfully that 'He is the one who . . .'. Psalms 135 and 145 are good examples of this 'stronger' sense of 'bless'. Psalm 135 has *hallĕlû – yāh* as its *inclusio* but moves from an initial stanza that calls for YHWH to be praised to a final one that calls for him to be blessed. Psalm 145 uses 'bless' in its *inclusio*, with 'extol' in the first verse and 'praise' in the last. Both psalms are strongly affirmatory, making powerful assertions about YHWH as if there is a point to be proved. The same sense of 'bless YHWH' can be seen in 1 Chronicles 29.10–11 and 20–22:

> Therefore David blessed the LORD in the presence of all the assembly; David said, 'Blessed are you, O LORD, the God of our ancestor Israel, forever and ever. Yours, O LORD, are the greatness, the power, the glory, the victory, and the majesty; for all that is in the heavens and on the earth is yours; yours is the kingdom, O LORD, and you are exalted as head above all.'

> Then David said to the whole assembly, 'Bless the LORD your God.' And all the assembly blessed the LORD, the God of their ancestors, and bowed their heads and prostrated themselves before the LORD and the king. On the next day they offered sacrifices and burnt offerings to the LORD, a thousand bulls, a thousand rams, and a thousand lambs, with their libations, and sacrifices

in abundance for all Israel; and they ate and drank before the LORD on that day with great joy.

In verses 10–11 we see David 'blessing YHWH' at a fund-raising event for building the Temple. What he does is in fact to declare how great YHWH is. Here, to 'bless YHWH' is to declare his greatness (as in verse 11). Similarly in verses 20–22 David calls on the congregation to 'bless YHWH' and their response is to bow their heads, worship and offer sacrifices. Here 'blessing YHWH' is about acknowledging him, giving him due honour.

It seems, therefore, that 'blessing YHWH' is more than praising or thanking him.[2] It appears to be about affirming that YHWH is God and declaring what kind of God he is, or, in the words of Horst, 'to acknowledge someone in his position of power and in his claim to high dignity with all due formality' (in Kraus, 1989, p. 291). This sense is supported by the fact that in the overwhelming number of occurrences of this verb with 'God' as its object, the object word is the divine name YHWH and not the word 'God' (60 occurrences to 6). This sense is clear in passages like Exodus 18.10–12, Deuteronomy 8.11–20 and Joshua 22.33 and may have its origin in the promotion of YHWH as God for Israel in the course of the development of ancient Israel's theology (of which more below). The clearest example of people actually 'blessing YHWH' might then be the people's response to Elijah's dramatic mountain-top victory when they throw themselves on their faces and say, 'YHWH – he is God! YHWH – he is God!' (1 Kings 18.39, cf. Deut. 4.35 and Josh. 24.18). This is also the sense of the repeated 'Blessed are you' and its responses, principally 'Sing his praise and *exalt him* for ever' (my italics), in the Song of the Three Young Men (Dan. 3.28–68, LXX), used liturgically as the Benedicite. I suspect, however, that we will wait a long time before congregations reply '*Adonai* is God, *Adonai* is God' in response to 'Let us bless the Lord'.

5. In *verses 1–5*, the psalm opens with a poetic idiom in which the psalmist announces his intention in saying this psalm. For this idiom of addressing his 'soul', see also Psalm 104.1 and compare Psalms 25.1, 42.2, 57.8, 108.2 and 146.1. The purpose of the psalm is to 'affirm' YHWH and to say why it is YHWH who is to be 'affirmed'. In the first instance it is because 'he is the one who' has restored the blessings of shalom to the psalmist. The description of shalom in verses 3–4 in terms of forgiveness, healing, rescue, 'crowning with *ḥesed* and "mercy" (*raḥamim*)' and 'satisfying with good' can be added to those noted in Chapter 3. The sum total of these five benefits (or possibly the sixth benefit) is that of

'renewed youth like an eagle's'. The Hebrew word covers both eagles and vultures, and it is not hard to see why all the translations go for 'eagles', which also appear in 2 Samuel 1.23 and Isaiah 40.30–31. GNB talks of being 'strong' as an eagle and Coverdale's old English in BCP has 'young and lusty as an eagle', but most translations rightly leave us with the metaphor and our imaginations.

Verses 6–19 form the core of the psalm and consist of a depiction of YHWH using a number of traditional theological motifs. From personal well-being the psalmist widens his reasons for affirming YHWH to YHWH's benefits to the covenant community and the 'whole earth' (the 'all' of verse 19). Two of the key words from the first stanza (ḥesed and raḥămîm) are repeated at verses 8, 11 and 17 and at verses 8, 13 (twice) respectively in a stanza that moves from reference to YHWH's 'righteous acts' (his acts which put things right, ṣědāqôt – verses 6 and 17, though this is not obvious in NRSV's 'vindication' in verse 6 and 'righteousness' in verse 17) to a declaration that he is universal king. The key event that demonstrates YHWH's action on behalf of his people is identified in verse 7 by the reference to Moses and in verse 18 by the reference to 'covenant' and 'commandments'. No details are given and readers or hearers are expected to know the Exodus story and recognize it as their story. They are the 'oppressed' who continue to experience YHWH's ṣědāqôt and mišpāṭîm (verse 6), the 'people of Israel' who know about Moses (verse 9), the 'us' of verses 10, 12 and 14 who know about their 'sins', 'iniquities' and 'transgressions' (verses 10 and 12), YHWH's anger (verses 8b–9) and his 'amazing fatherly grace' which surpasses it (verses 8a, 10–14), and about the transience of life and the eternity of YHWH's ḥesed and ṣedāqāh.[3] They are 'those who fear YHWH' (verses 11, 13 and 17), a verbal phrase which is best translated as 'those who worship YHWH', just as the noun phrase ('the fear of YHWH') is probably best understood to mean 'Yahwistic religion'. They are the ones who 'keep his covenant' and 'remember to do his commandments' (verse 18). These verses, which are framed by one-word markers of the Exodus story ('Moses' in verse 7 and 'the covenant' in verse 18), are rich in important words from the theological vocabulary of the Old Testament ('steadfast love', 'merciful and gracious', 'slow to anger', 'righteousness', including in verse 8 a quotation of its 'core creed') and in traditional expressions ('the fear of the LORD', 'children's children', 'remember to do his commandments'). As hymns and prayers rarely spell out that to which they allude, so this hymn assumes that readers and hearers know the story and pick up the allusions.[4] Ending the stanza at verse 19, however, adds another dimension, which picks up the reference to humanity in general in verse 15 and concludes with the depiction of YHWH as 'king' of heaven and earth.

Intertextuality

Psalm 103 is a good example of 'intertextuality'. Coming in from literary studies, this word became part of the vocabulary of biblical studies in the 1980s and refers to the way in which texts depend on other texts for their meaning. Psalm 103 works, for example, because a word here, an expression there or a name somewhere else sets it within a bigger narrative and it draws meaning into itself from that bigger narrative. In turn, those who read this psalm will read that bigger narrative more richly when they read it again. The most obvious forms of intertextuality are the direct quotation and the allusion, but whether a passage quotes another one or not or alludes to another, so the theory goes, all texts in a given corpus are related and interdependent because writers make use, consciously or unconsciously, of the texts that were there before them and readers make connections between the texts they know. A frequently used word here is *bricolage* (or 'collage'), which suggests that texts are created out of bits of other texts. See Koptak (2008), 'Intertextuality', in *DOTWPW*, pp. 325–32, and, for an advanced discussion, B. L. Tanner (2001).

Verses 20–22 are almost a precis of Psalm 148. Verse 19 makes the move from YHWH's authority over his covenant community to his authority in 'the heavens' and his cosmic rule, and verse 20 calls on the 'heavenly beings' and 'all his works' to affirm him. We met the 'Heavenly Court' in Chapter 6, and here again we see both how YHWH is regarded as supreme over all the 'unseen world' and how reticent the Old Testament is in describing it. The angels (described as 'mighty ones') 'do YHWH's bidding'. The Hebrew term is *mal'āk*, 'messenger', and when the message is from God the Old Testament usually translates the word as 'angel'. In Psalms we also find 'guardian angels' who protect God's people (for example, Pss 34.7 and 91.11, cf. 35.5) and 'destroying angels' who punished the Egyptians before they would let the Israelites go (Ps. 78.49). In later Jewish literature the picture becomes even more colourful and complex with grades of heavenly angels and 'cherubim', 'seraphim' and 'sons of God' drawn into the picture and the great ones named. Psalm 103 has not reached that stage yet, but it's on the way. In verse 20b they are called 'mighty heroes', using a common word for 'mighty ones' plus a word for strength, and NRSV's 'mighty ones' isn't quite strong enough. Verse 21 is perhaps best thought of as a call to the next rank down, to the larger number of YHWH's 'hosts' (as in the title 'YHWH of Hosts') and his 'ministers', a word used for servants, royal officials and priests. Verse 22 brings the psalm down to earth, but not simply to the human realm. It calls on everything that YHWH has made, that is, everything there is, in every place where he rules, *everywhere*, to affirm him as God (cf. Ps. 24.1–2). The *inclusio* includes the psalmist in this act of cosmic recognition.

6. According to Allen, this psalm 'takes the reader into the heart of Old Testament theology'. 'Old Testament Theology' is an emotive phrase. Allen's use of it, and mine, is simply shorthand for 'Old Testament talk about God'. The phrase has sometimes been used in Old Testament scholarship, however, as if it began with a hidden word, 'systematic'. In the twentieth century there was great debate about whether it was possible to write a '(systematic) theology of the Old Testament', that is, one that gathers up all the variety and diversity in Old Testament 'talk about God' into a comprehensive system. The usual answer was that it wasn't. The century ended, however, with some recognition that it was permissible for scholars to highlight those aspects of Old Testament talk about God that seem to them to be particularly significant, helpful and important, and for me Psalm 103 does precisely that. There is much that this psalm doesn't say, and, because its confidence in God and its pastoral tone contains none of the sharp questions to God, pointed contrasts between the 'righteous' and the 'wicked' and vitriolic attacks on Israel's enemies which feature in many other psalms, some will say that it is an untypical psalm. Be that as it may, Psalm 103 at least demonstrates how one unknown ancient Israelite theologian drew upon the theology available to him to produce a psalm that affirms above all else that YHWH is God and that 'his name and his nature is love'.

Old Testament theology

Where do you begin? How do you organize the material? How do you avoid writing your own theology that highlights those things that appeal most to you? It was questions like these that put a damper on 'Old Testament theology' as a subject in the latter years of the twentieth century after the two big books of Eichrodt and von Rad. This surfeit of riches was to form the temporary undoing of the whole enterprise. First, scholars began to wonder what else there was to say: but then that if two such different books can share the same title, perhaps the title is empty and what we have are subjective readings of the Old Testament? The difference in presentation was that Eichrodt used 'covenant' as his organizing principle, while von Rad used the shape of the Old Testament itself and the idea of God's 'saving acts' ('salvation history' or *Heilsgeschichte*). Questions were asked about other possibilities, but it became widely felt that this topic was at the mercy of scholars' personal preferences, and for the 1970s 'subjective' was a word that put the kiss of academic death on anything it touched. Then came Childs and his 'canonical criticism', and that threatened to seal the fate of Old Testament theology because, he argued, the Old Testament could only be read canonically, and that meant as the first part of the Christian Bible. The debate moved on, however, and in the late 1990s four major books arrived at once. James Barr (1999) discussed the difficulties and argued that the job was worth doing, and the other three (B. W. Anderson (1999), an American team production and Walter Brueggemann) deal with the problems in introductions before getting down to offering their takes on what they considered the main points of Old Testament theology to be. Since then Gerstenberger's *Theologies in the Old Testament* appeared in 2002, the first volume of Goldingay's major study appeared in 2003, with the second in 2006 and one more to follow, Rendtorff's large book appeared in 2005, and 2009 has seen the arrival of Rogerson's. All are different, but the discipline is clearly alive and well.

Voicing theology

Whether you consider psalms as hymns, prayers or chapters of torah, each psalm is 'talk about God'. Psalm 103 might take us to 'the heart of Old Testament theology', as Allen claims, and I would agree (Dawes, 2000, 2006), but every psalm voices theology in its talk to God or about God. Goldingay even goes so far as to say that 'theologically, the psalms are the densest material in the entire Old Testament', with a greater concentration of statements about God than anywhere else (Goldingay, 2006, vol. 1, p. 69). Add to that the recent work on Psalms as a whole (see Chapter 9), which adds a new dimension to thinking about the theology of the book, and there can be no doubt about the theological contribution of Psalms and its psalms, despite the fact that hymns and prayers are not the stuff of their work for most theologians and that many worshippers would be surprised to be told that they were doing theology when they were singing a worship song or reciting a prayer. In so far as commentaries expound, explain or exegete a psalm, therefore, they will be to one degree or another unpacking the theology of each psalm. A few (for example, Terrien and Goldingay) offer headed paragraphs on the theology of each psalm after its exposition. Here we will look at four more specific ways in which Psalms voices theology: by the forms, images and words of the psalms themselves and by the shape of the anthology in which they are found.

1 Individual psalms voice theology by their forms

All introductions to Psalms note that there are sub-genres in the anthology, whether they stay with those identified by Gunkel or tweak them, and that each sub-genre has its own distinctive ways of talking about God. Examining the characteristic ways that the different sub-genres talk about God is one way of describing the theology of Psalms adopted in a number of significant books, especially those of Vos and Travers. Among the introductions, Bullock's *Encountering the Book of Psalms* does the same, drawing out the theological contributions of each of the different sub-genres it identifies in its lengthy Part 3, entitled 'Encountering the Psalms as Literary and Theological Types'. This is preceded by a 19-page chapter devoted to the 'theological aspects' of Psalms (covering Israel and Creation, The Patriarchs in Retrospect, the Exodus, Sinai, Wilderness, Life in the Land, the Monarchy, the Exile and Return).

2 Individual psalms voice theology by their images

In Chapter 3 we saw something of the renewed interest in the images and meta-phors of Psalms, and W. P. Brown's *Seeing the Psalms* is the important book here. His approach is to identify the principal metaphors used in Psalms, and then to elucidate the theology in them. So he treats the metaphors of refuge, pathway, transplanted tree, 'sun of righteousness', the fear of drowning, animals, light and 'the anatomy of a personal God', and ends with a postscript headed 'A theology of prayer and *poesis*', in which he reminds his readers that 'prayer is the stuff of theology' and that metaphor is the power of the theological imagination (W. P. Brown, 2002, pp. 213–15).

3 Individual psalms voice theology by their words

You will have noticed that in this *Studyguide* I have often used transliterations of Hebrew words, that we have spent time looking at words like *ḥesed* and 'right-eousness' and that I have often included theological dictionary articles in the further reading suggestions. Not many introductions do this, but I plead three justifications: words matter; I have avoided the misuse of words about which James Barr chided us in the 1970s; and one of the most formative books on the Old Testament for me was Snaith's *The Distinctive Ideas of the Old Testament*, which discussed words and which I would still commend as essential reading.[5] That words matter ought to be as obvious as that images matter. That Hebrew contains some words that can be considered to be technical theological terms (just like Greek and English do) ought to be equally obvious, and of those words McCann writes, 'it is not an exaggeration to say that the most important theo-logical concept in the book of Psalms is represented by the Hebrew word חסד (*hesed*)' (*NIB*, vol. 6, p. 670).

Israel's 'core creed'?

> The LORD passed before him, and proclaimed, 'The LORD, the LORD, a God merciful and gracious, slow to anger, and abounding in steadfast love and faithfulness, keeping steadfast love for the thousandth generation (or 'for thousands'), forgiving iniquity and transgression and sin, yet by no means clearing the guilty, but visiting the iniquity of the parents upon the children and the children's children to the third and fourth generation.' (Ex. 34.6–7, NRSV).

Brueggemann cites this snippet as Israel's credo of adjectives and as God's 'self-disclosure' which is fundamental to Israel's 'daring vocabulary' in the Psalms (W. Brueggemann, 1997, pp. 215–18; 1995, pp. 45–9). Other commentators call these verses a 'formula' or 'confessional formula' and Hunter refers to it as '. . . the famous benediction enunciated most fully in Ex. 34.6–7' (Hunter, 2008, p. 121). In Judaism this passage is called 'Thirteen *Middot* (attributes) of God' and is used in synagogue worship on special holy days. Its age and origin are contested but it does appear to be something of a mini-creed which crops up in various places in the Old Testament and which echoes in many more. The wording varies and Exodus 34.6–7 is the fullest. The others are Numbers 4.18; Psalms 86.15; 103.8; 111.4; 145.8; Joel 2.13; Jonah 4.2; Nahum 1.3; Nehemiah 9.17 (cf. verse 31); 2 Chronicles 30.9. It also appears in a psalm from Qumran:

> I know, O Lord, that Thou art merciful and compassionate, long-suffering and rich in grace and truth, pardoning transgression and sin. Thou repentest of evil against them that love Thee, and keep Thy commandments, that return to thee with faith and wholeness of heart. (1QH8 lines 16f.)

At Exodus 34 this formula is set in the Exodus stories, and in most of the other 11 occurrences there is a reference to the Exodus nearby. This formula, therefore, seems to be very near to the heart of what the editors of the Old Testament understood about their God. Apart from its rather obscure introduction (who is doing the proclaiming and to whom?) the only translation issue is whether God's *ḥesed* is kept 'for thousands', which is the literal translation, or 'for/to the thousandth generation', which is the traditional Jewish interpretation followed by NRSV and NJPS.[6] This 'core creed' notes that God is 'slow to anger' and Psalm 103.8 that 'he will not always accuse, nor will he keep his anger for ever', understanding that God's anger is a sign that he takes sin and evil seriously, hating their devastating effects on human life and the life of the world. In the psalm or the 'core creed' it is not God's anger that is his last or greatest word but his committed, powerful, 'saving' and restoring 'love'.

4 Psalms voices theology by its shape

We shall see in the next chapter how much attention has recently been given to the shape of Psalms as a whole and what it might mean to read Psalms in its final form as one book. One result of this has been to see that the shape of Psalms itself voices theology. Walter Brueggemann's *The Message of the Psalms* might belong here, though it is essentially an unpacking of his threefold 'typology of function' in what is best seen as a work on the spirituality of Psalms. Crenshaw's short Chapter 6, 'Artistic and Theological Design', looks at various theories about the shape of Psalms and the theologies that they reflect (Crenshaw, 2001, pp. 96–105). The books by Mays and McCann are important here. In his commentary, Mays suggests that 'the LORD rules' (from Pss 93; 95; 97) is the 'organising confession' of the Psalter and that the psalms belong to the 'interim' period before that reign is consummated. Under that heading he lists 18 identifiable theological motifs in the Psalter (Mays, 1994b, pp. 29–36). This is a summary of his argument in *The Lord Reigns: A Theological Handbook to the Psalms* (1994a), which acknowledges its debt to the new work on the shape of Psalms. McCann does so even more fully, devoting Part 1 of his *A Theological Introduction to the Book of Psalms: The Psalms as Torah* (1993a) to the shape of the book. For him the Psalter is 'instruction' (torah) and the part headings illustrate his theme: 'Instruction for Praise and Praise as Instruction', 'Instruction for Prayer and Prayer as Instruction' and 'Instruction for Profession and Profession as Instruction'. For him 'Psalms ... instruct(s) the people of God about God, about themselves and the world, and about the life of faith' (p. 21). That Psalms is to be read as a book of torah, 'teaching' or 'instruction' and that theology is a core component of that teaching is an accepted conclusion of this new approach, and there is a large measure of consensus that 'ʏʜᴡʜ rules' or, possibly misleadingly, 'eschatology' is central to the theology taught.[7]

Another way of looking at how psalms voice theology can be seen in a variety of current introductions and commentaries, in which the writers either list the themes that they see in Psalms or edit that list in one way or another. For example:

- Curtis pays explicit attention to 'God in the Psalms: some key terms and themes', and looks at God's names and titles, God's nature, the covenant relationship and 'God, the Godly and the Godless' in 3 of his 17 pages of introduction (Curtis, pp. xxiii–xxxvi).
- Day heads his paragraphs on 'the theology of the psalms': 'Yahweh and the Gods', 'Yahweh as Creator', 'Yahweh's mighty deeds in history', 'Yahweh's attributes', 'Yahweh's presence', 'Humanity', 'Sheol and Life after Death', 'Universalism', 'the King', 'Sacrifice' and 'Ethics and the Law' (Day, 1990, pp. 123–36).
- Goldingay offers a focused six pages on 'The Psalms as Theology' with the headings 'God: Involved, Creator, Sovereign, at Home', 'King and Messiah' and 'Life and Death', before a concluding look at the theological aspect of the relationship of Psalms to the New Testament (Goldingay, 2006, vol. 1, pp. 69–75).

Others offer words of caution at this point:

- Lucas warns against imposing a systematic theology on Psalms but recognizes a number of themes: the understanding of God (Creator, Lord of History, descriptions of Yahweh, Yahweh's steadfast love, the presence of Yahweh, Yahweh and the nations), the understanding of humanity, life after death, sacrifice, imprecations in Psalms, the understanding of kingship and the messianic hope (Lucas, 2003, pp. 52–64).
- Hunter devotes the 27 pages of his Chapter 6 to 'Theological, Philosophical and Anthropological Reflections' and says that this cumbersome title is a deliberate reminder that the Psalter is open to a variety of readings (Hunter, 2008, pp. 108–35).
- Gillingham (1994) concludes with two short but powerful sections. 'Towards a theological interpretation of the Psalter' identifies six paradoxical elements:

'the God of Israel' and the 'God of all nations', 'God of the powerful' and 'God of the powerless', 'God and cultic worship' and 'God and inner devotion', 'God of judgement' and 'God of salvation', 'God of the living' and 'God of the dead' and 'God of the individual' and 'God of the community'. The three-page conclusion 'Theology and Poetry' takes the reader back to her opening chapters on interpreting poetry and the role of poetry as the medium of theology (Gillingham, 1994, pp. 270–8).

Here we can begin to see that the same problems exist in writing about 'the theology of Psalms' as in attempting to write on the theology of the Old Testament. Different writers identify different key themes and organize their material in significantly different ways, which we also see in another book-length treatment of the theology of Psalms and in chapters on Psalms in two 'Old Testament theologies':[8]

- Kraus gives one of the fullest treatments of the theology of Psalms in any contemporary commentary, arguing that the heart of the theology of the book is that 'Yahweh Sebaoth is present in the sanctuary in Jerusalem'. The psalms of praise celebrate that, and the laments arise where that reality is challenged (Kraus, 1988, pp. 68–81). In his *Theology of the Psalms* (1992), written to accompany his commentary, he expands on this in seven chapters: who is the God whom the psalms address and of whom they speak?; the people of God; the sanctuary and its worship; the king; the enemy powers; the individual in the presence of God and the psalms in the New Testament.
- Kraus begins by quoting from von Rad's chapter on Psalms (von Rad, 1962, vol. 1, ch. D). His two quotations that Psalms reflects Israel's response to 'Yahweh's two interventions for salvation' and that 'when these saving events happened to her, Israel did not keep silent' (von Rad, 1962, vol. 1, p. 355) illustrate von Rad's approach, which is to discuss the theology of Psalms under the heading of 'Israel before Yahweh' and to show how its responses to God's actions centre on the traditions around Moses, Exodus and the land on the one hand, and David and the monarchy on the other.
- Rendtorff too cites von Rad in his exploration of the theology of Psalms as Israel's 'response' in his major new book, *The Canonical Hebrew Bible: A Theology of the Old Testament* (2005). He recognizes that both the diversity of sub-genres in the collection and its final shape contribute to expressing its

theology, but declines to abstract a 'theology of psalms' beyond describing the theology evident in those two areas.

It is clear from all this that Psalms is a theologically rich anthology, which is perhaps not surprising if it shares characteristics of a hymn book, a book of prayers, or a 'catechism', with a preface in Psalm 1 which labels the collection as 'torah', 'teaching' or 'instruction'. The variety of its ways of talking about and to God should perhaps be no surprise either, at least to those whose understanding of theology recognizes the place of diversity and provisionality in all talk about God. Those, on the other hand, who want neat definitions and precise formulations will find Psalms as frustratingly reluctant to offer them as the Bible as a whole. Mays, and others, make a strong bid that 'YHWH is king' is the central theological image in Psalms, and they may well be right. If one presses further and asks what sort of king he is, to my mind at least a rather more important question, then words like *hesed* and the quotes from and allusions to the 'core creed' provide fruitful avenues to explore.

Other psalms that voice theology

Given that every psalm voices theology, this list contains only those that seem to me to focus on teaching or reflecting on or rehearsing the big theological themes of what God is like and what he has done. In addition to Psalm 103 my list would be Psalms 8, 37, 46, 48, 58, 68, 77, 78, 81, the full set of 'YHWH is king' psalms (93–100), 104, 105, 106, 107, 114, 115, 125, 127, 135 and 136.

Changing ideas about God

'Who is like YHWH our God? (Ps. 113.5)

'I am YHWH your God, who brought you out of the land of Egypt, out of the house of slavery; you shall have no other gods before (or 'besides') me.' (Ex. 20.2–3; Deut. 5.6–7)

'Ancient Israel' lived in a world of many faiths, local and international. It is also true that its own understandings of them and of its own god or gods developed over the centuries. Among those who are prepared to admit this, it is generally agreed that ancient Israel's perspectives on 'other faiths' and on the nature of its own god or gods developed from polytheism to monotheism via a recognizable intermediate position. It is also agreed that it is mistaken to think that this was either a co-ordinated or a smooth process.

Israel's earliest understandings of God are lost in history, but there is little reason to think that they were anything other than polytheistic; that Israelites worshipped a variety of gods and saw their gods as some among many. That is not, of course, how the story is told in the Old Testament, but it is now widely held that other gods were worshipped by ancient Israelites alongside YHWH and that evidence for this is found in the Old Testament itself. It is suggested that the names of some of these other gods remain as alternative names for YHWH, for example 'the God of Abraham' (Ex. 3.16), 'the Fear of Isaac' (Gen. 31.42), 'God of Bethel', 'el 'elyon ('God Most High') and 'el šaddai', as we saw in Chapter 5. But there is also something else.

To do

It is just after 586 BC. Jerusalem has fallen. The Temple has been destroyed. The leaders of Judah have been exiled to Babylon. So who are you going to blame? Read Jeremiah 44.15–19 and 20–23.[9]

The Bible was, to put it crudely but none the less accurately, written, edited and published by the 'winners', in this case the Deuteronomists, the preachers and teachers of Yahwism. Theirs are the views that constitute the orthodox theology of the Old Testament and that are portrayed in it as the faith and theology of Ancient Israel. It is natural and inevitable, therefore, to find views of God held by ancient Israelites that did not conform to their views described as heresy or apostasy. For them YHWH is 'The One', one in himself and one alone, the only, unique and 'jealous' God who will share his divine status with no other. The classic statement of this is in the Shema (Deut. 6.4), and the chapters of Deutero-Isaiah fill it out, poetically and polemically.

The Shema

The Shema (called after its opening word, *šĕma'* – 'hear') is the affirmation of faith that orthodox Jews make going in and out of their homes and in almost every service of worship in the synagogue. Its importance cannot be overstated. These are the words that a good Jew would want to be the last words of his or her dying breath.

> Hear, O Israel: The LORD is our God, the LORD alone. You shall love the LORD your God with all your heart, and with all your soul, and with all your might. (Deut. 6.4)

In synagogue services this verse is usually read with at least Deuteronomy 6.5–8 and is sometimes expanded to include Deuteronomy 11.13–21 and Numbers 15.37–41. The four core words are *yhwh 'ĕlôhēnû yhwh 'eḥād* ('YHWH our-God YHWH one'), but a glance at the footnotes in any translation will show that the meaning of this mysterious and holy phrase is not agreed. There are at least three other ways of translating it: 'The LORD our God is one LORD', 'The LORD our God, the LORD is one' and 'The LORD is our God, the LORD is one'. The Shema clearly means that YHWH is to be the only God that Israel should worship, but what else it means is not clear. Does it mean that YHWH is the only God there is? Or that he is unique among the other gods in some way? Or that he is somehow complete in himself, whole and entirely self-sufficient? Note the fascinating element of reticence and mystery in this basic affirmation: YHWH can neither be named aloud nor defined! This is refreshingly quite unlike western Christianity's passion for detailed theological definition as seen in its creeds.

Even the Old Testament itself, however, admits that this classic position was not arrived at without a struggle. A constant thread in its narrative and a frequent feature in the preaching of its prophets is that the Israelites were greatly attracted by and to the gods and culture of their neighbours. The royal heroes in this struggle, according to the Deuteronomic Historians cum Storytellers, were the reforming kings Hezekiah and Josiah who around 720 BC (see 2 Kings 18.1–8) and 620 BC (see 2 Kings 22—23) respectively purged the nation and the national shrines of the gods and liturgical paraphernalia of what they saw as this alien culture. Hosea is particularly useful in enabling us to see more of this alternative religion and theology with its condemnation of the worship of Baal ('Lord', especially the Lord of Storm, Rain and, therefore, of the Harvest: hence the strong polemic in Hos. 2.8) in the Northern Kingdom in the mid-eighth century BC. Archaeological discoveries have helped us see more of what was happening. Discoveries at Elephantine, a fourth-century BC military fort on the Nile at Aswan, garrisoned by Jewish mercenaries and equipped with its own Jewish temple, reveal that a goddess (Anat-Yaho or Anat-Bethel) was worshipped there alongside YHWH. Discoveries at Kuntillet 'Ajrud in the Sinai and Khirbet el-Qom near Hebron have found references to 'Yahweh and his Asherah'. Discoveries of 'Asherah (or Astarte) figurines' have been made at a number of Israelite sites. The conclusion appears to be that a number of gods identified with different people and places in Israel were worshipped in ancient Israel, some of whom were indigenous to Israel rather than foreign imports, and one of whom was YHWH.

There is, inevitably, a complicating factor here. There are two goddesses with similar names in the Canaanite pantheon: Asherah (the Canaanite mother goddess, chief consort of the High God El) and Astarte (or Ashtart, the Canaanite version of the Assyrian Ishtar, 'Queen of Heaven', the goddess of fertility, love and war, the consort of Baal). These two appear to be conflated at times in the Old Testament, and then there is a further confusion because *'ăšērâ* is a feminine singular word, which is usually given a masculine plural, *'ăšērîm*, and that word denotes both her and the wooden cult objects that were her symbol. AV translates it as '(sacred) grove/s' everywhere, but newer translations are more accurate, so NRSV has 'sacred pole/s' in some places and the name of the goddess in others. Ashtoreth (AV)/Astarte (NRSV) appears correctly as the goddess of the Sidonians, worshipped by Solomon in 1 Kings 11.5. The plural of the word (*'aštārôt*) occurs in other places, but its translation varies, for example, in Judges 2.13 AV has 'Ashtaroth' and NJB has 'Astartes', apparently referring to the consort of Baal, but NRSV has 'the Astartes', NIV 'the Ashtoreths' and REB and NJPS 'the ashtaroth'. The bottom line is that the words refer to two goddesses and a sacred pole, all of which evoked the disapproval of the Deuteronomists. We do not know the rituals or theology associated with the worship of Asherah and/or Astarte in the privacy of an Israelite home, just as we know little about the 'household gods' (*těrāpîm*) that feature in the story of Jacob and his wives (Gen. 31.19). Nor is it clear how they were worshipped in the public domain, for example how the sacred poles were used. Despite that, the evidence suggests that polytheism was alive and well in ancient Israel before the Exile.

The 'interim position' is usually called 'monolatry' (the worship of only one god) or 'henotheism' (from the Greek terms for 'one' and 'god'), though it should be clear by now that any talk of 'stages' in this development is problematic. This position asserts that 'YHWH is Israel's own and only God who demands its exclusive obedience' (just as Chemosh of the Moabite Stone was the God of Moab etc.). A good story making this point is Joshua's covenant-making ceremony at Shechem (Josh. 24), and the Shema and the First Commandment (Ex. 20.2–3; Deut. 5:6–7) both express this viewpoint. The question of who will be Israel's God forms the story line in the Elijah narratives. Deciding that is the purpose of the contest between Elijah as YHWH's champion and the prophets of Baal, which results in a climax of sorts on the summit of Mount Carmel when the people acclaim YHWH in the words 'YHWH indeed is God, YHWH indeed is God' (1 Kings 18.39). More is at stake here than the purity of Israel's worship or theology. The question of who will be Israel's only God has an ethical dimension, as seen in the story of Naboth's vineyard (1 Kings 21). If Queen Jezebel and her god succeed here, the story goes, then Israel's traditions of social justice and equality are finished, for the ideology, world-view and social system associated with Baal are alien to those of YHWH (cf. Ps. 81.9–10).

The final position is that of monotheism, 'the LORD is God, there is no other' (Deut. 4.35–39). This position is presented most clearly and dogmatically in Deutero-Isaiah with its repeated insistence on YHWH as the only God (Isa. 40.25; 41.4; 42.5–9; 43.8–13; 44.6ff., 24; 45.5ff., 18f.; 46.9 etc.) and its scorn of all other so-called gods as idols (for example, Isa. 40.18–20; 41.6ff., 21–24; 44.9–20; cf. Ps. 135.15–18). This is not, however, the only form of monotheism in the Old Testament because there is that less radical strand that considers YHWH to be the only True God or the Supreme God (for example, Ex. 15.11; Pss 84.7; 86.8; 95.3; 97.6–9), which finds places for other divine beings in his Heavenly Council (Ps. 82 etc.), even if traces of Deutero-Isaiah's scorn come into its references to them from time to time (for example, Pss 96.4–5; 97.7; 135).

Regardless of historical questions, however, including the accuracy or otherwise of this supposed 'development', or even the difference between the various expressions of monotheism discernible in its pages, the Old Testament in its final form has a single and powerful agenda on this issue, which is to insist on Israel's total and sole allegiance to its covenant God, YHWH, as expressed classically in the First Commandment. This is introduced by the formula that serves to introduce the whole Decalogue, that the one who gives this teaching is YHWH, Israel's saviour God, who in his grace has already delivered them from slavery and is leading them into freedom. This action also establishes his claim to the exclusive loyalty of Israel, that he alone will be their God and they alone will be his people (Ex. 19.4–6, 29.45f.), and indicates his character as a 'jealous' God who will tolerate no rival (Ex. 20.5). The second commandment follows it to say that Israel shall not worship any kind of representation of any god or even possibly of YHWH himself either. 'Before me' or 'besides me' are the variant translations of the literal 'to my face' (i.e., 'in my presence') and reflect two different nuances which some have seen in that phrase, understanding it to rule out the worship of any other god in preference to the worship of YHWH or alongside that worship. The plain meaning of these texts exclude other gods from Israel's spirituality. Psalm 82 and its picture of the Most High presiding over a Council of lesser gods and sitting in judgement on them reads strangely in both Judaism and Christianity, unless you remythologize it into God enthroned among the 'angels and archangels' etc. as both faiths do. The basis of his action against them is, however, clear and simple. They have failed to uphold and deliver social justice (*mišpāt*, verses 2–4). This psalm, which resists all attempts to classify it and identify its provenance, asserts that all gods and the religious systems and theologies that promote them are to be measured against a single yardstick: do they make it possible for their worshippers to practise their humanity by doing *mišpāt*? It insists that this is the priority of the Most High, by whatever name he is known.

To do

Has anything in this chapter excited you? What? Why? Has anything in it challenged you? What? How? Has anything in it worried you? What? Why? Has anything in it influenced the way you will read the Old Testament in future?

Suggestions for further reading

Asherah etc.

Albertz, R. (1994), *A History of Israelite Religion in the Old Testament Period*, London: SCM Press, vol. 1, pp. 85–87, 194, 211.

Day, J. (1992), 'Asherah', in *ABD*, vol. 1, pp. 483–7.

Day, J. (1992), 'Ashtoreth', in *ABD*, vol. 1, pp. 491–4.

Hess, R. S. (2007), *Israelite Religions*, Grand Rapids MI: Baker-Apollos.

*Sturgis, M. (2001), *It Ain't Necessarily So*, London: Headline.

Old Testament Theology

Anderson, B. W. (1999), *Contours of Old Testament Theology*, Minneapolis MN: Fortress Press.

Barr, J. (1999), *The Concept of Biblical Theology: An Old Testament Perspective*, London: SCM Press.

*Barton, J. (2002), 'Old Testament Theology', in Rogerson (ed.), *Beginning Old Testament Study*, pp. 94–113.

Birch, B. C., Brueggemann W., Fretheim, T. E and Petersen, D. L. (1999), *A Theological Introduction to the Old Testament*, Nashville TN: Abingdon Press.

Brueggemann, W. (2008), *Old Testament Theology*, Nashville TN: Abingdon Press.

Brueggemann, W. (1997), *Theology of the Old Testament*, Minneapolis MN: Fortress Press.

Coggins, R. (2001), *Introducing the Old Testament*, rev. edn, Oxford: Oxford University Press, pp. 140–52.

*Dawes, S. B. (2006), *Let us Bless the Lord: Rediscovering the Old Testament through Psalm 103*, Peterborough: Inspire; now available at www.stephendawes.com

Eichrodt, W. (1961), *Theology of the Old Testament*, 2 vols, London: SCM Press.

Goldingay, J. (2003), *Old Testament Theology: Vol. 1 Israel's Gospel*, Downers Grove IL: InterVarsity Press Academic, pp. 15–41.

Fretheim, T. E. (2005) *God and World in the Old Testament*, Nashville TN: Abingdon Press.

Gerstenberger, E. S. (2001), *Theologies in the Old Testament*, Edinburgh: T&T Clark

Moberly, R. W. (1999), 'Theology of the Old Testament', in Baker and Arnold (eds), *The Face of Old Testament Studies*, pp. 452–78.

Rendtorff, R. (2005), *The Canonical Hebrew Bible: A Theology of the Old Testament*, Leiden: Deo.

Reventlow, H. G. (2001), 'Modern Approaches to Old Testament Theology', in Perdue (ed.), *The Blackwell Companion*, pp. 221–40.

Rogerson, J. W. (2009), *A Theology of the Old Testament: Cultural Memory, Communication and Being Human*, London: SPCK.

von Rad, G. (1962), *Old Testament Theology*, 2 vols, Edinburgh: Oliver and Boyd.

mišpāṭ

Schultz, R. (1996), 'Justice', in *NIDOTTE*, vol. 4, pp. 837–46.

The theology of Psalms

*Day, J (1990), *Psalms: Old Testament Guides*, Sheffield: Sheffield Academic Press, pp. 123–44.

*Hunter, A. G. (2008), *An Introduction to the Psalms*, London: T&T Clark, pp. 108–35.

Kraus, H.–J. (1992), *Theology of the Psalms*, Minneapolis MN: Fortress Press.

Mays, J. L. (1994a), *The Lord Reigns: A Theological Handbook to the Psalms*, Louisville KY: Westminster John Knox Press.

*Mays, J. L. (1994b), *Psalms*, Interpretation Commentary Series, Louisville KY: Westminster John Knox Press, pp. 29–36.

McCann, J. C. (1993b), *A Theological Introduction to the Book of Psalms*, Nashville TN: Abingdon Press.

Rendtorff, R. (2005), *The Canonical Hebrew Bible: A Theology of the Old Testament*, Leiden: Deo, pp. 317–36.

Travers, M. E. (2003), *Encountering God in the Psalms*, Grand Rapids MI: Kregel.

Vos, C. G. A. (2005), *Theopoetry of the Psalms*, London: T&T Clark.

9

New studies in Psalms

What is this chapter about?

In this chapter we look at the two 'new' (always a relative term in anything to do with religion and religious institutions) and developing areas in Psalms study at the moment. First, under the heading 'Many psalms – one book', we explore what happens if we change our focus from looking at individual psalms to reading the book as a whole. In the second, under the heading 'Reception history (or "From then till now")' we look at the current interest in how psalms have been used over the centuries.

How is it organized?

- The chapter is in two parts under those two headings.
- There is a single text box entitled, 'Three collections', on the psalms of Asaph, Korah and the Songs of Ascents.
- There is only the usual final 'To do' box inviting you to reflect on the content of the chapter.
- The chapter ends with suggestions for further reading in both areas.

What should I be able to do by the end of it?

- Appreciate the new focus in Psalms study on reading Psalms as one book.
- Recognize the contribution of Gerald Wilson to Psalms study.

- Understand what is meant by 'reception history' (or *Rezeptionsgeschichte* or *Wirkungsgeschichte*).
- Begin to appreciate the rich afterlife of psalms and the Psalter.
- Recognize that 'interpretation' is an integral part of all reading, and that interpretations of texts can vary considerably in different times and cultures.

Many psalms – one book

Way back in Chapter 1, in the third 'To do' box to be precise, I asked you to read Psalms from beginning to end. I also commented that you might find the idea of doing that a bit odd. When I have suggested reading Psalms from chapter 1 to chapter 150 to classes of students, the common reaction has been for them to ask why. In other classes they were prepared to do that with Genesis or Amos, if I pushed them beyond the snippetizing of the Bible that is encouraged by church lectionaries and Bible-reading notes, but the idea of doing that with Psalms seemed strange. The reason it feels counter-intuitive, I suggest, is that we have all taken for granted that psalms are hymns or prayers, and no one reads a hymn book or an anthology of prayers from beginning to end. If we sing hymns we might, or might not, be aware of the structure of our hymn book, and if we have one we might, or might not, have noticed how our favourite anthology of prayers is organized, but in both cases our focus is normally on the hymns we sing and the prayers we pray and not on the 'shape' of the book in which they are found. And that is the way it was in Psalms study until the 1980s.

Prior to then it was commonly observed:

- there are doublets in Psalms: Psalm 14 = Psalm 53; Psalm 40.13–17 = Psalm 70.1–5; Psalm 108 = Psalm 57.7–11 + Psalm 60.5–12;
- Psalms is divided into five 'Books' (1—41, 42—72, 73—89, 90—106 and 107—150), the first four of which conclude with a doxology. At this point there would often be the quotation from Midrash on Psalms 1.2 that 'As Moses gave five books of laws to Israel, so David gave five books of Psalms to Israel', suggesting a complementarity between Psalms and the Torah;
- in Book 2 the use of the Hebrew word for God (*'ĕlôhîm*) vastly outnumbers the use of the divine name YHWH, whereas in the other four books it is the other way round, hence Book 2 is often called the 'Elohistic Psalter';

- after the benediction at the end of Book 2 there is a note that 'The prayers of David son of Jesse are ended', even though 'David psalms' are found in the following three books and one is specifically titled a 'prayer of David' (Ps. 86);
- Psalms contains identifiable named 'collections' of psalms: the 'Korah psalms', the 'Asaph Psalms' and the 'Songs of Ascents', plus two blocks of 'David Psalms' (Pss 3—41, assuming 9 and 10 to be one psalm and considering 33 as a possible insertion as it has no title, and Pss 51—71). At this point attempts were frequently made or noted to explore who the Korahites and Asaphites might have been, what their particular interests were, and so on;

Three 'collections'

The Korahite Psalms
Eleven psalms have titles that mention Korah, 'the Korahites' or 'the Sons of Korah' (Pss 42; 44—49; 84; 85; 87—89). One of these is also attributed to Heman the Ezrahite (Ps. 88). They appear to be some sort of 'collection' of psalms from the same musical school, as it were. In one case, perhaps, we even have the author's name, Heman. The rest simply use the 'school' name, much as people used to talk about 'Sankey's hymns', and meant all the hymns in that famous hymn book, including those written by everyone else, or as today we might talk about 'Iona' hymns. Surprisingly Korah gets no mention in the lists of key Temple personnel in Chronicles. The name appears only in a list in 1 Chronicles 6.22. The Korahites are mentioned as the first of the divisions of 'gatekeepers' in 1 Chronicles 26.1 and seem to have been promoted to singers in the next century (2 Chron. 20.19). There has been much speculation about where this 'collection' came from and who this 'school' were, from Goulder's suggestion that they came from Dan (in the far north) to Miller's that they come from the far south (Goulder, 1982, pp. 16–22; J. M. Miller, pp. 58–68).

The Asaph Psalms
The 12 Asaph psalms are found in a group of 11 at the beginning of Book 3 (Pss 73—83) with an outlier at Ps. 50. Asaph is one of the big names among the Temple personnel, and he appears first as Heman's brother and co-appointee of David with him and Ethan in 1 Chronicles 6.39, and then with Ethan and Heman in the trio of singers in

1 Chronicles 15.19 who are to sound the bronze cymbals. In 1 Chronicles 16.4 he is the leader of the Levites 'before the ark of the Lord'. His descendants continue in office as singers (Neh. 7.44) and these psalms probably come from them. The same issues arise with the preposition l^e in the headings of these psalms as with the David psalms. There are a number of distinctive features to these psalms, including stress on 'judgement', references to YHWH's 'mighty deeds' in the past, more references to Israel as YHWH's 'flock' than in the rest of the psalms put together, and a particular interest in 'Joseph', which might suggest a possible northern origin for this collection.

The Songs of Ascents
Psalms 120—134 are headed 'Songs of Ascents' in most translations. Almost every sub-genre of psalm is found in the set but they share a common interest in 'Zion'. The usual understanding is that they are 'pilgrim songs' or processional songs, for use by those 'going up' to Jerusalem for a festival. A minority view based on the fact that the word translated 'ascents' more often means 'stairs' is that they are a series of songs to be sung in Temple liturgies on the fifteen Temple steps.

- some psalms are grouped by other specific headings, for example Psalms 52—55 are all *Maskils* of David, and Psalms 56—60 are all *Miktams* of David;
- some psalms seem to be linked by catchwords or similar phraseology: for example, Psalms 1 and 2 are conjoined by the *inclusio*, 'Happy . . .', the final words of Psalm 32 and the first of Psalm 33 are very close, and Psalms 103 and 104 have the same opening lines (looking for links of this kind is sometimes called the 'microtextual approach');
- in addition to the 'Songs of Ascents', Psalms 113—118 is another group of psalms which later came to be recognized as a liturgical set (the 'Hallel' or 'Egyptian Hallel');
- there are identifiable groups of psalms linked by their themes: the 'YHWH is king' psalms (Pss 93—99), the 'Hallelujah psalms' (Pss 146—150) and possibly another set of 'Hallelujah psalms' in Psalms 111—117;
- there are bunches of psalms with the same 'voice', especially laments in the 'I' form, for example Psalms 3—7; 25—28; 54—57; 69—71; 140—143;

- there may be a change of mood through Psalms, in the movement from the 'laments', which predominate in the first half of the book, to the 'praises' with which it ends (though this should not be overemphasized, given that block of four laments in Pss 140—143).

From observations like these it was clear that Psalms is a composite book and that there must have been a process by which its various component parts were put together, but it was widely held that little could be said about the process. A. A. Anderson's three and a bit pages headed 'Compilation and Formation of the Psalter' (1972, vol. 1, pp. 24–8) outline what could be said, but he begins with the frank admission that, 'The formation of the Psalter must have undergone a complicated process which can no longer be reconstructed with any certainty' (p. 25). The same conclusion is spelled out at slightly greater length by Westermann (1981, pp. 250–8). As to the shape of the book as a whole, Anderson's 1972 commentary is silent.

That, however, was then, and things are rather different now. David Howard writes about the changes that have come about like this:

> [A] shift has taken place, and the prevailing interest in Psalms studies has to do with questions about the composition, editorial unity and overall message of the Psalter as a book, a literary and canonical entity that coheres with respect to its structure and message. Regardless of the authorship and provenance of individual psalms, or the prehistory of various collections within the Psalter, these were eventually grouped into a canonical book in the post-exilic period. Studies now abound that consider the overall structure of the book, the contours of its disparate parts and how they fit together, or the 'story-line' that runs from Ps. 1 to Ps. 150. (Johnston and Firth, p. 24)

This change is usually credited to Brevard Childs' agenda of reading the Old Testament 'canonically', by which he meant taking the final form of all its books seriously and then reading the book in its setting in the Bible as a whole (Childs, 1979; for his treatment of Psalms, see pp. 504–25). Not everyone has welcomed his agenda, and it is not without its flaws. For example, which 'canonical' shape and setting are we to consider, given that the Hebrew Bible's canonical shape and setting is different from that of both the 'Protestant' and 'Roman Catholic/ Orthodox' Christian Bibles? The variety of canons on offer reminds us that any talk about 'the Bible' or any assertion that 'The Bible says …' should immediately provoke the reader or listener to ask the simple but penetrating question, 'Which Bible?' Nevertheless, Childs has left two legacies in Psalms study. The first, not new to Childs but one that he boosted and secured, is the recognition that the placing of Psalm 1 at the beginning of Psalms is a deliberate and highly significant editorial decision that defines Psalms as a Torah book for meditation and study, a decision then reinforced in Psalm 19 and principally in Psalm 119. Mays and McCann, as we saw in Chapter 8, pursue this insight. The second is that there is now considerable interest in reading Psalms as one book, or in adopting a 'macrostructural approach', as it is sometimes called. Most credit, though a few scholars might call it blame, for taking these two suggestions seriously and giving shape to the debate must be given to Gerald Wilson.

Wilson's *The Editing of the Hebrew Psalter* appeared in 1985. In it he argued that there is a recognizable shape in Psalms. He began by considering collections of hymns from the ancient Near East and then applied insights from that study to Psalms, beginning there by taking its division into five books seriously. He argued that the presence of 'royal' psalms at what he called the 'seams' in the first three books was significant (Ps. 2 at the beginning of Book 1, Ps. 72 at the end of Book 2 and Ps. 89 at the end of Book 3, also suggesting that Ps. 41 at the end of Book 1 could be considered to be a 'royal' psalm). He claimed that this was the clue to the structure of the whole book: Books 1 and 2 celebrate YHWH's covenant with David but by the end of Book 3 the failure of that covenant, from the human side, has become apparent; thus Book 4 forms the editorial centre of the Psalter in its proclamation that YHWH is King, and Book 5 sets out the ways in which Israel can celebrate that and trust in his sovereignty. Other contributions followed in which he developed his ideas. Recognizing the weakness of considering Psalm 41 as a royal psalm, he concluded that Books 1 and 2 were already combined into a single Davidic collection (marked by that 'prayers of David are ended' note at the end of Ps. 72), which then gave two blocks of material (Pss 2—72 and 73—89), which are marked at their seams by 'royal' psalms.[1] He then developed his argument and suggested that it was possible to see two 'frames' in Psalms, the 'Royal Covenant Frame' (consisting of Pss 2, 72, 89; 144) and a 'Final Wisdom Frame' (consisting of Pss 1, 73, 90, 107 and 145, which he considered to be the first psalms in Books 1, 3, 4 and 5, and the final psalm in Book 5 proper). His conclusion was that in the final form of the book the Wisdom frame takes precedence over the Royal, thus making Psalms a 'wisdom' book, a book of teaching about how to live as a faithful subject of ᴙʜᴡʜ.[2] Among his last publications before his sudden death in 2005 is the essay in Johnston and Firth summarizing the debate (pp. 229–46). It concludes with a section on the theological implications of this shape, that

- 'all psalms can be adopted as models of individual prayer';
- 'the shape of the Psalter encourages an individual approach of meditation and study of the Psalter as a whole';
- 'in this careful shaping and arrangement of psalms and Psalter . . . these very human words *to* God have made the shift to become God's word to *us*';
- the shift from dominant lament to praise and thanksgiving indicates that while we are 'called to live in a real world of undeniable suffering and pain', God's final word is not lament but praise;
- 'the shift from individual lament to corporate praise/thanksgiving that takes place within the Psalter when read from beginning to end' points up the importance of the community of faith;
- 'the emphasis of the final form is that Yahweh is king'.

Some early reactions to Wilson were sceptical. Day, writing the Society for Old Testament Study student guide on Psalms in 1990, politely reflected that it was difficult to avoid the impression that this overarching message had been imposed on Psalms (Day, 1990, p. 111). Whybray (1996) was trenchant in his dismissal of the notion that kingship has any place in the shaping of Psalms, suggesting instead that the book is shaped by 'Wisdom' themes, to which others reacted by pointing out that these are not as easy to find as he thinks they are. A more recent and more gently critical voice is that of Curtis, who concludes that 'attempts to demonstrate an overarching scheme have not generally been found to be conclusive' (Curtis, p. xxiv). In contrast, however, David Mitchell (who disagrees significantly with Wilson's theological conclusions, as we shall see) can cite an impressive list of scholars in a long footnote and conclude:

Thanks to Wilson's work, there arose a scholarly consensus that the Psalms were redacted around a purposefully developing sequence of ideas. Instead of a jumble of unrelated lyrics, they became instead an oratorio, forming together a literary context for their mutual interpretation. And so Wilson became, in Isaac Newton's celebrated phrase, one of the giants upon whose shoulders we all stood.[3]

McCann offers a neat and accessible summary of Wilson's basic suggestion in his introduction to Psalms in *The New Interpreter's Bible* ('The Editorial Purpose of the Psalter', pp. 659–64). He recognizes that links between individual psalms should not be forced, but 'follows Wilson's lead', as he puts it, in drawing the reader's attention to those 'patterns that seem too striking to be co-incidental' (p. 659). On pages 664–5, however, commenting on Psalms 1 and 2 as an introduction to the Psalter, he moves into a contested area of Wilson's thought.

Wilson's position, sustained to the end despite some tweaks in response to David Mitchell, is that the shape and theology of Psalms teaches that the Davidic kingship is to be regarded as a failure which has now been replaced by the kingship of YHWH, and so the life of faith in YHWH is to be lived fully in the present moment in the way of Torah wisdom. A number of scholars, but principally Mitchell, regard this as an inadequate reading of Psalms. Mitchell begins from the common understanding that Psalms 1 and 2 together form the introduction to Psalms, joined as they are by that 'Happy' *inclusio*, and that the message of Psalms is set by the twin themes of Torah (Ps. 1) and Messiah (Ps. 2). He also accepts Wilson's identification of the 'royal' psalms at the 'seams' of the Psalter, but draws a different conclusion from it. He accepts that they do indeed indicate that the Davidic monarchy has been a failure, but argues that that failure does not write off the 'messianic' motif, as Wilson thinks it does, but reinterprets it and introduces a clearly eschatological theme. After all, a detail of the argument goes, are not the final eight psalms in the Psalter proper before its concluding and climactic Hallelujahs in Psalms 146—150, David psalms? Mitchell's argument is worked out in detail in *The Message of the Psalter*, and its thesis is set out in the subtitle, 'An Eschatological Programme in the Book of Psalms'. He uses the eschatological programme of Zechariah 9—14 as an interpretative key and makes much of the 'messianic hopes' of post-exilic Judaism. The key point is that unlike Wilson who sees the kingship of YHWH as something that makes the Davidic kingship redundant, Mitchell sees the kingship of YHWH as the ground for the renewal of the Davidic kingship in the form of a new 'anointed one'. Hence, for him, Psalms is 'prophetic' literature, pointing forwards to a new messiah, rather than didactic or wisdom literature as suggested by Wilson. So in his 2006 article he writes:

between us we indicated the way to two quite different understandings of the redactional agenda of the Psalms: I, eschatologico-messianic, pointing to a coming son of David; he, historico-didactic and non-messianic, pointing Israel to a future without the house of David. (p. 527)

Mitchell's thesis follows the agenda set by Childs. In that reading, the royal psalms are treasured in the Psalter 'as a witness to the messianic hope which look[s] for the consummation of God's kingdom through his Anointed One' (Childs, p. 517). Its conclusion is that 'the final form of the Psalter is highly eschatological in nature; it looks forward to the future and passionately yearns for its arrival' (Childs, p. 518).[4]

In his later survey of recent Psalms study Howard observes that 'Wilson's recent work seems to allow more room for an eschatological (re)reading of the royal psalms' but also that 'he maintains the thrust of his original arguments in favour of a dominant wisdom framework' and calls that, rather questionably, 'a rapprochement of sorts' (Johnston and Firth, p. 27). Wilson's own essay in that book acknowledges the points made by Mitchell but holds to his fundamental 'wisdom' and Torah stance. This debate is set to continue.[5]

Walter Brueggemann's name crops up in this discussion too. In Chapter 7 we looked at his 'typology of function', which sees a movement from psalms of orientation through psalms of disorientation to psalms of reorientation, but this is not a theory about the shape of Psalms in its final form. His contribution to that debate is found in an article entitled 'Bounded by Obedience and Praise: the Psalms as Canon'.[6] Writing in 1991 near the beginning of the debate, he acknowledged that Childs had 'legitimated the question concerning the literary shape and theological intentionality of the book of psalms as a whole' (p. 189). So he set out to explore 'how one gets from one end of the Psalter to the other' (p. 190), and that exploration gave him the title of the article because Psalms begins in Psalm 1 with 'obedience' and ends in Psalm 150 with 'praise'. The movement is from 'duty' to 'delight' (p. 193). It is not, however, a simple and delightful journey because the way is marked by 'candour about suffering' (here he focuses on Ps. 25) and 'gratitude about hope' (here his focus is on Ps. 103), through experiences which raise urgent questions about God's ḥesed (pp. 196–9). So he identifies Psalm 73 as the pivotal psalm in the theological structure of Psalms.

A quite different sort of attempt to explain the order and shape of Psalms has been made on the basis of its alleged ancient use in a triennial cycle of Torah readings in the synagogue. The thesis was that there were 150 weekly portions of Torah, each of which had its own accompanying psalm. The consensus view, however, is that there is no evidence to support the various theories which have attempted to make this case (see Day, 1990, p. 110, and Wilson, 1986, p. 85).

There have also been developments since A. A. Anderson's 1972 commentary on what might be called the 'logistic' rather than the 'theological' aspects of this question, and these centre on Qumran. We noted in Chapter 6 that Qumran has supplied what look like different 'collections' of the canonical psalms. *The Dead Sea Scrolls Bible* notes that there are 'five different arrangements evident in the Psalms scrolls' at Qumran: the 150 psalm arrangement known to us, that of 11QPs[a] and three 'smaller' ones (*DSSB*, pp. 507–8). From this it appears that Books 1–3 of Psalms were 'all present and correct' at Qumran in their present canonical order, but the same cannot be said of Books 4 and 5. For example, Wilson boldly states that the major Qumran Psalms Scroll (11QPs[a]) adds the 11 compositions we noted in Chapter 6 and omits:

- the opening psalms of Book 4 (Pss 90—92);
- Psalms 94—100, which include the 'YHWH is king' psalms that are crucial to the shape of Psalms for both Wilson and Mitchell;
- the psalms that link Books 4 and 5 (Pss 106—108), and so this Psalter does not have a 5-book structure;
- the coronation psalm (110);
- Psalms 111—116.[7]

Notice, therefore, how this changed shape, which eliminates the kingship of YHWH promotes a different theological reading of Psalms from that of the full Psalter in either Wilson's or Mitchell's readings. The main point to note, however, is that the existence of these different arrangements at Qumran adds further data and further complexity to the attempt to establish the processes by which the collection as we have it reached its final form.

The activity of reading Psalms as one book is alive and well and the discussions this rather counter-intuitive practice have generated have been lively and promise to continue to be so. It is very much a work in progress. It seems to me, however, that there is room for three cautionary notes.

- Because human beings are inveterate makers of meaning, it is possible, with imagination, to find patterns in any disparate collection of texts.
- It is not always clear that this debate is sufficiently alert to the distinction between what readers read, what is present in the text, and what writers or editors intend. Are the 'structural facts' on which so much of this debate hangs, from the presence of 'royal' psalms at the 'seams' to verbal details, really those of the text itself and/or its editors, or are they the 'readings of readers'?
- Fully aware of the debate, Goldingay baldly states that 'The Psalter does not work like Genesis or Isaiah' (2003, p. 37), and while that may be putting it too dogmatically, his quotes from the *Midrash on Psalms* on Psalm 3 give food for thought:

> As to the exact order of David's Psalms, Scripture says elsewhere: *Man knoweth not the order thereof* (Job 28.13). R. Eleazar taught: The sections of Scripture are not arranged in their proper order. For if they were arranged in their proper order, and any man so read them, he would be able to resurrect the dead and perform other miracles. For this reason the proper order of the sections of Scripture is hidden from mortals and is known only to the Holy One, blessed be He, who said: '*Who, as I, can read and declare it, and set it in order*' (Isa. 44.7).

> When R. Joshua ben Levi sought to arrange the Psalms in their proper order, a heavenly voice came forth and commanded: 'Do not rouse that which slumbers.'

Reception history (or 'From then till now')

The latest addition to Psalms study is 'reception history' (or *Rezeptionsgeschichte* or *Wirkungsgeschichte*). This quote from the Series Editors' Preface to the newly appearing Blackwell Bible Commentaries, 'the first series to be devoted primarily to the reception history of the Bible', justifies the series and reception history itself like this: 'how people have interpreted, and been influenced by, a sacred text like the Bible is often as interesting and historically important as what it originally meant' (Gillingham, 2008, p. xi).

A reception history of Psalms, therefore, looks at how Psalms has been read and used over the millennia and explores its 'influence on literature, art, music and film, its role in the evolution of religious beliefs and practices, and its impact on social and political developments' (Gillingham, 2008, p. xi).

The titles of two other books are also helpful in explaining this new area of study: *The Psalms through Three Thousand Years* (Holladay, 1993) and *Psalms in Community: Jewish and Christian Textual, Liturgical and Artistic Traditions* (Attridge and Fassler, 2003). In something completely different (*The Bible for Dummies*), Geoghegan and Homan set out the scope of this investigation in the titles of their two chapters in Part V, 'That was Then, This is Now: Discovering the Bible's Enduring Influence', which are 'The Bible in the Abrahamic Faiths: Judaism, Christianity and Islam' and 'Michelangelo, Milton and Movies: Art, Literature, Life and the Bible'. Finally, the publisher's blurb for the new multi-volume *Encyclopedia of the Bible and its Reception* (*EBR*) puts it like this and promises much:

> *EBR* also documents the history of the Bible's reception in the Christian churches and the Jewish Diaspora; in literature, art, music, and film; in Islam, as well as in other religious traditions and current religious movements, Western and non-Western alike.

The scope of this new project is obviously enormous, and in welcoming it, it would be wrong to suggest that no one took any academic notice of the use of Psalms or psalms over the centuries before reception history arrived on the scene. There were church historians who took an interest in different aspects of the production, translation, promotion, interpretation and use of the Bible, as evidenced in the variety of chapters and concerns in the three volumes of *The Cambridge History of the Bible* (published in 1970, 1963 and 1969 respectively). There was also interest shown in university departments of English literature, as can be seen in the index of the 2009 *Blackwell Companion to the Bible in English Literature*, or by historians of music or art, as in Leveen's *The Hebrew Bible in Art* (1944): but few Old Testament scholars would have gone there, except possibly as a hobby. A book which both Hunter and Gillingham identify as a lonely forerunner of this new interest rather proves the point. Rowland

Prothero's *The Psalms in Human Life* (1903), which illustrates how psalms are 'inextricably mingled' with national and private life, and celebrates their place in the spiritual life of people from the infancy of Christianity to the Boer War, was not written by a professional biblical scholar but by a 'learned Victorian'.[8] It leaves an important impression, but soon becomes something of a tedious read lightened only by the occasional gem.

'Reception history' begins from the simple observation that writers and speakers have no control over their words once they have gone public. Senders of indiscreet private emails discover this to their cost, and most preachers have had the disconcerting conversation in which they are told how helpful a particular sermon has been, when they know full well that they said something quite different if not opposite to what is being so fulsomely praised. In this sense the reception history of a text or saying begins immediately, and the process can take what is said or written into strange places. Some have suggested that we can see this in the way in which an ancient Canaanite hymn to Baal has been taken over by the Israelites and reapplied in Psalms to the worship of YHWH (Ps. 29: Anderson discusses the suggestions on p. 233 of volume 1 of his commentary). It is obvious that the process is under way in Psalms, however, with the gathering of individual psalms into collections, and then into the Psalter as a whole. Psalms whose *raison d'être* and *Sitz-im-Leben* was liturgical take on new meanings as chapters in a book of torah meditation. So do 'royal' psalms when kings are dead and monarchy extinct. Thus, it is often observed, those psalm titles that locate a particular psalm at a specific moment of David's life are transforming those psalms into prayers for faithfulness 'through all the changing scenes of life' in which we can all make 'David's prayers' our own. This is one of the meanings of the term 'the 'democratization of the psalms', the other being the proliferation of translations made available by the printing revolution in the fifteenth century. We see further movements in the Septuagint and its translation of the psalm titles, for example, in translating the Hebrew noun (*lamměnaṣēaḥ*, 'to the Leader/Choirmaster') by *eis to telos* ('for completion'/'to the end'), it gives the psalms concerned an eschatological twist. Gillingham notes all this right at the beginning of her commentary by subheading her opening pages 'from composition to compilation to translation' (Gillingham, 2008, p. 5).

An outline of Gillingham's approach will help us to see the parameters and possibilities of this young discipline. In volume 1 of the two volumes on Psalms in the new Blackwell series, she approaches the task by looking generally at how

Psalms has been used in different periods. In volume 2 she promises a look at the reception history of each psalm. At the outset she regrets that her commentary has the drawback of being a 'word-centred' survey and one that inevitably illustrates her own 'particularity' (Gillingham, 2008, p. 1). It is also, it must be said, a commentary that is almost entirely confined to the reception history of Psalms in Judaism and Christianity. Volume 1 divides its survey into six periods, with a chapter (for some reason without any number on the opening page of the chapters) on each:

- the eleventh century BCE to the fifth century CE
- the fifth to the eleventh centuries
- the eleventh to the fifteenth centuries
- the fifteenth to the seventeenth centuries
- the eighteenth and nineteenth centuries
- the twentieth to twenty-first centuries.

Gillingham notes that each of these different periods will 'suggest different changes of emphasis in the reception of psalmody in both Jewish and Christian traditions' (Gillingham, 2008, p. 2), and so she lists five different 'types of reception history':

- reception through *exposition*, which focuses on how psalms are explained in commentaries and their like;
- reception through *instruction*, which looks at how the moral and spiritual teaching of psalms is applied in sermons or devotional literature;
- reception through *liturgy*, which considers how psalms feature in public worship and private prayer;
- reception through *translation*, which explores what happens to psalms in translations ancient and modern;
- reception through *aesthetic representation*, which discusses the use of psalms in literature, music, architecture and art.

The title of Chapter 2 simply includes the dates of the period and the three types of reception covered in it, but in other chapters the title identifies a particular theme of the period covered. The title of Chapter 1, for example, indicates that it will cover translation, exposition, instruction and liturgy and adds 'and the

Prophetic Bias', referring to what the author identifies as a major developing trend in the use of psalms in that early period. The headings to Chapters 4 and 6, which cover the fifteenth to seventeenth centuries and our own day, mention none of Gillingham's five types of reception but focus entirely on the overarching themes of 'Democratization and Dissemination' and 'Pluralism and Ecumenism' respectively.

Given that the possibilities of this area are almost literally boundless, we will close this chapter by a look at one of the earliest examples of 'reception by exposition', and a brief look at contemporary reception, with apologies to those who would have liked to linger longer here and explore more areas.

One of the most accessible places to explore the early reception history of Psalms is the New Testament, where the 'exposition' type of reception is prominent. Christianity began its life as a 'messianic Jewish sect' and in its preaching, teaching and writing used the conventions for interpreting 'Scripture' already in use in such movements, such as can be seen in the Dead Sea Scrolls. Gillingham explains and summarizes this approach by calling it 'prophetic' (Gillingham, 2008, pp. 14–23). In this way of reading old texts, readers in a new context move beyond the original sense of the passage and reapply it to their new situation. The classic Old Testament prophets, for example, are transformed in this rereading from preachers and spokespeople who announce God's will to their contemporaries, often with a warning or threat about what will happen pretty soon if those contemporaries don't mend their ways, or a promise that better days are about to dawn because God has listened to their cries for help, into predictors of a much further-away future, namely, the time in which the interpreter is living. The principle of interpretation at work is that old texts mean more than might have been understood by their first speakers or authors and by their original readers or hearers, as we saw in the Habakkuk commentary from Qumran in Chapter 6. You can hardly open the New Testament before you see Matthew using old texts in this way, and the practice is endemic in the New Testament where Psalms and Isaiah are the Old Testament books most extensively mined for new, messianic, meanings and applications. Quotes from Psalms are used to establish many things, but among them the messianic status and qualifications of Jesus are prominent. If we take Mark as an example, Psalm 2 is cited at 1.11 and 9.7, Psalm 118 at 11.9–10 and 12.10–11, Psalm 110 at 12.36 and alluded to in 14.62, and Psalm 22 at 15.24, 15.34, and alluded to in 15.29 (Watts, pp. 25–45). Day points out that about one-third of the Old Testament quotations in the New Testament are from Psalms, and among them Psalms 2, 22, 69, 110 and 118 are 'particularly important' (Day, 1990, p. 137). Steve Moyise, *The Old Testament in the New*, offers access to this area in an opening chapter headed 'Text and Interpretation in the First Century', followed by chapters headed 'The Old Testament in Mark' and 'Paul' and so on. *The Psalms in the New Testament*, edited by Moyise and M. J. J. Menken, begins with an introductory chapter on 'The Psalms in Early Jewish Literature in the Light of the Dead Sea Scrolls' (by G. J. Brooke), before detailed chapters looking at 'The Psalms in Mark's Gospel' and so on. The New Testament expounds Psalms as a book of future promises now in the process of being fulfilled and of texts about the Messiah. Its psalms are interpreted 'christologically' and it is read as a book that points to Jesus Christ, using the reading strategies and methods of interpreting 'Scripture' already in use at Qumran.

Finally, what of today? Gillingham's last chapter mentions the four big names we have met throughout this book (Gunkel, Mowinckel, Westermann and Brueggemann), together with many more, including Alter, Berlin, Eaton and Wilson. The academic 'reception' of Psalms, in its many forms, is an important facet of the whole. It is, however, far from the only one. One of the biggest revolutions in biblical study in the last 30 years, or as we might put it in the context of this chapter, one of the most interesting new areas of the reception of the Bible in this period, has been in the way in which the Bible has been read and used by people at the margin. The first 'voices from the margin', to use the title of Sugirtharajah's important book, *Voices from the Margin: Interpreting the Bible in the Third World* (1995), were those of liberation theology and of the feminist writers. In liberation theology it was the Exodus narratives that attracted the attention of the poor Christians in the *favellas* of Rio or Sao Paolo, who read them as their story about their God and their freedom.[9] Feminist readers of the Old Testament began to discover the hidden women of that patriarchal text and read them back into the narratives from which they had been excluded.[10] After that has come a whole range of 'interested' readings, that is, readings of the Old Testament from particular perspectives that consciously and deliberately read with those interests in mind: political readings, green readings, womanist readings, third-world readings, multicultural readings, post-colonial readings and queer readings, to name only a few, and there is no sign of the development slowing down. In something of a reaction, books are now even advertised as 'Christian readings' or 'theological readings', prompting one reviewer to comment wryly that after reading one such 'theological reading' he felt like that fictional character who suddenly realized that he had been speaking prose all his life. Traditional 'devotional' readings continue to be written too, of course. Another contemporary feature is that dialogue between different faith communities is opening up new possibilities of sharing insights on the Bible from different faith perspectives. Gillingham's conclusion, however, that 'feminist studies of psalmody are very much in their infancy' (Gillingham, 2008, p. 284) applies much more widely, for readings of Psalms feature relatively little so far in this rich variety of 'interested readings', with the exception, as one would expect, of those 'spiritual' or 'devotional' readings. The entries on Psalms in the *Women's Bible Commentary* (by Kathleen Farmer), *The IVP Women's Bible Commentary* (by Gwyneth Raikes) and the *Global Bible Commentary* (by David Tuesday Adamo) are good ways into two of these 'interested' readings, and all three will alert white, western, Christian, 'male' readers (who are not, of course, all men) to the very different messages and meanings that are obtainable from Psalms when that book is read from another place. Adamo's 'therapeutic' reading from his African context, which demonstrates the use of the 'potent words' of the psalms to effect cures, is one of the most radically different 'receptions' of Psalms that I have encountered and it is very different from what he calls the 'Eurocentric' readings of both academia and the colonial Church, among which, without doubt, he would include the feminist readings of Farmer and Raikes.

This area too is very much a work in progress:

- Its archaeological aspect, unearthing ancient usages of psalms, especially esoteric ones in exotic places, will always fascinate.
- Updating Prothero's agenda of seeing how psalms have been used in the 'devotional lives' of the great and good, and of the not-so-great but often better, will also be of value to those who are interested in how spirituality and religion affect human lives, either for good or ill.
- Observing how psalms are read in different cultures and contexts will always be of interest to those who want to understand the worlds in which other people live and learn lessons from them.
- Moving the study of psalms beyond words into the areas of music, art, dance, liturgy or drama will have real appeal to many.
- This new development in Psalms study has a sharp edge to it. It is not simply an interesting exercise in historical research or cultural studies for those who

like that sort of thing. Its historical observations and its recognition of the modern 'democratization' of Psalms, with its plethora of readings, alert us to those big 'hermeneutical' questions that diversities of readings inevitably raise. Are we condemned by our observation of how Psalms has been read over the centuries to conclude that all readings, including those we label 'academic' and 'critical', are provisional, constrained by culture, circumstance and interest, and condemned to be seen as such by those who come later? If so, is this a bad thing, or a good one? Or neither, just the way it is?

Perhaps that is not a bad point at which to end this *Studyguide* because it focuses on what Psalms is about. We have seen that Psalms is a lively anthology, which voices praise, shalom, dissonance, penitence, hope, spirituality and theology. We have felt the vigour of its language, metaphors and attitudes and read its poems which speak of pain, distress and hopelessness and those which sing of peace, joy and laughter. We have seen that at the beginning it makes a programme-statement about where meaning and satisfaction are to be found in human life, and that at the end, when we have travelled in its pages 'through all the changing scenes of life, in trouble and in joy', it concludes with praise to God. And we have seen something of the many ways in which Psalms has been treasured, used and made contemporary over the centuries since it and its component poems first saw the light of day in ancient Israel. Whatever else may be said about Psalms, it is a book about real life, about the challenge real life presents to faith in a God whose name and nature is love, and about the reality of the blessing of that God in the midst of that real life. The psalmists and their editors struggled with the meaning of life and faith; their modern readers do so too and add a struggle of their own with the meaning of meaning. In their struggles words addressed to God and words spoken about him gave their writers, speakers and singers, and the faith community to which they belonged, songs, prayers and 'instruction' on which to 'meditate' and by which to voice their joys and sorrows, commitments and values, hopes and fears. The continued use of psalms through the ages testifies to the fact that that ancient book still does the same.

To do

Has anything in this chapter excited you? What? Why? Has anything in it challenged you? What? How? Has anything in it worried you? What? Why? Has anything in it influenced the way you will read the Old Testament in future?

Suggestions for further reading

The shape and shaping of Psalms

Brueggemann, W. (1991), 'Bounded by Obedience and Praise: the Psalms as Canon', in JSOT 50, pp. 63–92, reproduced in Brueggemann, *The Psalms and the Life of Faith*, pp. 189–213.

*Bullock, C. H. (2001), *Encountering the Psalms*, Grand Rapids MI, Eerdmans, pp. 57–71.

*Crenshaw, J. L. (2001), *The Psalms: An Introduction*, Grand Rapids MI, Eerdmans, pp. 98–105.

deClaissé-Walford, N. (1997), *Reading from the Beginning: The Shaping of the Hebrew Psalter*, Macon: Mercer University Press.

Grant, J. A. (2008), 'Editorial Criticism', in *DOTWPW*, pp. 149–56.

*Hunter, A. G. (2008), *An Introduction in the Psalms*, London: T&T Clark, pp. 36–9.

*Lucas E. (2003), *Exploring the Old Testament, vol. 3: The Psalms and Wisdom Literature*, London: SPCK, pp. 28–34.

McCann, J. C. (ed.) (1993a), *The Shape and Shaping of the Psalter*, Sheffield: JSOT Press.

*McCann, J. C. (1993–2002), 'The Shape and Shaping of the Psalter', in *NIB*, vol. 4, pp. 655–66. Do not confuse this article with the full-length book.

Mitchell, D. C. (1997), *The Message of the Psalter: An Eschatological Programme in the Book of Psalms*, Sheffield: Sheffield Academic Press.

Whybray, N. (1996), *Reading the Psalms as a Book*, Sheffield: Sheffield Academic Press.

Wilson, G. H. (1985, reissued 2004), *The Editing of the Hebrew Psalter*, Chicago: Scholars Press.

Wilson has developed his thinking in a number of articles: particularly accessible are

'The Use of Royal Psalms at the "Seams" of the Hebrew Psalter', in *JSOT* 35 (1986), pp. 85–94, and 'The Structure of the Psalter' in Johnston and Firth, *Interpreting the Psalms*, pp. 229–46.

Psalms down the ages

Attridge, H. W. and Fassler, M. E. (eds) (2003), *Psalms in Community: Jewish and Christian Textual, Liturgical and Artistic Traditions*, Leiden: Brill.

Beal, L. W. (2008), 'Psalms 3: History of Interpretation', in *DOTWPW*, pp. 605–13.

Brueggemann, D. A. (2005), 'The Evangelists and the Psalms', in Johnston and Firth, *Interpreting the Psalms*, pp. 263–78.

*Bullock, C. H. (2001), *Encountering the Book of Psalms*, Grand Rapids MI, Eerdmans, pp. 88–96.

*Day, J. (1990), *Psalms: Old Testament Guides*, Sheffield: Sheffield Academic Press, pp. 136–41.

*Eaton, J. (2003), *The Psalms: A Historical and Spiritual Commentary*, London: T&T Clark International, pp. 41–58.

*Geoghegan J. and Homan M. (2002), *The Bible for Dummies*, New York: Wiley; see ch. 24, 'The Bible in the Abrahamic Faiths: Judaism, Christianity and Islam', and ch. 25, 'Michelangelo, Milton and Movies: Art, Literature, Life and the Bible'.

Gillingham, S. (2008), *Psalms through the Centuries*, vol. 1, Oxford: Blackwell (vol. 2 forthcoming).

Holladay, W L. (1993), *The Psalms through Three Thousand Years*, Minneapolis MN: Fortress Press.

Moyise, S. (2001), *The Old Testament in the New*, London: Continuum.

Moyise, S. and Menken, M. J. J. (2004), *The Psalms in the New Testament*, London: Continuum.

Prothero, R. E. (1903), *The Psalms in Human Life*, London: Thomas Nelson (various editions since).

Reid, S. B. (1997), *Listening In: A Multicultural Reading of the Psalms*, Nashville TN: Abingdon Press.

Sawyer, J. F. A. (ed.) (2009), *A Concise Dictionary of the Bible: And its Reception*, Louisville KY: Westminster John Knox Press.

Seybold, K. (1990), *Introducing the Psalms*, Edinburgh: T&T Clark, pp. 213–46.

Wallace, H. N. (2005), *Words to God, Word from God*, Aldershot: Ashgate.

Waltke, B. K. and Houston, J. K. (2009), *The Psalms as Christian Worship: A Historical Commentary*, Grand Rapids MI: Eerdmans.

See the 'Bible – Old Testament books' index for the references to Psalms in R. Lemon, E. Mason, J. Roberts and C. Rowland (eds) (2009), *The Blackwell Companion to the Bible in English Literature*, Oxford: Wiley Blackwell.

DMBI is a good resource for exploring the contributions of 'famous names'.

There will also be the entry or entries on Psalms in the *Encyclopedia of the Bible and its Reception* (by Walter de Gruyter, in process of publication) when the relevant volume appears.

Notes

1 Opening the Book

1 For a careful discussion of issues around defining genre in Psalms, see Broyles, *Conflict of Faith and Experience*, pp. 22–7. Some commentators use 'genre' for the different 'types' or categories of psalms: laments, hymns, Songs of Zion etc. (see Chapter 3). I prefer to think of those categories as 'sub-genres', just as in the genre of the recipe there are sub-genres of pudding recipes, vegan recipes etc., and to reserve the word 'genre' for the more basic question of what kind of literature a psalm is.

2 Tremper Longman III, in Goldingay, *Old Testament Theology*, vol. 1, p. 9. Luther writes: '[Psalms] could well be called a "little Bible" since it contains, set out in the briefest and most beautiful form, all that is to be found in the whole Bible . . . in order that those who could not read the whole Bible through would have almost the whole of it in summary form, comprised in a single booklet' (Preface to the Revised Edition of the German Psalter (1531), reproduced in B. L. Woolf, *Reformation Writings of Martin Luther*, London: Lutterworth Press, 1956, pp. 267–71, at p. 268). See also the paragraph on *Luther and the Old Testament* (H. Bornkamm, 1948) in Seybold, *Introducing the Psalms*, p. 224.

3 See Clements, 'Mowinckel', in *DMBI*, pp. 757–62.

4 Gerstenberger (1988) has mounted a rather different challenge to this, which has not been widely accepted, suggesting that many psalms arose in family, neighbourhood or community settings rather than Temple ones.

5 Psalm 24 with possible rubrics added.

Inside the Temple
Worship Leader: The earth is the Lord's and all that is in it
Temple Choir: the world, and those who live in it
Worship Leader: for he has founded it on the seas
Temple Choir: and established it on the rivers

At the foot of the Temple mount
Procession Leader: Who shall ascend the hill of the LORD?
Procession Choir: And who shall stand in his holy place?
Procession Leader: Those who have clean hands and pure hearts
Procession Choir: Who do not lift up their souls to what is false and do not swear deceitfully
Procession Leader: They will receive blessing from the LORD
Procession Choir: and vindication from the God of their salvation
Procession Leader: Such is the company of those who seek him
Procession Choir: who seek the face of the God of Jacob

The procession moves to the Temple gate and the Procession Leader strikes the gate with his rod
Procession Leader: Lift up your heads, O Gates!
Procession Choir: And be lifted up, O ancient doors!
Procession Leader and Choir: that the King of glory may come in
Doorkeeper (from inside): Who is the King of glory?
Procession Leader: The LORD, strong and mighty
Procession Choir: the LORD, mighty in battle

The Procession Leader strikes the door for a second time
Procession Leader: Lift up your heads, O Gates!
Procession Choir: And be lifted up, O ancient doors!
Procession Leader and Choir: that the King of glory may come in
Doorkeeper (from inside): Who is the King of glory?
Procession Leader and Choir: The LORD of hosts
Doorkeeper, opening the doors: He is the king of glory.

The procession enters the Temple, preceded by a group of liturgical dancers with banners, and everyone sings, 'We will enter his gates with thanksgiving in our hearts, we will enter his courts with praise . . .'

The Dramatised Bible (Marshall Pickering, 1990) is more sober and gives the psalm a cast of three solo voices (Leader, Enquirer and Director) and a chorus of 'All'.
   6 It has been common in the last 50 years to dismiss any attempt to talk about what authors meant or intended. To do that was to be guilty of the 'intentional fallacy' – 'the mistaken belief that what the author intended is the "real", "final" meaning of the work *and that we can or should know what this is*' (Bennett and Royle, *Introduction to Literature, Criticism and Theory*, p. 7, my italics) – which in literary circles was

the unforgivable sin. Seeking the author's intention and naming that as the meaning of the text is, no doubt, both impossible and incorrect in many genres of literature, but in others, for example textbooks, recipes, instruction manuals and the Highway Code, recognizing and then appropriating the author's intention is essential for competent reading of such literature. In terms of the Bible, attempting to say what Job, Ecclesiastes or the Song of Songs mean on the basis of what their authors might have intended is indeed to fall foul of the 'intentional fallacy', but that can't be said of texts like the Ten Commandments or Amos 5.24. We know precisely what the author intended when he wrote, 'You shall not steal'. It was that his readers should understand that they should not steal, and that understanding that, they should not steal. He might, of course, as a property-owner, have been writing out of self-interest and his motives might go beyond an altruistic desire to promote shalom, but his intention is clear in and from the text. Again, it comes down to the recognition of genre, and, in genres like these, authorial intention is no fallacy.

7 The editorial notes in *NCTS* explain its use of italics in the psalm titles as follows: 'Text not represented in some way in the Hebrew original is signalled by italics. The absence of italics should not be construed to mean that the targum translates literally.'

8 Yes, I know that adds up to more than 100. The three psalms that mention Jeduthun also mention one of the others, and Psalm 88 also has two names in its title, and we can't count these psalms twice.

9 11QPs^a = 11Q5. The traditional method used in naming Qumran material is to give the number of the cave in which the manuscript was found, 'Q' for Qumran, then the name of the book and any further clarification. So 11QPs^a is the first (denoted by the ^{a}) Psalms scroll found at Qumran in Cave 11. A new system is being introduced, which numbers this scroll as 11Q5.

10 'Only with the personalization of the originally anonymous Holy Scriptures and the distribution of the text-complexes under the names of great authors, Moses, David, Solomon, and the prophets, Ezra, etc., did the Psalms too come to be given an "author", a simplification which may have had dogmatic advantages, but which in the long run has been at the cost of historical plausibility and has led to ideological entrenchment.' Seybold, *Introducing the Psalms*, p. 38. See also Goldingay, *Old Testament Theology*, vol. 1, pp. 27–8.

11 The translation problem is sharpened here because it is always harder to translate a single word standing alone, as the words do in the psalm headings, than it is to translate words put together in sentences.

12 I have already quoted from Seybold's preface. The other important point he makes in that wise page and a half refers to his cover illustration of a fragment of Psalm 103 from Qumran, which is, he says, 'a symbol of our fragmentary knowledge

of the Psalms'. We can see a number of things and deduce some more, 'but there is a great deal which is no longer available to us'. Seybold, *Introducing the Psalms*, p. v.

2 Voicing praise

1 For music and musical instruments in the Bible, see the entries by Matthews and Jones in 'Music and Musical Instruments', in *ABD*, vol. 4, pp. 930–9, and Werner, 'Musical Instruments', in *IDB*, vol. 3, pp. 469–76. To help you through Jones' list, the musical instruments mentioned in Ps. 150 are, in order of appearance: *šôpār*, *nēbāl*, *kinnôr*, *tōp* – he regards NRSV's 'lute' (*minnîm*) as a general reference to 'strings' rather than to a specific instrument – *ʿūgāb* and two types of *ṣelṣelîm*.

2 *God Who Acts* was the title of an influential book in the mid-twentieth century by G. E. Wright and was also something of a motto for the 'Biblical Theology Movement' of that time.

3 The Moabite Stone was discovered in 1868 and is now reconstructed in the Louvre. It commemorates the victories of King Mesha of Moab over Israel around 830 BC, and attributes these victories to Chemosh, the God of Moab, fighting for his people against their enemies. This extract shows the belief that Chemosh had acted both to save Moab and to punish it,

> I am Mesha, son of Chemosh . . . king of Moab. My father was king over Moab thirty years and I became king after my father. And I made this sanctuary for Chemosh at Qrchh, a sanctuary of salvation; for he saved me from all the kings and let me see my desire upon my adversaries. Omri, king of Israel, oppressed Moab many days, for Chemosh was angry with his land. And his son succeeded him, and he too said, 'I will oppress Moab.' In my days he spoke thus, but I saw my desire upon him and upon his house, when Israel perished utterly for ever . . . And the king of Israel had built Jahaz and he dwelt in it while fighting against me. But Chemosh drove him out before me (*DOTT*, pp. 196–7)

4 See the extended comment in Chapter 3.

5 See Parrish, 'Brueggemann', in *DMBI*, pp. 242–7.

6 For examples, see the extended comment on translating the psalms in Chapter 5.

7 For a useful summary of the issues, see Lucas, *Exploring the Old Testament*, ch. 2.

8 Berlin, 'Poetry' in *OCB*, pp. 597–9, and *The Dynamics of Biblical Parallelism*; Gillingham, *Poems and Psalms*, pp. 14 and 21.

9 Kugel, *The Idea of Biblical Poetry*. Gillingham discusses the question of whether or not there is such a thing as Hebrew poetry as distinct from Hebrew prose and offers four general and nine specific characteristics (*Poems and Psalms*, ch. 2). She

summarizes Kugel's position by saying that he suggests 'that Hebrew verse is simply a developed prose style with rhetorical tendencies' (p. 32). For another list of characteristics, see Lucas, *Exploring the Old Testament*, pp. 73–4.

10 Gillingham offers the suggestion that 'seconding' might be a better word than 'parallelism' and suggests three types of seconding in psalms 1, where A = B, 2, where A > B, that is, A carries the main point that B qualifies, and 3, where A < B, that is, where A introduces B which is the main point (pp. 78–82). A. A. Anderson speaks of three kinds of parallelism – complete, incomplete and formal – but rather gives the game away by saying that strictly speaking 'formal' is no parallelism at all (1972, vol. 1, pp. 41–2). Howard (2005) quotes Alter with approval that 'the second "verset" of a couplet (goes) beyond the first in any of a number of ways, only one of which might be synonymity (and that only rarely). Others include complementarity, focusing, heightening, intensification, specification, consequentiality, contrast and disjunction' (Johnston and Firth, p. 32).

3 Voicing shalom

1 That psalm is a pastiche of phrases or verses from 11 biblical psalms: of Pss 120.1 and 31.22 in verse 2, Pss 69.2 and 42.7 in verse 3, Pss 31.22 and 5.7 in verse 4, Pss 69.1 and 18.4 in verse 5, Ps. 103.4 in verse 6, Pss 143.5 and 88.2 in verse 7, Ps. 31.6 in verse 8, and Pss 116.17f. and 3.8 in verse 9.

2 Haran, *Temples and Temple Service in Ancient Israel*, remains the best handbook. The old standby de Vaux, *Ancient Israel: Its Life and Institutions*, is still useful, and Sanders, *Judaism*, has some helpful chapters. 'The Temple in First Century CE Judaism' is a good essay by Martin Goodman in Day, *Temple and Worship in Biblical Israel*. Gerstenberger, *Psalms*, pp. 5–33, offers a general introduction to these questions stressing how little we know.

3 By the 'Crimond version' I mean the metrical version of Ps. 23 by William Whittingham (1524–79), altered by Francis Rous (1579–1659) and others, which is usually sung to the tune 'Crimond'. Tracing its lineage is an interesting exercise in 'source criticism', while deciding who is to be credited with its tune is best left to the lawyers. Its users are unaware of both questions and none the worse for that. It reads in full:

1 The Lord's my Shepherd, I'll not want / He makes me down to lie
   In pastures green; He leadeth me / The quiet waters by.

2 My soul He doth restore again / And me to walk doth make
   Within the paths of righteousness / E'en for His own name's sake.

3 Yea, though I walk in death's dark vale / Yet will I fear no ill;
  For Thou art with me, and thy rod / And staff me comfort still.

4 My table thou hast furnished / In presence of my foes;
  My head Thou dost with oil anoint / And my cup overflows.

5 Goodness and mercy all my life / Shall surely follow me,
  And in God's house for evermore / My dwelling-place shall be.

4 For more on the 'construct' and the translation issues this grammatical feature raises, see the extended comment in Chapter 5 (pp. 105–6).

5 *DBI* is a good resource to see, for example, how 'sheep, shepherd' and 'banquet' are used here and elsewhere in the Old Testament.

6 The contemporary debate on this is extensive, but the 1980s books by Sallie McFague and Janet Martin Soskice in the suggestions for further reading are among the generative texts.

7 See the comment on this 'core creed' in chapter 8.

8 This is Hunter's summary of Gunkel's main 'types' with their identifying motifs (Hunter, *An Introduction to the Psalms*, pp. 49f.):

a. Hymns
  (i) call to praise
  (ii) reasons for praise (1. The Lord is great; 2. The Lord is good)
  (iii) Alleluiah!
b. Psalms of the enthronement of YHWH
c. Communal complaints:
  (i) invocation
  (ii) complaint
  (iii) review of God's past help
  (iv) petition
  (v) praise or vow to praise
d. Royal psalms
e. Individual complaints with the same motifs as communal ones
f. Individual thanksgiving songs:
  (i) introduction (1. summons; 2. initial summary)
  (ii) call to praise
  (iii) account (Narrative) (1. crisis in retrospect; 2. rescue)
  (iv) praise or vow to praise.

9 All the seven writers in Johnston's Appendix classify Ps. 23 as a 'Confidence Psalm', with six of them placing it in the sub-category of 'Confidence Psalm of the Individual' (along with Pss 4, 11, 16, 62, 91, 121, 131). Most commentators agree with that broad classification. For Brueggemann it is a psalm of reorientation (W. Brueggemann, *The Psalms and the Life of Faith*, p. 31); for Westermann a psalm of praise (Westermann, *Praise and Lament in the Psalms*, p. 75).

4 Voicing dissonance

1 For the ways in which the psalms can be categorized or divided into 'types', see the extended comment at the end of Chapter 3.

2 I introduce it by saying that this is the first of the two creation parables with which the Bible begins. I use the word 'parable' because congregations know how to understand parables, i.e. the story is fiction and the message is very important.

3 NJPS capitalizes each second-person pronoun referring to God in this psalm, and reading it in that version it is very clear how directly God is being addressed in this psalm: *You*, *Your*, *Yours* and *Yourself* occur 34 times in that translation.

4 I use the word 'dissonance' aware of Walter Brueggemann's 'disorientation' and Philip Johnston's strong case for 'distress' (Johnston and Firth (eds), *Interpreting the Psalms*, ch. 3). For me, 'disorientation' risks understating the sheer physicality of suffering, and 'distress' risks underplaying the theological dimension, hence my preference for 'dissonance', which encompasses both elements.

5 See Limburg, 'Westermann', in *BMBI*, pp. 1043–8.

6 Two popular books that explore these questions are Harold Kushner, *When Bad Things Happen to Good People*, from a Jewish perspective, and Philip Yancey, *Where is God when it Hurts?* from a Christian one.

7 There are almost none. The sharpest known to me is not found in any current hymn book. It is 'When wilt Thou save the people? / O God of mercy, when?' by Ebenezer Elliot (1781–1849), which was no. 909 in the *Methodist Hymn Book* of 1933. It was given stage treatment in the musical *Godspell*.

8 Theodicy is one of the biggest theological issues facing Christianity and Judaism, and always has been. It permeates the Bible in general and Psalms in particular. On that ground I justify the inclusion of this reflection which I have used in classes on theodicy with the South West Ministry Training Course for a number of years. It contains a joke from my A-level RE teacher. Some things are so bad you never forget them: the joke I mean, not the teacher.

5 Voicing penitence

1 The designation of Pss 6, 32, 38, 51, 102, 130 and 143 as the 'seven penitential psalms' is an ancient one in Christian circles, going back at least to Augustine
(Gillingham, *Psalms through the Centuries*, p. 113). There is, however, nothing penitential about three of them (Pss 6, 102, 143), which are properly identified as 'laments'
and as such contain no sense that the person making the lament is anything other
than an innocent victim.

2 Two of the characters in the imaginative reflection at the end of Chapter 4.

3 Num. 15.27–31 contrasts forgivable and unforgivable failure in terms of those
who sin 'unintentionally' and those who act 'high-handedly'. Lev. 4—6 also discusses
unintentional failure. This terminology is interesting but the qualification in Num.
15.30 that this sin with a 'high-' or 'raised-hand' involves 'despising' the 'word of the
LORD' as well as breaking his commandment, and the fact that Lev. 6.1–5 can include
major sins like bearing false witness and theft among 'unintentional' sins, suggests
that what really makes the difference is the deliberate intention wilfully to disobey
God.

4 The text of the Hebrew Bible was eventually fixed by Jewish scholars (the
'Masoretes') between the sixth and ninth centuries AD, who also added tiny points
above, beneath or in between the large consonants to indicate the vowels which had
not been included in Hebrew manuscripts up to then. See Penkower, 'The Development of the Masoretic Bible', in *The Jewish Study Bible*, pp. 2077–84. BHS uses this text
as it is found in the Leningrad Codex copied by Samuel ben Jacob in AD 1008 or 1009,
which is the oldest dated manuscript of the complete Hebrew Bible we have. It is 'a
broadly reliable guide to a textual tradition going back into the pre-Christian period'
(Goldingay, *Old Testament Theology*, vol. 1, p. 11). How this manuscript ended up in
the Leningrad Public Library is probably a question best not asked.

5 The opening of Ps. 23 in Jim Cotter's superb reflection, *Through Desert Places*
(1989). He covers Pss 51—100 in *By Stony Paths* (1991) and Pss 101—150 in *Towards
the City* (1993).

6 Voicing hope

1 During the twentieth century the debate about where you could place a 'real
history begins here' marker in the Old Testament story moved it steadily forwards
(or is it backwards?), from Abraham, via Moses and the Exodus, to the 'United Monarchy', and got increasingly acrimonious as it went. The 'Minimalists' or 'Revisionists'
questioned whether there was any 'Israel of History' as distinct from 'Biblical Israel'
until very late indeed. The 'Maximalists' insisted that at least from the twelfth century

BC you could talk in these terms, though you did need to recognize that the story was presented from a particular point of view and used its own conventions of storytelling. Both groups are serious biblical scholars, and none read the Old Testament stories as straight, literal and factual descriptions of what really was what. Mills, *Historical Israel: Biblical Israel*, provides a good introduction to the questions. Finkelstein and Silberman, *The Bible Unearthed*, provides a very readable statement of the 'Minimalist' viewpoint and its archaeological basis. Provan, Long and Longman, *A Biblical History of Israel*, defends the 'Maximalist' position. A via media with regard to the 'united monarchy' is offered by William Dever in 'Histories and Non-histories of Ancient Israel: the Question of the United Monarchy', Day (ed.), *In Search of Ancient Israel*, ch. 4.

2 Mowinckel, *Psalms*, vol. 1, ch. 5; A. R. Johnson, *Sacral Kingship in Ancient Israel*; Eaton, summarized in *The Psalms* (2003), pp. 22–5. Other scholars have given the 'Autumn Festival' a different focus: for example, Weiser saw it as a festival of Covenant Renewal of the Sinai Covenant, and Kraus a Royal Zion festival celebrating YHWH's choice of Zion and his blessings on the Temple and city (see Lucas, *Exploring the Old Testament*, pp. 13–19; Johnston and Firth (eds), *Interpreting the Psalms*, pp. 128–32; Hunter, *An Introduction to the Psalms*, 2008, pp. 92–4).

3 In many of these cases NRSV adds a footnote along the lines of this one to the Song of Hannah: 'It was the custom of biblical editors to insert poems into prose books to increase artistic and religious appeal. The poems may be older or later than the contexts into which they are inserted. In this case the poem seems to be considerably later.'

4 *NETS*. An older translation by G. B. Gray, in Charles (ed.), *The Apocrypha and Pseudepigrapha of the Old Testament*, vol. 2, pp. 631–52, can be found at a number of locations online, such as http://wesley.nnu.edu/biblical_studies/noncanon/ot/pseudo/psalms-solomon.htm. A new translation and introduction by R. B. Wright is available in Charlesworth, *The Old Testament Pseudepigrapha*, vol. 2, pp. 639–70.

5 Swanson, 'Qumran and the Psalms', in Johnston and Firth (eds), *Interpreting the Psalms*, p. 248.

6 The words in the square brackets are hypothetical reconstructions.

7 In his introduction to this chapter, Seybold points out that faced with the discovery of large amounts of ancient oriental psalmody scholars have had to face the question of what is special about Psalms which led to its continued use over several millennia when the rest disappeared. With respect, I would have thought the answer to that was obvious – Psalms remained in use because the faith community which produced it continues to exist and also gave birth to another faith community which treasures its ancient texts.

7 Voicing spirituality

1 The 'western text' of Acts 13.33 quotes Ps. 2.7 and says that it is from the first psalm. In Jewish tradition there is a quote from Rabbi Johanan: 'Every chapter that was particularly dear to David he commenced with "Happy" and terminated with "Happy". He began with "Happy," as it is written, "Happy is the man," and he terminated with "Happy," as it is written, "Happy are all they that take refuge in him"' (Tractate Berakot 9b). As these references are to the first verse of Ps. 1 and the last of Ps. 2 it looks as if Rabbi Johanan considered them as one psalm.

2 The differences between Pss 14 and 53 are minor except in the naming of God (YHWH in 14 and 'Elohim in 53). The existence of two versions of the same psalm and the fact that the second is included in what is usually called the 'Elohistic Psalter' (Pss 42—83) is another piece in the jigsaw of the history of the compilation of Psalms (see Chapter 9). BCP has extra verses in Ps. 14 which come from LXX.

3 Pss 14 and 53 are both 'David' psalms. The famous medieval Jewish commentator *Rashi* (Rabbi Schlomo son of Isaac, 1040–1105) regarded Ps. 14 as David's prophetic (in the 'predicting the future' sense of that term) word about the destruction of Solomon's Temple in 586 BC, and Ps. 53 as his prophetic word about the destruction of Herod's Temple in AD 70. *Radak* (Rabbi David Kimchi, 1160–1235) thought that David was just repeating himself.

4 The literature on the 'New Perspective' is extensive. For a succinct introduction, see F. Thielman, 'Law', in Hawthorne, Martin and Reid (eds), *Dictionary of Paul and his Letters*, pp. 529–42, especially pp. 529–32 and the extensive bibliography given on p. 542. Paul's own view on 'the Law' is, however, far from agreed. For useful introductions, see Zeisler, *Pauline Christianity*, ch. 6; Horrell, *An Introduction to the Study of Paul*, ch. 6; and Harris, *SCM Core Text: Paul*.

8 Voicing theology

1 For an exploration of this see, Dawes, 'Let us Bless the Lord'.

2 Biblical statistics are as suspect as any other, but an incontrovertible point is that there are not many instances of the use of 'Bless-,' 'Praise-' and 'Thank the LORD' in synonymous parallel in the Old Testament. The total occurrences of 'Bless the LORD' are about 60, those of 'Praise the LORD' about 80 and 'Thank the LORD' about 50: but the total of parallels is only 6 and of other collocations only another handful, about a dozen out of around 180 occurrences. At the very least this enables us to say that the verbs *bārak*, *hālal* and *hôdāh* plus the divine name are hardly full synonyms or freely interchangeable, for if that were the case one would expect many more parallels and collocations. The three phrases belong to the same semantic field, that of the worship

or praise of God: but they do not have the same meaning. They are related: but they are not identical.

3 Note the images in verses 11–15: metaphors of height and distance for the towering greatness of YHWH's *ḥesed* and the extent of his forgiveness, the metaphor of a father's care, and the metaphors of dust (as in Isa. 40.1–17) and grass (as in Isa. 40.6–7) from nature for human frailty and the transience of human life. In Christianity dust is much more likely, however, to suggest human 'dirtiness' than its 'almost-nothingness', and in England's 'green and pleasant land' there is nothing more permanent than grass. Hence the need for translators to translate images rather than simply repeat them.

4 Explicit references to the Exodus feature in only 12 psalms (66, 68, 77, 78, 81, 95, 99, 103, 105, 106, 114, 136) and only in three of them is the story retold in any detail (78, 105, 106). It is impossible to say whether references to God's law, the covenant and commandments, pursuing enemies who get their comeuppance, quaking mountains crowned with smoke and God feeding his people are allusions to the Exodus or simply more general motifs. Interestingly, references to Zion feature in considerably more psalms.

5 James Barr made important criticisms of the foibles (such as the excessive use of 'etymology' and the practice of talking about the 'root' meaning of Hebrew words) of the early volumes of 'Kittel'/*TDNT* (*Theological Dictionary of the New Testament*) which appeared in English from 1964 on, since which scholars have been nervous about attributing too much to words standing alone (Barr, *Comparative Philology and the Text of the Old Testament*). Snaith, *Distinctive Ideas of the Old Testament*, reprinted by a number of publishers including Paternoster in their Biblical and Theological Classics series (1997), among other themes, discusses the holiness of God, the righteousness of God, the salvation of God (including here a study of *Tsedeq/ tsedaqah* in Second Isaiah) and the covenant love of God (including here a look at *chesed*).

6 The same issue is found in the Ten Commandments at Ex. 20.6 and Deut. 5.10. Deut. 7.9–11 is usually cited to justify the inclusion of 'generation', the result of which is to make a specific contrast with its usage in the second half of the saying. The first half stresses YHWH's 'love', using a variety of ordinary-language words plus the technical theological term *ḥesed* twice. Including 'generation' in the first half, it is suggested, puts God's 'anger' in the second into perspective. His punishment might last for three or four generations, but his 'blessing' lasts for a thousand generations! The same point is made in a slightly different way in Ps. 30.5: 'For his anger is but for a moment: his favour is for a lifetime. Weeping may linger for the night, but joy comes with the morning.'

7 I say 'possibly misleadingly' because in biblical studies generally the term 'eschatology' is reserved for ideas about the 'end' rather than about the present realities of the rule of God.

8 A search through other Old Testament 'theologies' reveals little as they are not organized by biblical books.

9 Jeremiah, taking the official 'Deuteronomist' party line, insists that the disaster is entirely the result of the people of Jerusalem and Judah failing to honour YHWH in their worship and their living. They have failed to follow his commandments and walk in his ways, polluted his worship, lived by alien values and lifestyles and adopted a culture and world-view inimical to YHWH. It's all the people's fault! The women of Jerusalem disagree. They say that the disaster is entirely the result of King Josiah failing to honour the Queen of Heaven in the worship of the Temple. He, encouraged by the Deuteronomists and aided by prophets like Jeremiah, failed to honour her and walk in her ways, ended her worship, imposed new values and lifestyles and adopted a revisionist culture and world-view inimical to the true old gods and the true old religion. It's all the fault of Josiah and his cronies! The editor of Jeremiah 44 has given us a window here into a quite different religious world from the one we are accustomed to see.

9 New studies in Psalms

1 Wilson, 'The Use of Royal Psalms at the "Seams" of the Hebrew Psalter', in *JSOT* 35, pp. 85–94.

2 Wilson, 'Shaping the Psalter' in McCann (ed.), *The Shape and Shaping of the Psalter*.

3 Mitchell, 'Lord, Remember David', pp. 526–48. The quote is from p. 526.

4 In Chapter 6 I mentioned N. T. Wright's words of caution as a New Testament scholar about exaggerating the 'messianic expectations' of post-exilic Judaism. That warning needs to be remembered in this debate too.

5 Perhaps the tension between the 'eschatologico-messianic' and the 'historico-didactic' modes (to use Mitchell's jargon) is endemic in Christianity and Judaism (if not in all religions in one form or another). Once it became clear that the return of Jesus to bring about the End ('eschaton') was not going to happen, early Christianity settled into the latter mode, but the other has bubbled up repeatedly in the history of the Church. Mainstream churches regularly repeat the bit in the Creed about Jesus 'coming again' and make annual gestures towards 'The End' at Advent, but for them the 'historico-didactic' is the default position. At the same time strange eschatological movements keep on coming (and then going).

6 First published in *JSOT* 50 (1991), pp. 63–92; reprinted in *The Psalms and the Life of Faith*, pp. 180–213. Page references are given from this version. DeClaissé-Walford explores the same theme.

7 In Johnston and Firth (eds), *Interpreting the Psalms*, p. 242. In the same book Swanson paints a much more complex and less clear picture of the contents of this manuscript (pp. 250–1).

8 Rowland Prothero (1851–1937) was a lawyer, historian and sometime Fellow of All Souls. He played cricket for Hampshire. For 20 years he was Agent for the Duke of Bedford. For a short time he was MP for the University of Oxford and President of the Board of Agriculture for the second half of the 1914–18 war. He was a writer and among his books are histories of English agriculture and lives of Arthur Stanley and Lord Byron. He ended his life as First Baron Ernle of Chelsea, a title that reflected his aristocratic roots.

9 For an introduction to liberation theology and its ways of reading and using the Bible, see Segovia, 'Reading the Bible Ideologically: Socioeconomic Criticism', in McKenzie and Haynes, *To Each its Own Meaning*, pp. 283–306, and Coggins, *Introducing the Old Testament*, pp. 94–100 and the reading suggested there.

10 For an introduction to feminist readings of the Bible, see Fewell, 'Reading the Bible Ideologically: Feminist Criticism', in McKenzie and Haynes, *To Each its Own Meaning*, pp. 268–82; Loades, 'Feminist Interpretation', in Barton (ed.), *The Cambridge Companion to Biblical Interpretation*, pp. 81–94 and the reading suggested there; plus Tamez, 'Women's Rereading of the Bible', in Sugirtharajah, *Voices from the Margin*, pp. 48–57.

Glossary

Acrostic   Poem in which the first verse begins with the first letter of the alphabet, the second with the second, and so on; for example, Psalm 34.

Alliteration   Repetition of the sound of consonants.

Apocrypha   Term for the books found in the Greek and Latin Bibles, which were removed from the Old Testament at the Reformation because they were not in the Hebrew Bible and which are printed as a supplement in some 'Protestant' Bibles.

Assonance   Repetition of vowel sounds.

Atonement   Theories about and liturgies for restoring the right relationship between God and humanity.

Canon/canonical   Official list of authorized and approved books, or to do with such a list.

Cult   Term used in older studies for liturgy.

Deuteronomic History   The single narrative made up of the books of Joshua, Judges, Samuel and Kings.

Deuteronomic orthodoxy   The dominant theology in the Old Testament. Another term for Yahwism/Yahwistic orthodoxy. See the box in Chapter 5.

Doxology   From the Greek words *doxa* (glory) and *logos* (word), an affirmation in which God is praised.

Ellipsis   Or 'gapping'. A common feature of Hebrew poetry in which a verb is omitted from the second line of a pair of lines.

Exegesis   Explanation of a biblical passage. See the box in Chapter 2.

Genre   Technical term for types or categories of literature.

Haggadah   The 'inspirational' material in the Torah. See the explanatory box in Chapter 7.

Halakah   The 'rules' or 'commands' in the Torah. See the explanatory box in Chapter 7.

Hebrew Bible   The official 'Holy Scripture' of Judaism, consisting of three sections: Torah (The Law), with its five books of Genesis to Deuteronomy; Nevi'im (The Prophets), with its four books of the 'Former Prophets' (Joshua, Judges, Samuel and Kings) and four of the 'Latter Prophets' (Isaiah, Jeremiah, Ezekiel, the Twelve); and Kethuvim (The Writings) with the rest of the books familiar to readers of the Protestant Old Testament.

Hermeneutics   How we understand, interpret and find meaning in what we hear or read.

Hermeneutic of suspicion   'Suspicious interpretation.' Why is this text telling me this? What is it trying to do to me? Whose interest is being served here?

Hermeneutic of trust   'Trustful interpretation.' I know what this text is trying to sell me, I know the product, and the salesperson; and I intend to buy into it.

Historical-critical method   The standard way in academic circles, between the 1850s and the 1980s, of studying the Bible. Its aim was to understand these ancient texts in their original meanings.

Ideology   Position or point of view that a text is seeking to promote or that underlies it.

Inclusio   Technical term in poetry for a word, phrase or sentence that both introduces and concludes a passage.

Intertextuality   How all texts depend on other texts for their meaning. See the box in Chapter 8.

Irony   Figure of speech (trope), which states something in order to suggest something quite different. As such 'irony' is the basic tone of the lament whose constant references to God's powerful presence serve to point up his absence.

Lament   Type of psalm. Not to be confused with mourning songs (especially the sort played on bagpipes). See the box in Chapter 4.

Messiah   'Anointed', a term for the kings of David's line, and their hoped-for successor. See the box in Chapter 6.

Metaphor   Trope (figure of speech) which likens something to something else without using the word 'like' (phrases that use 'like' or 'as' are similes): e.g. 'God is my rock.' See Chapter 2.

Metonymy   Figure of speech (trope) which uses a word instead of something else: for example, psalmists often use 'my soul' when they mean themselves, or refer to the 'sea' when they mean 'the forces of chaos, evil and death'.

Old Testament (or First Testament) The first part of the Christian Bible, containing different books in different Christian traditions.

Onomatopoeia Use of words that sound like what they describe.

Parallelism Usual term for the common binary technique used in Hebrew poetry. See Chapter 2.

Paranomasia Technical term for a 'play on words'.

Parataxis Feature in Hebrew poetry where lines are butted together without conjunctions.

Peshitta Syriac translation probably produced in the third century AD. See the box in Chapter 1.

Pseudepigrapha Generic name for an indeterminate number of ancient Jewish religious books occupying the next circle out, as it were, from the Apocrypha. See the box in Chapter 6.

Rhetoric How an argument works; how a speech or text performs its task.

Septuagint The Greek Bible, which was produced in several versions from the third century BC onwards. See the box in Chapter 1.

Shema Name for Deuteronomy 6.4, a key liturgical affirmation used in Judaism. See the box in Chapter 8.

Sheol The place of the dead.

Sitz-im-Leben 'Situation in life' – technical term for the settings in life in which particular types of biblical material first took shape.

Synecdoche Trope (figure of speech) which uses a part of something to refer to the whole of it: for example, the many references in Psalms to 'the hand of God' doing this or that, where plainer language might just say 'God'.

Targum(s) The usually rather free translations of the Hebrew Bible into Aramaic produced from the second century BC onwards, and eventually written down in two versions (the Babylonian and the Jerusalem). See the box in Chapter 1.

Theodicy From the Greek words *theos* (God) and *dikē* (justice/rightness), the shorthand term for the discussion of 'the problem of evil'. See the box in Chapter 4.

Torah An important word of several meanings, including 'teaching', 'instruction' and 'law'. See the extended comment in Chapter 7.

Trope Technical term for a 'figure of speech'. It is often said that there are four major tropes: metaphor, metonymy, synecdoche and irony.

Vulgate Jerome's Latin Bible. See the box in Chapter 1.

Wisdom   An alternative and distinctive theological approach identifiable in the Old Testament. See Chapter 7.

Yahwism/Yahwistic orthodoxy   Another term for Deuteronomic orthodoxy.

Zion   An alternative and symbolic name for Jerusalem.

A Guide to Commentaries on Psalms

There is no end to the writing of commentaries, even though publishers appear and disappear regularly. Tremper Longman III (2003), *Old Testament Commentary Survey*, Leicester: InterVarsity Press, is worth consulting. Do not forget that commentaries are not 'value-neutral'. Every commentary, whether academic or ecclesial, is written from a particular point of view to promote a position and to sell an academic or devotional product.

Many commentaries are produced by religious publishers for 'devotional' use and reading. Some of these are 'uncritical' and of little use for study purposes. Some, however, are written by biblical scholars who attempt to utilize the insights of their biblical scholarship in their commentaries 'for general use' and these commentaries can make good 'entry' material into the world of Psalms.

Coggan, D. (1995), *Psalms*, 2 vols, Oxford: Bible Reading Fellowship, is part of The People's Bible Commentary series which aims to nurture mind and heart. It is a commentary that treats the psalms traditionally and explores their meanings for today.

Knight, G. A. F. (1983), *Psalms*, 2 vols, Edinburgh: St Andrew Press, is part of the Daily Study Bible series, which aims to do the kind of introductory and popular work for the Old Testament that William Barclay had done so splendidly for the New in the 1950s. It is a solidly competent paragraph-by-paragraph and psalm-by-psalm exposition.

Limburg, J. (2000), *Psalms*, Louisville KY: Westminster John Knox Press, is part of the Westminster Bible Companion series, which tries to be relevant and accessible with a message for Christians today. It is alert to contemporary issues in Psalms study but treats them and all critical questions lightly.

Commentaries produced primarily to help students read Psalms can be graded according to university module 'levels' (although in reality these levels vary between institutions).

Level 1 commentaries describe and explain the principal critical issues.

Alter, Robert (2007), *The Book of Psalms: A Translation with Commentary*, New York and London: W. W. Norton and Co. is a fresh translation by a major literary critic with a helpful short introduction and footnotes on issues raised in particular verses.

Broyles, C. C. (1999), *Psalms*, Peabody MA: Hendrickson, in the New International Biblical Commentary series, based on the NIV, is conservative but lively and is a good candidate for the most generally workmanlike and useful commentary at this level.

Clifford, R. J. (2002/03), *Psalms*, 2 vols, Nashville TN: Abingdon Press, in the Abingdon Old Testament Commentary series, is a competent traditional-style commentary which barely mentions the issues discussed in Chapter 9.

Curtis, A. (2004), *Psalms*, Peterborough: Epworth, in the Epworth Commentary series, is aimed primarily at preachers, but is a short, snappy and thoroughly up-to-date entrance-level commentary strongly commended for student use at level 1.

Davidson, R. (1998), *The Vitality of Worship*, Edinburgh: Handsel, is not strictly speaking a commentary at all, but is offered by the publishers as the Psalms volume in their International Theological Commentary series, which aims to 'transcend the parochialism of Western civilisation'. Anything by Davidson is good and this is no exception, but it is not a commentary.

Eaton, J. H. (2003), *The Psalms: A Historical and Spiritual Commentary with an Introduction and New Translation*, London: T&T Clark International, reflects Eaton's lifetime engagement with Psalms and his indebtedness to Mowinckel.

Kidner, D. (1973/75), *Psalms*, 2 vols, Leicester: InterVarsity Press, in the Tyndale Old Testament Commentary series, comes from a conservative base and provides a 'sound and solid' commentary on the text of the psalms in the light of the scholarship of its day.

Mays, J. L. (1994b), *Psalms*, Louisville KY: Westminster John Knox Press, is 'A Bible Commentary for Teaching and Preaching' in the Interpretation Commentary series, which aims to bridge the gap between academic and less critical approaches. Do not confuse this series with the very devotional Interpretation Bible Studies series from the same publishers.

Rogerson, J. W. and McKay, J. W. (1977), *Psalms*, 3 vols, Cambridge: Cambridge University Press, in the Cambridge Bible Commentary series, which was published to accompany the publication of the NEB in the 1960s and 1970s, is a good example of the moderate scholarship of its day made accessible in a clear and straightforward way.

To these can be added the lengthy sections on Psalms in the *New Interpreter's Bible* and the *Oxford Bible Commentary*:

McCann, J. C. (1966) 'The Book of Psalms', in *The New Interpreter's Bible: A Commentary in Twelve Volumes*, Nashville TN: Abingdon Press, vol. 4, pp. 641–1280.

Rodd, C. S. (2001) 'Psalms' in Barton, J. and Muddimann, J. (eds), *The Oxford Bible Commentary*, Oxford: Oxford University Press, pp. 355–405.

Level 2 commentaries offer more depth and fuller discussion of critical issues.

- The *Anchor Bible* series, published by Doubleday and begun in the 1950s, is still coming out. The three volumes on Psalms by Michel Dahood in this solidly academic and meaty series from the USA were published in 1966, 1968 and 1970 and are notorious for seeing Ugarit and Ugaritic as the solution to every question. They also predate our Chapter 9 issues.
- *Berit Olam* is a new series published by Michael Glazier/The Liturgical Press (its parallel New Testament series is called *Sacra Pagina*). It offers a variety of 'literary readings' and is especially strong on a close reading of the poetry of the psalms as the subtitle of the series 'Studies in Hebrew Narrative and Poetry' suggests. The volume on Psalms is by Konrad Schaefer and was published in 2001.
- The *New Cambridge Bible Commentary* is a new series from Cambridge University Press, gradually emerging since 2004 to replace the old *Cambridge Bible Commentary* series and move to this higher level. There is no volume on Psalms available yet, but it will be worth looking out for.

- The *New Century Bible Commentary* went through a number of publishers after it was first produced in the 1960s and recently disappeared altogether, which is sad because it was a thoroughly useful series. The two volumes on Psalms by A. A. Anderson, which appeared in 1972, are worth seeking out for their detailed treatment of each psalm, though this commentary is, of course, pre-Chapter 9.
- The *Old Testament Library* series was published by SCM Press in the 1960s as the British flagship of mainstream Old Testament studies aimed at ministers, teachers and the 'thinking layperson'. The series has been taken over by Westminster John Knox Press and some of the classics are available from them, though at a price, and they are adding new titles too. The commentary on Psalms by A. Weiser, published in 1962, was, however, not a classic.
- The *Shorter Commentary* series, now appearing, is a shorter version of the updated *ICC Commentaries* (see below) minus the highly technical stuff. There is no volume on Psalms as yet.
- The *Smith and Helwys Bible Commentary* series is another new series making its appearance, though its volume on Psalms has not yet appeared.

Level 3 commentaries use Hebrew and that does deter some students, but much can be gained from these commentaries with perseverance by students without any knowledge of that language.

- Blackwell Bible Commentaries are not commentaries in the traditional sense. They aim to trace the 'reception-history' of the books in question, as we saw in Chapter 9. The two volumes on Psalms are by Susan Gillingham. Volume 1 (2008) is a detailed historical survey of the use of Psalms, and volume 2 (yet to appear) will trace the use of each psalm down the centuries.
- Goldingay, J. (2006), *Psalms*, Grand Rapids MI: Baker Academic, Baker Commentary on the Old Testament Wisdom and Psalms, is a refreshing three volumes that is thoroughly up to date, academically rigorous, and yet unafraid to conclude its discussion of each psalm with a 'Theological Implications' section which can get quite preachy in the best sense of that word. Highly recommended.
- The *Hermeneia* series (subtitled 'A Critical and Historical Commentary on the Bible') is published by Fortress Press and based on a German model. It is very thorough in a historical-critical mode. There will be three volumes on

Psalms, of which volume 2, covering Psalms 51—100, by F.-L. Hossfeld and E. Zenger, appeared in 2005.

- The *International Critical Commentary* series first appeared at the beginning of the twentieth century and older volumes are being replaced in an ongoing programme. There is no replacement for the 1907 volume on Psalms yet.
- H.-J. Kraus, *Psalms 1—59* (1988) and *Psalms 60—150* (1989), together with the companion volume, *Theology of Psalms* (1996 [1992]), Minneapolis MN: Fortress Press, form a rigorous trio.
- The *Word Biblical Commentary* series, published by Word Publishing (Waco), usually (but not always) represents a conservative perspective on the historical-critical model. There are three volumes on Psalms (P. C. Craigie (1986), *Psalms 1—50*; M. E. Tate (1990), *Psalms 51—100*; and L. C. Allen (1987), *Psalms 101—150*) and these are a must for any serious engagement with Psalms.

Other commentaries referred to in this *Studyguide* are:

Addis, W. E. (1919), 'The Psalms', in Peake, A. S. (ed.), *Peake's Commentary on the Bible*, London: Thomas Nelson, pp. 366–96.

Anderson, G. W. (1962), 'The Psalms', in Black, M. and Rowley, H. H. (eds), *Peake's Commentary on the Bible: Completely Revised and Reset*, London: Thomas Nelson, pp. 409–43.

Eaton, J. H. (1967), *Psalms*, Torch Bible Paperbacks, London: SCM Press.

Kirkpatrick, A. F. (1906), *The Book of Psalms*, Cambridge: Cambridge University Press.

Terrien, S. L. (2003), *The Psalms: Strophic Structure and Theological Commentary*, Grand Rapids MI: Eerdmans.

General Bibliography

Abegg, M., Flint, P. and Ulrich, E. (1999), *The Dead Sea Scrolls Bible*, New York: HarperSanFrancisco.

Achtemeier, E. R. (1962), 'Righteousness in the OT', in Buttrick, G. A. (ed.), *The Interpreter's Dictionary of the Bible*, Nashville TN: Abingdon Press, vol. 4, pp. 80–5.

Achtemeier, P. (ed.) (1997), *HarperCollins Bible Dictionary*, San Francisco CA: HarperCollins.

Addis, W. E. (1919), 'The Psalms', in Peake, A. S. (ed.), *A Commentary on the Bible*, London: Thomas Nelson, pp. 366–96.

Albertz, R. (1994), *A History of Israelite Religion in the Old Testament Period*, 2 vols, London: SCM Press.

Alexander, P. (1992), 'Targum, Targumim', in Freedman, D. N. (ed.), *The Anchor Bible Dictionary*, New York: Doubleday, vol. 6, pp. 320–31.

Allen, L. C. (1987), *Psalms 101—150*, Word Biblical Commentary, Waco TX: Word.

Alter, R. (1985), *The Art of Biblical Poetry*, New York: Basic Books.

Alter, R. (2007), *The Book of Psalms: A Translation with Commentary*, New York and London: W. W. Norton and Co.

Alternative Service Book 1980, The (1980), London: Hodder and Stoughton.

Anderson, A. A. (1972) *Psalms*, 2 vols, New Century Bible, London: Oliphants.

Anderson, B. W. (1962), 'God, names of', in Buttrick, G. A. (ed.), *The Interpreter's Dictionary of the Bible*, Nashville TN: Abingdon Press, vol. 2, pp. 407–17.

Anderson, B. W. (1999), *Contours of Old Testament Theology*, Minneapolis MN: Fortress Press.

Anderson, B. W. (2000), *Out of the Depths*, Louisville KY: Westminster John Knox Press.

Anderson, G. A. (1992), 'Sacrifice: Old Testament', in Freedman, D. N. (ed.), *The Anchor Bible Dictionary*, New York: Doubleday, vol. 5, pp. 870–86.

Anderson, G. W. (1962), 'The Psalms', in Black, M. and Rowley, H. H. (eds), *Peake's*

Commentary on the Bible: Completely Revised and Reset, London: Thomas Nelson, pp. 409–43.

Anderson, G. W. (ed.) (1979), *Tradition and Interpretation*, Oxford: Oxford University Press.

Ashby, G. (1988), *Sacrifice*, London: SCM Press.

Attridge, H. W. and Fassler, M. E. (eds) (2003), *Psalms in Community: Jewish and Christian Textual, Liturgical and Artistic Traditions*, Leiden: Brill.

Atwell, E. A. (2004), *The Sources of the Old Testament*, London: T&T Clark.

Baer, D. A. and Gordon, R. P. (1996), '2874 הדר', in VanGemeren, W. A. (ed.), *The New International Dictionary of Old Testament Theology and Exegesis*, Grand Rapids MI: Eerdmans, vol. 2, pp. 211–18.

Baker, D. W. and Arnold, B. T. (eds) (1999), *The Face of Old Testament Studies: A Survey of Contemporary Approaches*, Grand Rapids MI: Baker.

Barr, J. (1968), *Comparative Philology and the Text of the Old Testament*, Oxford: Oxford University Press.

Barr, J. (1999), *The Concept of Biblical Theology*, London: SCM Press.

Bartholomew, C. and West, A. (eds) (2001), *Praying by the Book*, Carlisle: Paternoster Press.

Barton, J. (1996), *Reading the Old Testament*, 2nd edn, London: Darton, Longman and Todd.

Barton J. (ed.) (1998), *The Cambridge Companion to Biblical Interpretation*, Cambridge: Cambridge University Press.

Barton, J. (2002), 'Old Testament Theology', in Rogerson, J. W. (ed.), Beginning Old Testament Study, London: SPCK, pp. 94–113.

Barton, J. (2007), *The Nature of Biblical Criticism*, Louisville KY: Westminster John Knox Press.

Barton, J. and Bowden, J. (2004), *The Original Story: God, Israel and the World*, London: Darton, Longman and Todd

Barton, J. and Muddimann, J. (eds) (2001), *Oxford Bible Commentary*, Oxford: Oxford University Press.

Beal, L. W. (2008), '5. Psalms in the Modern Period', in Longman, T. and Enns, P. (eds), *Dictionary of the Old Testament: Wisdom, Poetry and Writings*, Downers Grove IL: InterVarsity Press Academic, pp. 608–13.

Bellinger, W. H. (1990), *Psalms: Reading and Studying the Book of Praises*, Peabody MA: Hendrickson.

Bennett, A. and Royle, N. (1999), *Introduction to Literature, Criticism and Theory*, 2nd edn, Harlow: Prentice Hall.

Berlin, A. (1985), *The Dynamics of Biblical Parallelism*, Bloomington IN: Indiana University Press.

Berlin, A. (1993–2002), 'Introduction to Hebrew Poetry', in *The New Interpreter's Bible*, various editors, Nashville TN: Abingdon Press, vol. 4, pp. 301–15.

Berlin, A. (1993), 'Poetry', in Metzger, B. M. and Coogan, M. D. (eds), *The Oxford Companion to the Bible*, Oxford: Oxford University Press, pp. 597–9.

Berlin, A. (2004), 'Reading Biblical Poetry', in Berlin, A. and Brettler, M. Z. (eds), *The Jewish Study Bible*, Oxford: Oxford University Press, pp. 2097–104.

Berlin, A. and Brettler, M. Z. (2004) (adapted), 'The Modern Study of the Bible', in Berlin, A. and Brettler, M. Z. (eds), *The Jewish Study Bible*, Oxford: Oxford University Press, pp. 2084–96.

Berlin, A. and Brettler, M. Z. (eds) (2004), *The Jewish Study Bible*, Oxford: Oxford University Press.

Beyerlin, W. (1978), *Near Eastern Religious Texts Relating to the Old Testament*, London: SCM Press.

Birch, B. C., Brueggemann W., Fretheim, T. E. and Petersen D. L. (1999), *A Theological Introduction to the Old Testament*, Nashville TN: Abingdon Press.

Black, M. and Rowley, H.H. (eds) (1962), *Peake's Commentary on the Bible: Completely Revised and Reset*, London: Thomas Nelson.

Botterweck, G. J. et al. (eds) (1974–2006), *Theological Dictionary of the Old Testament*, 16 vols, Grand Rapids MI: Eerdmans.

Bradley, I. (1995), *The Power of Sacrifice*, London: Darton, Longman and Todd.

Bratcher, R. G. (1993) '(Translations) English Language Versions', in Metzger, B. M. and Coogan, M. D. (eds), *The Oxford Companion to the Bible*, Oxford: Oxford University Press, pp. 758–63.

Braude, W. G. (1959), *The Midrash on Psalms*, 2 vols, New Haven CT: Yale University Press.

Brenton, L. (1844), *The Septuagint Version: Greek and English*, London: Samuel Bagster and Sons; various editions since.

Brettler, M. Z. (1989), *God is King: Understanding an Israelite Metaphor*, Sheffield: Sheffield Academic Press.

Brock, S. P. (1992), 'Peshitta', in 'Versions, Ancient (Syriac)', in Freedman, D. N. (ed.), *The Anchor Bible Dictionary*, New York: Doubleday, vol. 6, pp. 794–5.

Brock, S. P. (1993), '(Translations) Ancient Languages', in Metzger, B. M. and Coogan, M. D. (eds), *The Oxford Companion to the Bible*, Oxford: Oxford University Press, pp. 752–4.

Brooke, G. J. (2004), 'The Psalms in Early Jewish Literature in the Light of the Dead Sea Scrolls', in Moyise, S. and Menken, M. J. J. (eds), *The Psalms in the New Testament*, London: Continuum, ch. 1.

Brown, C. (ed.) (1975), *The New International Dictionary of New Testament Theology*, 3 vols, Exeter: Paternoster Press.

Brown, M. J. (2000), *What They Don't Tell You: A Survivor's Guide to Biblical Studies*, Louisville KY: Westminster John Knox Press.

Brown, R. E., Fitzmyer J. A. and Murphy R. E. (eds) (2000), *New Jerome Biblical Commentary*, New Jersey: Prentice Hall.

Brown, W. P. (2002), *Seeing the Psalms: A Theology of Metaphor*, Louisville KY: Westminster John Knox Press.

Broyles, C. C. (1988), *The Conflict of Faith and Experience in the Psalms*, Sheffield: Journal for the Study of the Old Testament Press.

Broyles, C. C. (1999), *Psalms*, New International Biblical Commentary, Peabody MA: Hendrickson.

Broyles, C. C. (2008), 'Lament: Psalms of', in Longman, T. and Enns, P. (eds), *Dictionary of the Old Testament Wisdom*, *Poetry and Writings*, Downers Grove IL: InterVarsity Press Academic, pp. 384–99.

Brueggemann, D. A. (2005), 'The Evangelists and the Psalms', in Johnston, P. S. and Firth, D. G. (eds) (2005), *Interpreting the Psalms: Issues and Approaches*, Leicester: Apollos, pp. 263–78.

Brueggemann, D. A. (2008), 'Psalms 4: Titles', in Longman, T. and Enns, P. (eds), *Dictionary of the Old Testament Wisdom*, *Poetry and Writings*, Downers Grove IL: InterVarsity Press Academic, pp. 613–21.

Brueggemann, W. (1980), 'Psalms and the Life of Faith: A Suggested Typology of Function', Journal for the Study of the Old Testament 17, pp. 3–32; reproduced in Clines, D. J. A. (ed.) (1997), *The Poetical Books: a Sheffield Reader*, Sheffield: Sheffield Academic Press, pp. 35–66.

Brueggemann, W. (1984), *The Message of the Psalms*, Minneapolis MN: Augsburg.

Brueggemann, W. (1986), 'The Costly Loss of Lament', Journal for the Study of the Old Testament 36, pp. 57–71; reprinted in Brueggemann, W., *The Psalms and the Life of Faith*, ed. Miller, P. D., Minneapolis MN: Fortress Press, pp. 98–111.

Brueggemann, W. (1988), *Israel's Praise: Doxology against Idolatry and Ideology*, Philadelphia: Fortress Press.

Brueggemann, W. (1991), 'Bounded by Obedience and Praise: The Psalms as Canon', Journal for the Study of the Old Testament 50, pp. 63–92; reproduced in Brueggemann, W., *The Psalms and the Life of Faith*, ed. Miller, P. D., Minneapolis MN: Fortress Press, pp. 189–213.

Brueggemann, W. (1995), *The Psalms and the Life of Faith*, ed. Miller, P. D., Minneapolis MN: Fortress Press.

Brueggemann, W. (1997), *Theology of the Old Testament*, Minneapolis MN: Fortress Press.

Brueggemann, W. (2002), *Spirituality of the Psalms*, Minneapolis MN: Fortress Press (an abridged version of *The Message of the Psalms*).

Brueggemann, W. (2003), *An Introduction to the Old Testament: The Canon and Christian Imagination*, Louisville KY: Westminster John Knox Press.

Brueggemann, W. (2008), *Old Testament Theology*, Nashville TN: Abingdon Press.

Bullock, C. H. (2001), *Encountering the Book of Psalms*, Grand Rapids MI: Baker Academic.

Buss, M. J. (2007), 'Gunkel', in McKim, D. K. (ed.), *Dictionary of Major Biblical Interpreters*, Downers Grove IL: InterVarsity Press USA, pp. 499–503.

Buttrick, G. A. (ed.) (1962), *The Interpreter's Dictionary of the Bible*, 4 vols, Nashville TN: Abingdon Press.

Carson, D. A., France, R. T., Motyer, A. and Wenham, G. J. (eds) (1994) *New Bible Commentary: 21st-Century Edition*, Nottingham: InterVarsity Press.

'Characteristics of Hebrew Poetry' (1991) (unattributed), in Metzger, B. M. and Murphy, R. E. (eds), *The New Oxford Annotated Bible*, Oxford: Oxford University Press, pp. 392–7.

Charles, R. H. (ed.) (1911), *The Apocrypha and Pseudepigrapha of the Old Testament*, Oxford: Clarendon Press.

Charlesworth, J. H. (1983, 1985), *The Old Testament Pseudepigrapha*, 2 vols, New York: Doubleday.

Childs, B. S. (1979), *Introduction to the Old Testament as Scripture*, London: SCM Press.

Chilton B. et al. (eds) (2008), *Cambridge Companion to the Bible*, Cambridge: Cambridge University Press.

Clements R. E. (2007), 'Mowinckel', in McKim, D. K. (ed.), *Dictionary of Major Biblical Interpreters*, Downers Grove IL: InterVarsity Press USA, pp. 757–62.

Clifford, R. J. (2002/03), *Psalms*, 2 vols, Abingdon Press Old Testament Commentary, Nashville TN: Abingdon Press.

Coggan, D. (1995), *Psalms*, 2 vols, The People's Bible Commentary, Oxford: Bible Reading Fellowship.

Coggins, R. (2001), *Introducing the Old Testament*, rev. edn, Oxford: Oxford University Press.

Coggins, R. J. and Houlden, J. L. (eds) (1990), *Dictionary of Biblical Interpretation*, London: SCM Press.

Cohen, A. (1945), *The Psalms*, Hindhead: Soncino Press.

Collins, J. J. (2005), *The Bible after Babel: Historical Criticism in a Postmodern Age*, Grand Rapids MI: Eerdmans.

Collins, J. J. (2007), *A Short Introduction to the Hebrew Bible*, Minneapolis MN: Fortress Press.

Common Worship: Services and Prayers for the Church of England (2000), London: Church House Publishing.

Coogan, M. (2008), *The Old Testament: A Very Short Introduction*, Oxford: Oxford University Press.

Cotter, J. (1989), *Through Desert Places: A Version of Psalms 1—50*, Sheffield: Cairns Publications.

Cotter, J. (1991), *By Stony Paths: A Version of Psalms 51—100*, Sheffield: Cairns Publications.

Cotter, J. (1993), *Towards the City: A Version of Psalms 101—150*, Sheffield: Cairns Publications.

Cover, R. C. (1992), 'Sin: Old Testament', in Freedman, D. N. (ed.), *The Anchor Bible Dictionary*, New York: Doubleday, vol. 6, pp. 31–40.

Craigie, P. C. (1986), *Psalms 1–50*, Word Biblical Commentary, Waco: Word.

Craven, T. (1992), *The Book of Psalms: Message of Biblical Spirituality 6*, Collegeville MN: The Liturgical Press.

Crenshaw, J. L. (1993), 'Wisdom Literature', in Metzger, B. M. and Coogan, M. D. (eds), *The Oxford Companion to the Bible*, Oxford: Oxford University Press, pp.801–3.

Crenshaw, J. L. (2001), *The Psalms: An Introduction*, Grand Rapids MI: Eerdmans.

Crenshaw, J. L. (2005), *Defending God: Biblical Responses to the Problem of Evil*, Oxford: Oxford University Press.

Crim, K. (ed.) (1976), *The Interpreter's Dictionary of the Bible Supplementary Volume*, Nashville TN: Abingdon Press.

Culler, J. (1997), *Literary Theory: A Very Short Introduction*, Oxford: Oxford University Press.

Curtis, A. (2004), *Psalms*, Epworth Commentary, Peterborough: Epworth Press.

Dahood, M. (1966, 1968, 1970), *Psalms*, 3 vols, The Anchor Bible, New York: Doubleday.

Davidson, R. (1983), *The Courage to Doubt*, London: SCM Press.

Davidson, R. (1998), *The Vitality of Worship*, Edinburgh: Handsel.

Davies, J. (2008), 'Theodicy', in Longman, T. and Enns, P. (eds), *Dictionary of the Old Testament Wisdom, Poetry and Writings*, Downers Grove IL: InterVarsity Press Academic, pp. 808–17.

Davies, J. G. (ed.) (1986), *A New Dictionary of Liturgy and Worship*, London: SCM Press.

Dawes, S. B. (1995), 'Let Us Bless the Lord: An Invitation to Affirm the Living God', *The Expository Times*, July, vol. 106, no. 10, pp. 293–6.

Dawes, S. B. (2000), *Let Us Bless the Lord: A Study of Old Testament Theology in Psalm 103*, Truro: Southleigh; now available at www.stephendawes.com.

Dawes, S. B. (2006), *Let us Bless the Lord: Rediscovering the Old Testament through Psalm 103*, Peterborough: Inspire; now available at www.stephendawes.com.

Day, J. (1990), *Psalms: Old Testament Guides*, Sheffield: Sheffield Academic Press.

Day, J. (1992), 'Asherah', in Freedman, D. N. (ed.), *The Anchor Bible Dictionary*, New York: Doubleday, vol. 1, pp. 483–7.

Day, J. (1992), 'Ashtoreth', in Freedman, D. N. (ed.), *The Anchor Bible Dictionary*, New York: Doubleday, vol. 1, pp. 491–4.

deClaissé-Walford, N. (1997), *Reading from the Beginning: The Shaping of the Hebrew Psalter*, Macon: Mercer University Press.

de Jonge, M. (1992), 'Messiah', in Freedman, D. N. (ed.), *The Anchor Bible Dictionary*, New York: Doubleday, vol. 4, pp. 777–87.

de Lange, N. (1986), *Judaism*, Oxford: Oxford University Press.

Dell, K. (2000), *Get Wisdom, Get Insight*, London: Darton, Longman and Todd.

Dever, W. (2004), 'Histories and Non-histories of Ancient Israel: The Question of the United Monarchy', in Day, J. (ed.), *In Search of Ancient Israel*, London: T&T Clark, pp. 65–94.

de Vaux, R. (1961), *Ancient Israel: Its Life and Institutions*, London: Darton, Longman and Todd.

de Vries, S. (1962), 'Sin, Sinners', in Buttrick, G. A. (ed.), *The Interpreter's Dictionary of the Bible*, Nashville TN: Abingdon Press, vol. 4, pp. 361–7.

Dillard, R. B. and Longman, T. (1995), *An Introduction to the Old Testament*, Leicester: Apollos.

Drane, J. (2000), *Introducing the Old Testament*, Oxford: Lion.

Dunn, J. D. G. and Rogerson, J. (eds) (2004), *Eerdman's Commentary on the Bible*, Grand Rapids MI: Eerdmans.

Eaton, J. H. (1967), *Psalms*, Torch Bible Paperbacks, London: SCM Press.

Eaton, J. H. (1976), *Kingship and the Psalms*, London: SCM Press.

Eaton, J. H. (1990), 'Kingship' in Coggins, R. J. and Houlden, J. L., (eds), *Dictionary of Biblical Interpretation*, London: SCM Press, pp. 379–82.

Eaton, J. H. (2003), *The Psalms: A Historical and Spiritual Commentary with an Introduction and New Translation*, London: T&T Clark International.

Eaton, J. H. (2004), *Meditating on the Psalms*, London: Continuum.

Eaton, J. H. (2006), *Psalms for Life*, London: SPCK.

Edwards, T. M. (2005), 'The Targum of Psalms', in Johnston, P. S. and Firth, D. G.

(eds), *Interpreting the Psalms: Issues and Approaches*, Leicester: Apollos, pp. 279–94.

Ehrlich, C. S. (1993), 'Israelite Law', in Metzger, B. M. and Coogan, M. D. (eds), *The Oxford Companion to the Bible*, Oxford: Oxford University Press, pp. 421–3.

Eichrodt, W. (1961), *Theology of the Old Testament*, 2 vols, London: SCM Press.

Elliger, K. and Rudolph, W. (eds) (1967–77), *Biblia Hebraica Stuttgartensia*, Stuttgart: Deutsche Bibelgesellschaft.

Emerton, J. A. (1993), 'Names of God in the Hebrew Bible', in Metzger, B. M. and Coogan, M. D. (eds), *The Oxford Companion to the Bible*, Oxford: Oxford University Press, pp. 548–9.

'English Versions of the Bible' (1991) (unattributed), in Metzger, B. M. and Murphy, R. E. (eds), *The New Oxford Annotated Bible*, Oxford: Oxford University Press, pp. 400–6.

Enns, P. (1996), 'Law of God', in VanGemeren, W. A. (ed.), *The New International Dictionary of Old Testament Theology and Exegesis*, Grand Rapids MI: Zondervan, vol. 4, pp. 893–900.

Eshel, E. (2004), 'The Bible in the Dead Sea Scrolls', in Berlin, A and Brettler, M. Z. (eds), *The Jewish Study Bible*, Oxford: Oxford University Press, pp. 1920–8.

Evans, R. (1999), *Using the Bible*, London: Darton, Longman and Todd.

Fee, G. D. and Hubbard, R. L. (eds) (2010), *The Eerdmans Companion to the Bible*, Grand Rapids MI: Eerdmans.

Fee, G. D. and Stuart, D. (2003), *How to Read the Bible for All Its Worth*, new edn, Grand Rapids MI: Zondervan.

Fewell, D. (1999), 'Reading the Bible Ideologically: Feminist Criticism', in McKenzie, S. L. and Haynes, S. R., *To Each its Own Meaning*, Louisville KY: Westminster John Knox Press, pp. 268–82.

Finkelstein, I. and Silberman N. A. (2001), *The Bible Unearthed*, New York: Simon and Schuster.

Fiorenza, Elisabeth Schüssler (2009), *Democratizing Biblical Studies*, Louisville KY: Westminster John Knox Press.

Firth, D. G. (2005), *Surrendering Retribution in the Psalms*, Milton Keynes: Paternoster Press.

Flint, P. W. (2005), 'The Prophet David at Qumran', in Henze, M. (ed.), *Biblical Interpretation at Qumran*, Grand Rapids MI: Eerdmans, pp. 158–67.

Fokkelman, J. P. (2001), *Reading Biblical Poetry: An Introductory Guide*, Louisville KY: Westminster John Knox Press.

Freedman, D. N. (ed.) (1992), *The Anchor Bible Dictionary*, 6 vols, New York: Doubleday.

Freedman, D. N. (ed.) (2000), *Eerdman's Dictionary of the Bible*, Grand Rapids MI: Eerdmans.

Fretheim, T. E. (2005), *God and World in the Old Testament*, Nashville TN: Abingdon Press.

Futato, M. D. (2007), *Interpreting the Psalms: An Exegetical Handbook*, Grand Rapids MI: Kregel.

Futato, M. D. (2008), 'Hymns', in Longman, T. and Enns, P. (eds), *Dictionary of the Old Testament Wisdom, Poetry and Writings*, Downers Grove IL: InterVarsity Press Academic, pp. 300–5.

Gaster, T. H. (1962), 'Sacrifices and Offerings', in Buttrick, G. A. (ed.), *The Interpreter's Dictionary of the Bible*, Nashville TN: Abingdon Press, vol. 4, pp. 147–59.

Geoghegan J. and Homan M. (2002), *The Bible for Dummies*, New York: Wiley.

Gerstenberger, E. S. (1988), *Psalms: Part 1, with an Introduction to Cultic Poetry*, Grand Rapids MI: Eerdmans.

Gerstenberger, E. S. (2002), *Theologies in the Old Testament*, Edinburgh: T&T Clark.

Gerstenburger, E. S. (2001), 'The Psalter', in Perdue, L. G. (ed.), *The Blackwell Companion to the Hebrew Bible*, Oxford: Blackwell, pp. 402–17.

Gillingham, S. E. (1994), *The Poems and Psalms of the Hebrew Bible*, Oxford: Oxford University Press.

Gillingham, S. E. (1998), *One Bible, Many Voices*, London: SPCK.

Gillingham, S. E. (2008), *Psalms through the Centuries*, vol. 1, Oxford: Blackwell.

Goldingay, J. (2003), *Old Testament Theology: Vol. 1 Israel's Gospel*, Downers Grove IL: InterVarsity Press Academic.

Goldingay, J. (2006), *Old Testament Theology: Vol. 2 Israel's Faith*, Downers Grove IL: InterVarsity Press Academic.

Goldingay, J. (2006), *Psalms*, 3 vols, Baker Commentary on the Old Testament Wisdom and Psalms, Grand Rapids MI: Baker Academic.

Good, E. M. (1962), 'Peace in the OT', in Buttrick, G. A. (ed.), *The Interpreter's Dictionary of the Bible*, Nashville TN: Abingdon Press, vol. 3, pp. 704–6.

Gooder, P. (2009), *Searching for Meaning: An Introduction to Interpreting the New Testament*, London: SPCK.

Goodman M. (2007), 'The Temple in First Century CE Judaism', in Day, J. (ed.), *Temple and Worship in Biblical Israel*, Edinburgh: T&T Clark.

Goodrick, E. W and Kohlenberger, J. R. (eds) (1999), *New International Bible Concordance*, Grand Rapids MI: Zondervan.

Gorman, M. J. (2008), *Elements of Biblical Exegesis*, rev. edn, London: Hendrickson.

Gordon, R. P. (1993), '(Translations) The Targums', in Metzger, B. M. and Coogan, M. D. (eds), *The Oxford Companion to the Bible*, Oxford: Oxford University Press, pp. 754–5.

Goulder, M. D. (1982), *The Psalms of the Sons of Korah*, Sheffield: Journal for the Study of the Old Testament Press.

Goulder, M. D. (1990), *The Prayers of David (Psalms 51–72)*, Sheffield: Sheffield Academic Press.

Goulder, M. D. (1998), *The Psalms of the Return*, Sheffield: Sheffield Academic Press.

Grant, J. A. (2005), 'The Psalms and the King', in Johnston, P. S. and Firth, D. G. (eds), *Interpreting the Psalms: Issues and Approaches*, Leicester: Apollos, pp. 101–18.

Grant, J. A. (2008), 'Editorial Criticism', in Longman, T. and Enns, P. (eds), *Dictionary of the Old Testament Wisdom, Poetry and Writings*, Downers Grove IL: InterVarsity Press Academic, pp. 149–56.

Greenspoon, L. J. (2004), 'Jewish Translations of the Bible', in Berlin, A. and Berettler, M. Z. (eds), *The Jewish Study Bible*, Oxford: Oxford University Press, pp. 2005–20.

Halpern, B. (1993), 'Kingship and Monarchy', in Metzger, B. M. and Coogan, M. D. (eds), *The Oxford Companion to the Bible*, Oxford: Oxford University Press, pp. 413–16.

Haran, M. (1978), *Temples and Temple Service in Ancient Israel*, Oxford: Oxford University Press.

Harrelson, W. J. (1962), 'Law in the OT', in Buttrick, G. A. (ed.), *The Interpreter's Dictionary of the Bible*, Nashville TN: Abingdon Press, vol. 3, pp. 77–89.

Harris, G. (2009), *SCM Press Core Text: Paul*, London: SCM Press.

Hastings, A. M., Mason, A. and Pyper, H. (eds) (2000), *The Oxford Companion to Christian Thought*, Oxford: Oxford University Press.

Hayes, J. H. and Holladay, C. R. (2007), *Biblical Exegesis: A Beginner's Handbook*, 3rd edn, Louisville KY: Westminster John Knox Press.

Healey, J. P. (1992), 'Peace – Old Testament', in Freedman, D. N. (ed.), *The Anchor Bible Dictionary*, New York: Doubleday, vol. 5, pp. 206–7.

Hempel, J. (1962), 'Psalms, Book of', in Buttrick, G. A. (ed.), *The Interpreter's Dictionary of the Bible*, Nashville TN: Abingdon Press, vol. 3, pp. 942–58.

Henze, M. (ed.) (2005), *Biblical Interpretation at Qumran*, Grand Rapids MI: Eerdmans.

Hess, R. S. (2007), *Israelite Religions*, Grand Rapids MI: Baker-Apollos.

Holdsworth, J. (2005), *SCM Press Studyguide to the Old Testament*, London: SCM Press.

Holladay, W L. (1993), *The Psalms through Three Thousand Years*, Minneapolis MN: Fortress Press.

Horrell, D. (2000), *An Introduction to the Study of Paul*, London: Continuum.

Hossfeld, F.-L. and Zenger, E. (2005), *Psalms 2*, Hermeneia Series, Minneapolis MN: Fortress Press.

Howard, D. M. (1999), 'Recent Trends in Psalms Study', in Baker, D. W. and Arnold, B. T. (eds), *The Face of Old Testament Studies: A Survey of Contemporary Approaches*, Grand Rapids MI: Baker, pp. 329–68.

Howard, D. M. (2005), 'The Psalms and Current Study, in Johnston, P. S. and Firth, D. G. (eds), *Interpreting the Psalms: Issues and Approaches*, Leicester: Apollos, pp. 23–40.

Hunter, A. G. (1999), *Psalms*, Old Testament Readings, London: Routledge.

Hunter, A. G. (2008), *An Introduction to the Psalms*, London: T&T Clark.

Hutchinson, J. H. (2005), 'The Psalms and Praise', in Johnston, P. S. and Firth, D. G. (eds), *Interpreting the Psalms: Issues and Approaches*, Leicester: Apollos, pp. 85–100.

Jacob, E. (1962), 'Death', in Buttrick, G. A. (ed.), *The Interpreter's Dictionary of the Bible*, Nashville TN: Abingdon Press, vol. 1, pp. 802–3.

Janis, S. (2008), *Spirituality for Dummies*, 2nd edn, Hoboken: Wiley Publishing.

Johnson, A. R. (1967), *Sacral Kingship in Ancient Israel*, 2nd edn, Cardiff: University of Wales Press.

Johnson, B. (1974–2006), 'צדק etc', in Botterweck, G. J. et al. (eds), *Theological Dictionary of the Old Testament*, Grand Rapids MI: Eerdmans, vol. 12, pp. 239–64.

Johnston, P. S. (2002), *Shades of Sheol: Death and Afterlife in the Old Testament*, Leicester: Apollos.

Johnston, P. S. (2005), 'Appendix 1: Index of Form-Critical Categorizations', in Johnston, P. S. and Firth, D. G. (eds), *Interpreting the Psalms: Issues and Approaches*, Leicester: Apollos, pp. 295–300.

Johnston, P. S. (2005), 'The Psalms and Distress', in Johnston, P. S. and Firth, D. G. (eds), *Interpreting the Psalms: Issues and Approaches*, Leicester: Apollos, pp. 63–84.

Johnston, P. S. (2008), 'Afterlife', in Longman, T. and Enns, P. (eds), *Dictionary of the Old Testament Wisdom, Poetry and Writings*, Downers Grove IL: InterVarsity Press Academic, pp. 5–8.

Johnston, P. S. and Firth, D. G. (eds) (2005), *Interpreting the Psalms: Issues and Approaches*, Leicester: Apollos.

Jones, I. (1992), 'Musical Instruments', in 'Music and Musical Instruments', in

Freedman, D. N. (ed.), *The Anchor Bible Dictionary*, New York: Doubleday, vol. 4, pp. 934–9.

Keel, O. (1978), *The World of Biblical Symbolism*, London: SPCK.

Keel, O. (1997), *The Symbolism of the Biblical World: Ancient Near Eastern Iconography and the Book of Psalms*, Winona Lake: Eisenbrauns.

Kidner, D. (1973/75), *Psalms*, 2 vols, Tyndale Old Testament Commentary, Leicester: InterVarsity Press.

Kirkpatrick, A. F. (1906), *The Book of Psalms*, Cambridge: Cambridge University Press.

Klingbeil, M. G. (2008), 'Iconography', in Longman, T. and Enns, P. (eds), *Dictionary of the Old Testament Wisdom*, *Poetry and Writings*, Downers Grove IL: InterVarsity Press Academic, pp. 621–31.

Knight, G. A. F. (1983), *Psalms*, 2 vols, Daily Study Bible, Edinburgh: St Andrew Press.

Koch, K. (1974–2006), 'חטא *chata*' etc', in Botterweck, G. J. et al. (eds), *Theological Dictionary of the Old Testament*, Grand Rapids MI: Eerdmans, vol. 4, pp. 309–19.

Koch, K. (1974–2006), 'עון *'awon* etc', in Botterweck, G. J. et al. (eds), *Theological Dictionary of the Old Testament*, Grand Rapids MI: Eerdmans, vol. 10, pp. 546–62.

Koptak, P. E. (2008), 'Intertextuality', in Longman, T. and Enns, P. (eds), *Dictionary of the Old Testament Wisdom*, *Poetry and Writings*, Downers Grove IL: InterVarsity Press Academic, pp. 325–32.

Kraus, H.-J. (1966), *Worship in Israel*, Oxford: Blackwell.

Kraus, H.-J. (1988, 1989), *Psalms*, 2 vols, Minneapolis MN: Fortress Press.

Kraus, H.-J. (1992), *Theology of the Psalms*, Minneapolis MN: Fortress Press.

Kroeger, C. C. and Evans, M. J. (eds) (2001), *The IVP Women's Bible Commentary*, Downers Grove IL: InterVarsity Press.

Kugel, J. L. (1981), *The Idea of Biblical Poetry*, New Haven CT: Yale University Press.

Kushner, H. S. (2002), *When Bad Things Happen to Good People*, new edn, London: Pan.

Kwakkel, G. (2008), 'Righteousness', in Longman, T. and Enns, P. (eds), *Dictionary of the Old Testament Wisdom*, *Poetry and Writings*, Downers Grove IL: InterVarsity Press Academic, pp. 663–8.

LeFebvre, M. (2005), 'Torah-Meditation and the Psalms: The Invitation of Psalm 1', in Johnston, P. S. and Firth, D. G. (eds), *Interpreting the Psalms: Issues and Approaches*, Leicester: Apollos, pp. 213–25.

Lemon, R., Mason, E., Roberts, J. and Rowland C. (eds) (2009), *The Blackwell Companion to the Bible in English Literature*, Oxford: Wiley Blackwell.

Lewis, C. S. (1961), *Reflections on the Psalms*, London: Collins Fontana.

Limburg, J. (1992), 'Psalms, Book of', in Freedman, D. N. (ed.), *The Anchor Bible Dictionary*, New York: Doubleday, vol. 5, pp. 522–36.

Limburg, J. (2000), *Psalms*, Westminster Bible Companion, Louisville KY: Westminster John Knox Press.

Limburg, J. (2007), 'Westermann', in McKim, D. K. (ed.), *Dictionary of Major Biblical Interpreters*, Downers Grove IL: InterVarsity Press USA, pp. 1043–8.

Loades, A. (1998), 'Feminist Interpretation', in Barton, J. (ed.) *The Cambridge Companion to Biblical Interpretation*, Cambridge: Cambridge University Press, pp. 81–94.

Longman, T. (1988), *How to Read the Psalms*, Downers Grove IL: InterVarsity Press USA.

Longman, T. (2005), 'The Psalms and Ancient Near Eastern Prayer Genres', in Johnston, P. S. and Firth, D. G. (eds), *Interpreting the Psalms: Issues and Approaches*, Leicester: Apollos, pp. 41–59.

Longman, T. (2008), 'Psalms 2: Ancient Near Eastern Background', in Longman, T. and Enns, P. (eds), *Dictionary of the Old Testament Wisdom, Poetry and Writings*, Downers Grove IL: InterVarsity Press Academic, pp. 593–605.

Longman, T. and Enns, P. (eds) (2008), *Dictionary of the Old Testament: Wisdom, Poetry and Writings*, Downers Grove IL: InterVarsity Press Academic.

Lucas, E. (2003), *Exploring the Old Testament, vol. 3: The Psalms and Wisdom Literature*, London: SPCK.

Lucas, E. (2008), 'Poetics: Terminology of', in Longman, T. and Enns, P. (eds), *Dictionary of the Old Testament Wisdom, Poetry and Writings*, Downers Grove IL: InterVarsity Press Academic, pp. 520–5.

Lucas, E. (2008), 'Wisdom Theology', in Longman, T. and Enns, P. (eds), *Dictionary of the Old Testament Wisdom, Poetry and Writings*, Downers Grove IL: InterVarsity Press Academic, pp. 901–12.

Magonet, J. (1994), *A Rabbi Reads the Psalms*, London: SCM Press.

Martin-Achard, R. (1992), 'Resurrection – Old Testament', in Freedman, D. N. (ed.), *The Anchor Bible Dictionary*, New York: Doubleday, vol. 5, pp. 680–4.

Matthews, V. H. (1992), 'Music', in 'Music and Musical Instruments', in Freedman, D. N. (ed.), *The Anchor Bible Dictionary*, New York: Doubleday, vol. 4, pp. 930–4.

Mays, J. L. (ed.) (1990), *Harper's Bible Commentary*, San Francisco: HarperSanFrancisco.

Mays, J. L. (1994a), *The Lord Reigns: A Theological Handbook to the Psalms*, Louisville KY: Westminster John Knox Press.

Mays, J. L. (1994b), *Psalms*, Interpretation Commentary series, Louisville KY: Westminster John Knox Press.

McCann, J. C. (1993–2002), 'The Book of Psalms', in *The New Interpreter's Bible*, various editors, Nashville TN: Abingdon Press, vol. 4, pp. 641–1280.

McCann, J. C. (1993–2002), 'The Shape and Shaping of the Psalter', in *The New Interpreter's Bible*, various editors, Nashville TN: Abingdon Press, vol. 4, pp. 655–66.

McCann, J. C. (ed.) (1993a), *The Shape and Shaping of the Psalter*, Sheffield: Journal for the Study of the Old Testament Press.

McCann, J. C. (1993b), *A Theological Introduction to the Book of Psalms*, Nashville TN: Abingdon Press.

McCarthy, M. (2000), 'Spirituality in a Postmodern Era', in Woodward, J. and Pattison, S. (eds), *The Blackwell Reader in Pastoral and Practical Theology*, Oxford: Blackwell.

McFague, S. (1982), *Metaphorical Theology*, Philadelphia: Fortress Press.

McKenzie S. L. and Graham M. P. (eds) (1998), *The Hebrew Bible Today*, Louisville KY: Westminster John Knox Press.

McKenzie S. L. and Haynes, S. R. (1999), *To Each its Own Meaning: An Introduction to Biblical Criticisms and their Applications*, Louisville KY: Westminster John Knox Press.

McKim, D. K. (ed.) (2007), *Dictionary of Major Biblical Interpreters*, Downers Grove IL: InterVarsity Press USA.

Mettinger, T. N. D. (1987), *In Search of God: The Meaning and Message of the Everlasting Names*, Philadelphia: Fortress Press.

Metzger, B. M. and Coogan, M. D. (eds) (1993), *The Oxford Companion to the Bible*, Oxford: Oxford University Press.

Metzger, B. M. and Murphy, R. E. (eds) (1991), *The New Oxford Annotated Bible*, Oxford: Oxford University Press.

Millard, A. R., Packer, J. I. and Wiseman, D. J. (eds) (1996), *New Bible Dictionary*, 3rd rev. edn, Nottingham: InterVarsity Press.

Miller, J. M. (1970), 'The Korahites of Southern Judah', Catholic Biblical Quarterly, vol. 32, pp. 58–68.

Miller, P. D. (1986), *Interpreting the Psalms*, Philadelphia: Fortress Press.

Mills, M. (1998), *Images of God in the Old Testament*, London: Cassell.

Mills, M. (1999), *Historical Israel: Biblical Israel*, London: Cassell.

Mitchell, D. C. (1997), *The Message of the Psalter: An Eschatological Programme in the Book of Psalms*, Sheffield: Sheffield Academic Press.

Mitchell, D. C. (2006), 'Lord, Remember David: G. H. Wilson and the Message of the Psalter', *Vetus Testamentum*, vol. LVI, no. 4, pp. 526–48.

Moberly, R. W. (1999), 'Theology of the Old Testament', in Baker, D. W. and Arnold, B. T. (eds), *The Face of Old Testament Studies: A Survey of Contemporary Approaches*, Grand Rapids MI: Baker, pp. 452–78.

Mowinckel, S. (1967), *The Psalms in Israel's Worship*, 2 vols, Oxford: Blackwell.

Moyise, S. (2001), *The Old Testament in the New*, London: Continuum.

Moyise, S. (2004), *Introduction to Biblical Studies*, 2nd edn, London: T&T Clark.

Moyise, S. and Menken, M. J. J. (2004), *The Psalms in the New Testament*, London: Continuum.

Murphy, R. E. (1992), 'Wisdom in the OT', in Freedman, D. N. (ed.), *The Anchor Bible Dictionary*, New York: Doubleday, vol. 6, pp. 920–31.

Murphy, R. E. (1993), 'Psalms, The Book of', in Metzger, B. M. and Coogan, M. D. (eds), *The Oxford Companion to the Bible*, Oxford: Oxford University Press, pp. 626–9.

Nel, P. J. (1996), '8966 שלם', in VanGemeren, W. A. (ed.), *The New International Dictionary of Old Testament Theology and Exegesis*, Grand Rapids MI: Zondervan, vol. 4, pp. 130–4.

New English Translation of the Septuagint (NETS) (2007), Oxford: Oxford University Press.

New English Translation of the Septuagint (NETS), online version, at http://ccat.sas. upenn.edu/nets.

New Interpreter's Bible, The (1993–2002), various editors, 12 vols, Nashville TN: Abingdon Press.

Newsletter for Targumic and Cognate Studies at http://www.targum.info.

Newsom, C. A. and Ringe, S. H. (eds) (1998), *Women's Bible Commentary*, Louisville KY: Westminster John Knox Press.

Nickelsburg, G. W. E. (1981), *Jewish Literature between the Bible and the Mishnah*, London: SCM Press.

Nida, E. A. (1992), 'Theories of Translation', in Freedman, D. N. (ed.), *The Anchor Bible Dictionary*, New York: Doubleday, vol. 6, pp. 512–15.

Nida, E. A. (1993), '(Translations) Theory and Practice', in Metzger, B. M. and Coogan, M. D. (eds), *The Oxford Companion to the Bible*, Oxford: Oxford University Press, pp. 750–2.

Parker, D. (1992), 'Vulgate', in Freedman, D. N. (ed.), *The Anchor Bible Dictionary*, New York: Doubleday, vol. 6, pp. 860–2.

Parrish, V. S. (2007), 'Brueggemann', in McKim, D. K. (ed.), *Dictionary of Major*

Biblical Interpreters, Downers Grove IL: InterVarsity Press USA, pp. 242–7.

Patte, D. (ed.) (2004), *Global Bible Commentary*, Nashville TN: Abingdon Press.

Peake, A. S. (ed.) (1919), *A Commentary on the Bible*, London: Thomas Nelson.

Penkower, J. S. (2004), 'The Development of the Masoretic Bible', in Berlin, A. and Brettler, M. Z. (eds), *The Jewish Study Bible*, Oxford: Oxford University Press, pp. 2077–84.

Perdue, L. G. (ed.) (2001), *The Blackwell Companion to the Hebrew Bible*, Oxford: Blackwell.

Peters, M. (1992), 'Septuagint', in Freedman, D. N. (ed.), *The Anchor Bible Dictionary*, New York: Doubleday, vol. 5, pp. 1093–1104.

Peterson, Eugene H. (2007), *The Message Bible*, Colorado Springs CO: NavPress.

Phillips, A. (2005), *Standing up to God*, London: SPCK.

Pietersma, A. (ed.) (2007), *New English Translation of the Septuagint*, Oxford: Oxford University Press.

Pritchard, J. B. (ed.) (1969), *Ancient Near Eastern Texts Relating to the Old Testament*, 3rd edn, Princeton: Princeton University Press.

Prothero, R. E. (1903), *The Psalms in Human Life*, London: Thomas Nelson.

Provan, I., Long, V. P. and Longman, T. (2003), *A Biblical History of Israel*, Louisville KY: Westminster John Knox Press.

Reid, S. B. (1997), *Listening In: A Multicultural Reading of the Psalms*, Nashville TN: Abingdon Press.

Reimer, D. J. (1996), '7405 צדק', in VanGemeren, W. A. (ed.), *The New International Dictionary of Old Testament Theology and Exegesis*, Grand Rapids MI: Zondervan, vol. 3, pp. 744–69.

Rendtorff, R. (2005), *The Canonical Hebrew Bible: A Theology of the Old Testament*, Leiden: Deo.

Reventlow, H. G. (2001), 'Modern Approaches to Old Testament Theology', in Perdue, L. G. (ed.), *The Blackwell Companion to the Hebrew Bible*, Oxford: Blackwell, p. 220–41.

Richards, K. H. (1992), 'Death – Old Testament', in Freedman, D. N. (ed.), *The Anchor Bible Dictionary*, New York: Doubleday, vol. 2, pp. 108–110.

Rodd, C. S. (2001), 'Psalms', in Barton J. and Muddiman, J. (eds), *The Oxford Bible Commentary*, Oxford: Oxford University Press, pp. 355–405.

Rogerson, J. W. (2002), *Beginning Old Testament Study*, rev. edn, London: SPCK.

Rogerson, J. W. (2009), *A Theology of the Old Testament: Cultural Memory, Communication and Being Human*, London: SPCK.

Rogerson, J. W. and McKay, J. W. (1977), *Psalms*, 3 vols, Cambridge Bible Commentary, Cambridge: Cambridge University Press.

Rose, M. (1992), 'Names of God in the OT', in Freedman, D. N. (ed.), *The Anchor Bible Dictionary*, New York: Doubleday vol. 4, pp. 1001–11.

Rowley, H. H. (ed.) (1951), *The Old Testament and Modern Study*, Oxford: Oxford University Press.

Rowley, H. H. (1967), *Worship in Ancient Israel*, London: SPCK.

Ryken, L. (1984), *How to Read the Bible as Literature*, Grand Rapids MI: Zondervan.

Ryken, L., Wilhoit, J. C. and Longman, T. (eds) (1998), *Dictionary of Biblical Imagery*, Downers Grove IL: InterVarsity Press USA.

Ryrie, A. (2004), *Deliver us from Evil*, London: Darton, Longman and Todd.

Sakenfield, K. D. (1992), 'Hesed', in 'Love – Old Testament', in Freedman, D. N. (ed.), *The Anchor Bible Dictionary*, New York: Doubleday, vol. 4, pp. 377–80.

Sanders, E. P. (1992), 'Law in Judaism in the NT Period', in Freedman, D. N. (ed.), *The Anchor Bible Dictionary*, New York: Doubleday, vol. 4, pp. 254–65.

Sanders, E. P. (1992), *Judaism: Practice and Belief 63BCE–66CE*, London: SCM Press.

Sanders, J. A. (1976), 'Torah', in Crim, K. (ed.), *The Interpreter's Dictionary of the Bible Supplementary Volume*, Nashville TN: Abingdon Press, pp. 909–11.

Sawyer, J. F. A. (ed.) (2009), *A Concise Dictionary of the Bible: And its Reception*, Louisville KY: Westminster John Knox Press.

Schaeffer, K. (2001), *Psalms*, *Berit Olam* Series, Collegeville MN: The Liturgical Press.

Schökel, L. A. (1988), *A Manual of Hebrew Poetics*, Rome: Pontifical Biblical Institute.

Schultz, R. (1996), 'Justice', in VanGemeren, W. A. (ed.), *The New International Dictionary of Old Testament Theology and Exegesis*, Grand Rapids MI: Zondervan, vol. 4, pp. 837–46.

Scullion, J. J. (1992), 'Righteousness – Old Testament', in Freedman, D. N. (ed.), *The Anchor Bible Dictionary*, New York: Doubleday, vol. 5, pp. 724–36.

Seebass, H. (1974–2006), 'פשע pešaʿ etc', in Botterweck, G. J. et al. (eds), *Theological Dictionary of the Old Testament*, Grand Rapids MI: Eerdmans, vol. 12, pp. 133–51.

Segovia, F. (1999), 'Reading the Bible Ideologically: Socioeconomic Criticism', in McKenzie S. L. and Haynes, S. R., *To Each its Own Meaning: An Introduction to Biblical Criticisms and their Applications*, Louisville KY: Westminster John Knox Press, pp. 268–82.

Seybold, K. (1990), *Introducing the Psalms*, Edinburgh: T&T Clark.

Smart, N. (1989), *The World's Religions*, Cambridge: Cambridge University Press.

Snaith, N. H. (1944), *The Distinctive Ideas of the Old Testament*, London: Epworth Press.

Soskice, J. M. (1985), *Metaphor and Religious Language*, Oxford: Clarendon Press.

Soulen, R. N. and Soulen, R. K. (2001), *Handbook of Biblical Criticism*, 3rd edn rev. and expanded, Louisville KY: Westminster John Knox Press.

Stendebach, F. J. (1974–2006), 'שׁלם šalom' in Botterweck, G. J. et al. (eds), *Theological Dictionary of the Old Testament*, Grand Rapids MI: Eerdmans, vol. 15, pp. 13–49.

Stern, P. (1993), 'Torah', in Metzger, B. M. and Coogan, M. D. (eds), *The Oxford Companion to the Bible*, Oxford: Oxford University Press, pp. 747–8.

Strawn, B. A. (2008), 'Imprecation', in Longman, T. and Enns, P. (eds), *Dictionary of the Old Testament Wisdom, Poetry and Writings*, Downers Grove IL: InterVarsity Press Academic, pp. 314–20.

Strong, J., Kohlenberger, J. R. and Swanson, J. A. (eds) (2004), *The Strongest Strong's Exhaustive Concordance of the Bible*, Grand Rapids MI, Zondervan.

Stuart, D. (2002), *Old Testament Exegesis*, 3rd rev. edn, Louisville KY: Westminster John Knox Press.

Stuhlmuller, C. D. (2002), *Spirituality of the Psalms*, Collegeville MN: The Liturgical Press.

Sturgis, M. (2001), *It Ain't Necessarily So*, London: Headline.

Sugirtharajah, R. S. (ed.) (1995) *Voices from the Margin*, new edn, New York: Orbis Books and London: SPCK.

Swanson, D. D. (2005), 'Qumran and the Psalms', in Johnston, P. S. and Firth, D. G. (eds), *Interpreting the Psalms: Issues and Approaches*, Leicester: Apollos, pp. 247–61.

Tamez, E. (1995), 'Women's Rereading of the Bible', in Sugirtharajah, R. S. (ed.), *Voices from the Margin*, new edn, New York: Orbis Books and London: SPCK, pp. 48–57.

Tanner, B. L. (2001), *The Book of Psalms through the Lens of Intertextuality*, New York: Lang.

Tate, M. E. (1990), *Psalms 51—100*, Word Biblical Commentary, Waco TX: Word.

Taylor, V. (1966), *The Gospel According to St Mark*, 2nd edn, London: Macmillan.

Terrien, S. L. (2003), *The Psalms: Strophic Structure and Theological Commentary*, Grand Rapids MI: Eerdmans.

Thielman, F. (1993), 'Law', in Hawthorne G. F., Martin R. P. and Reid D. G. (eds), *Dictionary of Paul and his Letters*, Downers Grove IL: InterVarsity Press, pp. 529–42.

Thomas, D. W. (1958), *Documents from Old Testament Times*, New York: Harper.

Travers, M. E. (2003), *Encountering God in the Psalms*, Grand Rapids MI: Kregel.

Tucker, W. D. (2008), 'Psalms 1: Book of', in Longman, T. and Enns, P. (eds),

Dictionary of the Old Testament Wisdom, Poetry and Writings, Downers Grove IL: InterVarsity Press Academic, pp. 578–93.

VanGemeren, W. A. (ed.) (1996), *The New International Dictionary of Old Testament Theology and Exegesis*, 5 vols, Grand Rapids MI: Zondervan.

Vermes, G. (1994), *An Introduction to the Complete Dead Sea Scrolls*, 3rd edn, London: SCM Press.

Vermes, G. (1997) *The Complete Dead Sea Scrolls*, complete edn, London: Allen Lane, Penguin.

von Rad, G. (1962), *Old Testament Theology*, 2 vols, Edinburgh: Oliver and Boyd.

Vos, C. J. A. (2005), *Theopoetry of the Psalms*; London: T&T Clark.

Wallace, H. N. (2005), *Words to God, Word from God: The Psalms in the Prayer and Preaching of the Church*, Aldershot: Ashgate.

Waltke, B. K. and Houston, J. K. (2009), *The Psalms as Christian Worship: A Historical Commentary*, Grand Rapids MI: Eerdmans.

Watson, W. G. E. (1984), *Classical Hebrew Poetry: A Guide to its Techniques*, Sheffield: Journal for the Study of the Old Testament Press.

Weiser, A. (1962), *Psalms*, Old Testament Library, London: SCM Press.

Werner, E. (1962), 'Musical Instruments', in Buttrick, G. A. (ed.), *The Interpreter's Dictionary of the Bible*, Nashville TN: Abingdon Press, vol. 3, pp. 469–76.

Westermann, C. (1976), 'Psalms, Book of', in Crim, K. (ed.), *The Interpreter's Dictionary of the Bible Supplementary Volume*, Nashville TN: Abingdon Press, pp. 705–10.

Westermann, C. (1981), *Praise and Lament in the Psalms*, Edinburgh: T&T Clark.

White, R. E. O. (1984), *A Christian Handbook to the Psalms*, Grand Rapids MI: Eerdmans.

Whitelam, K. W. (1992), 'King and Kingship', in Freedman, D. N. (ed.), *The Anchor Bible Dictionary*, New York: Doubleday, vol. 4, pp. 40–8.

Whybray, N. (1996), *Reading the Psalms as a Book*, Sheffield: Sheffield Academic Press.

Wilson, G. H. (1985, reissued 2004), *The Editing of the Hebrew Psalter*, Chicago: Scholars Press.

Wilson, G. H. (1986), 'The Use of Royal Psalms at the "Seams" of the Hebrew Psalter', Journal for the Study of the Old Testament 35, pp. 85–94.

Wilson, G. H. (1993), 'Shaping the Psalter: A Consideration of Editorial Linkage in the Book of Psalms', in McCann, J. C. (ed.), *The Shape and Shaping of the Psalter*, Sheffield: Journal for the Study of the Old Testament Press.

Wilson, G. H. (1996), 'Wisdom', in VanGemeren, W. A. (ed.), *The New International*

Dictionary of Old Testament Theology and Exegesis, Grand Rapids MI: Zondervan, vol. 4, pp. 1276–85.

Wilson, G. H. (2005), 'The Structure of the Psalter', in Johnston, P. S. and Firth, D. G. (eds), *Interpreting the Psalms: Issues and Approaches*, Leicester: Apollos, pp. 229–46.

Wren, B. (1989), *What Language Shall I Borrow? God-talk in Worship: A Male Response to Feminist Theology*, New York: Crossroad Books.

Wright, G. E. (1952), *God Who Acts*, London: SCM Press.

Wright, N. T. (1993), *The New Testament and the People of God*, London: SPCK.

Wright, R. B. (1985), 'Introduction to the Psalms of Solomon', in Charlesworth, J. H., *The Old Testament Pseudepigrapha*, New York: Doubleday, vol. 2, pp. 639–70.

Young, R. (reissued 2002), *Analytical Concordance to the Holy Bible*, London: Hendrickson.

Yancey, P. (1997), *Where is God When It Hurts?* Grand Rapids MI: Zondervan.

Zeisler, J. (1990), *Pauline Christianity*, rev. edn, Oxford: Oxford University Press.

Zenger, E. (1996), *A God of Vengeance? Understanding the Psalms of Divine Wrath*, Louisville KY: Westminster John Knox Press.

Zobel, H.-J. (1974–2006), 'חסד', in Botterweck, G. J. et al. (eds), *Theological Dictionary of the Old Testament*, Grand Rapids MI: Eerdmans, vol. 5, pp. 44–64.

Index of Bible References

Index of modern authors